RETHINKING DISABILITY

Acknowledgement

The development of this book was made possible through financial support from the National Institute on Disability and Rehabilitation Research. We wish to express our deepest gratitude. Many people contributed with their work, advice, and wisdom towards the growth and realization of this book. In alphabetical order they are Jocelyn Armstrong, Pamela Block, David Braddock, Clark Cunningham, René Devisch, Joan Erickson, LeAnn Fields, Carol Gill, Tamar Heller, Miriam Hertz, Lynda Leach, Kirsten McBride, David Mitchell, Martine Peeters, Allan Peshkin, Cindy Reiter, Tom Riley, Stephen Rubin, Mahir Şaul, Sharon Snyder, Sean Sweeney, Betty Taylor, Steven Taylor, and John Trach.

For their cordial touch and correct handling of the manuscript, we thank Huug Van Gompel and Theo Kengen.

Patrick Devlieger, Frank Rusch & David Pfeiffer
(Eds.)

Rethinking Disability
The emergence of new definitions,
concepts and communities

Garant

Antwerp-Apeldoorn

Third Printing: 2010

Patrick Devlieger, Frank Rusch & David Pfeiffer (Eds.)
Rethinking Disability
The emergence of new definitions, concepts and communities
Antwerp – Apeldoorn
Garant
2003

210 pp. – 24 cm
D/2003/5779/38
ISBN 978-90-441-1394-5

Cover design: Koloriet / Danni Elskens

© The authors & Garant Publishers

All parts of the book are protected by copyright. Every use beyond the narrow limitations of the copyright law is inadmissible without the prior permission from the copyright owners. This is also valid for photocopying, translations and microfilm copies as well as storage and utilisation in electronic systems.

Garant
Somersstraat 13-15, 2018 Antwerp (Belgium)
Koninginnelaan 96, 7315 EB Apeldoorn (The Netherlands)
Garant/Coronet Books, 311 Bainbridge Street, Philadelphia PA 19147 (USA)
Garant/Central Books, 99 Wallis Road, London E9 5LN (England)
info@garant.be – info@garant-uitgevers.nl
order@coronetbooks.com – bill@centralbooks.com
www.garant-uitgevers.eu

Contents

Part 1: Introduction — 7

Rethinking disability as same *and* different! Towards a cultural model of disability — Patrick Devlieger, Frank Rusch & David Pfeiffer — 9

In Memoriam Irving Kenneth Zola (1935-1994) — Carol S. Goldin — 17

Part 2: Toward Definitions and Conceptual Alignment — 23

Disability Values, Representations and Realities — Gary Albrecht — 27

Labeling in the Name of Equality: Political and Social Realities in the Schooling of Disabled Students — Venta Kabzems — 45

Understanding Disabilities:
The Emergence of Our Understanding of Sameness — Frank Rusch — 63

Can Disability Be Thought Of In Terms of Difference? — Henri-Jacques Stiker — 79

The Disability Studies Paradigm — David Pfeiffer — 95

Part 3: Emerging Disability Communities — 107

Examining the Fit Between Deafness and Disability — Susan Foster — 111

Winks, Blinks, Squints and Twitches: Looking for Disability and Culture Through My Son's Left Eye — Philip Ferguson — 131

The Common Agenda of Aging and Disabilities: Stalemate or Progress — Madelyn Iris — 149

From "Idiot" to "Person with Mental Retardation":
Defining Difference in an Effort to Dissolve It — Patrick Devlieger — 169

'Virtual' Support Groups: An Ethnographic Interpretation — Gerald Gold — 189

Contributors — 205

Index — 209

Part 1
Introduction

Rethinking disability as same **and** different!
Towards a cultural model of disability

Patrick Devlieger, Frank Rusch and David Pfeiffer

A fundamental assumption in contemporary Western discourse on disability is the assumption of the desirability of equality–understood as sameness or similarity (Ingstad and Reynolds-Whyte, 1995). Terminology, concepts, social policy, and disability ideology have developed according with this assumption. The concept of "handicap" is directly connected to the idea of equalization of chances (Stiker, 1997; 1999) and should be considered a concept of modern times. It appeared as a concept of public discourse in the United States around the turn of the 1900's, in Europe only after World War II, and in certain developing countries, as part of post-colonial ideologies, as late as the 1970's. In most of continental Europe, particularly in those countries with strong social security systems, the concept of handicap continues to dominate.

In the United States, "handicap" became loaded with negative connotations and banned as a central professional concept in the mid-1970's (Devlieger, 1999) to be replaced by "disability", a concept that intends, albeit in a negative way, to communicate "ability", reinforcing that which links persons with disabilities to a society where "can do" rather than assumed limitations is emphasized. Social policy for the enhancement of employment opportunities of persons with disabilities subscribes to this same idea. The ideology of normalization has influenced both research and practice toward achieving the goal that persons with disabilities are the same, not different. Core disciplines such as medicine, psychology, education, and rehabilitation have been the embodiments, both in shaping discourse and practice, in shaping a new understanding of sameness.

While these developments are critical to the quality of the lives of persons with disabilities, people with disabilities themselves have claimed the uniqueness of their history, and their personal and cultural identities as disabled. Their sense of difference has developed due to the oppression that they have and continue to face and due to the unique contributions they, as persons with disabilities, have made. Such contributions range from the sophistication in the development of language, such as sign language, to the enrichment of environments, technologies, and institutions as they are shaped from the interface with disability, and to the very mundane but essential roles we play as part of families and society. The field of disability studies, in its emerging phases, has illuminated these phenomena.

It appears that a rift could develop between the approaches of core disciplines and those disciplines that represent disability studies with neither side recognizing that persons with disability are both similar *and* different. These, however, appear to be the challenges of post post-modern times. In its emerging stages, core disciplines have at different stages of their development heralded either disability as difference or as sameness. Much of this development is informed by the development of sciences, but perhaps more important by historical momentum. Since the coming of the normalization movements, many core disciplines have supported integration and normalization as principles of sameness.

Disability studies have heralded an interesting mix of approaches that emphasize disability as either same or different. In relying upon a human rights perspective, similarity is obvious and in its presentation of the perspective of people with disabilities *as* disabled, through the development of identity, difference is the principle. This ambiguity is expected to continue. At present, the social sciences in their contribution to disability studies may be more informed and attempting of strengthening a discourse of disability-as-same while the humanities may be more informed of illuminating how disability has and can be represented and claimed in images of difference.

This text addresses an inclusive view in the portrayal of persons with disabilities as both similar *and* different, and it seeks to develop core models and concepts as a result of this view. In such a view, disciplines that emphasize similarity and/or difference must be included. "Oppression" has been a core concept in the development of women's studies and ethnic minority group studies and it will certainly also be applied in the development of disability studies. "Deviance and stigma" has been highly dominant in the social sciences. Destigmatization, through the work of self help groups, the deinstitutionalization and human rights movements, disability identity and cultural development , and even self-display have turned "deviance" into "difference".

With these developments in mind, the scholars in this book have reflected on their own research efforts, and accepted to contribute to an approach that supersedes the divisive currents; withstand the easy constructing of categorizing persons with disabilities as either similar or different; and in one that can bridge research and teaching.

Core Concepts...

People with disabilities have been portrayed and researched in many ways. These trends have always been ideological, reflecting the play of history in the relationship between a universal phenomenon, disability, and a context, from which the meaning of disability is constructed. In modernist times, the trend is toward effacing difference, the creation of the same. The postmodern era may have emphasized fragmentation and its celebration but we also start to recognize that such celebration may be hollow in view of the connections of disadvantage, poverty, disability, race, and class. In other times, we need other ways of thinking, bridging both modern and post-modern times, and even incorporating pre-modern views of disability. Such an opportunity is fully developing as societies have plunged in the information age. We would like to propose a "similar *and* different" view of disability for the information age. To reach this point, we must go through a stage that is currently in full development, the "similar *but* different" stage, which is essentially that of developing the culture of disability, in an urge of demanding respect for difference. Most fundamentally, in a "similar and different" view of disability, we recognize and cognize disability as part of our lives. We finally come around in understanding that disability was there, is here, and will be there. And while we have struggled in the era in which the concept of 'handicap' meant "access to service", and have evolved in the public debate to the concept of 'disability,' by which we essentially mean the ability-can do of persons with disabilities, we may be heading to an era of recognition, celebration, inclusion and study of a phenomenon that is an essential part of the human condition.

A stimulating distinction can be made between a pre-modern, modern and post-modern view of disability (Woodill, 1994). In a pre-modern view, disability in the mythical world is a message from an other-worldly reality; for the Hebrews it was a sign of imperfection that was incompatible with the sacred, and in early Christianity, the ambivalence of disability was one that needed healing because it was the result of sin. Curiously, in our contemporary technological world, there is resurgence to asking ancient questions and searching to answer ultimate questions to disability, sometimes summarized as "the 'why' of our lives". Such answers may lie in the development of disability cosmologies and in the development of a rehabilitation cosmology. A cosmology, in essence, sorts out and brings order, to disability as an event that is inherently disordering, creating chaos, by developing links between the experience of the disabled body and its environment, in the largest possible sense.

The modern view of disability, essentially that of sameness, is one in which people with disability are "fixed", "named and labeled", and then "forgotten" (Stiker, 1982). This modern stance has been corrected because of the inhumanity that resulted from its reduction and, perhaps even more, from the explosion of the spiral of knowledge and power, as it accumulated in institutional practice, curiously enough, from the first invasions of the information age. It was the fast and crude reporting on television that brought "forgotten disability" to the forefront, and ultimately brought institutions such as Willowbrook to their knees. The deinstitutionalization and the integration, mainstreaming, and inclusion movements that followed, however, were not a departure from a modernist ideal. Continuously relying on a scientific credo, making more of the same was now situated in the world, its ultimate aim still being to forget about the difference that disability constitutes. Rather than hiding and forgetting in the institutions, this second wave of modernist ideology has been to expose and to forget. In the normalization view, the person with the disability is always the problem, and, very often, also the victim.

In the post-modern stance, a schism has been introduced that is fundamental. The epistemological foundations of the modern stance, as they are found in empirical research, are being questioned. Disability is no longer "found", rather it is socially and culturally constructed. In the development of disability cultures, most famously pronounced by the Deaf communities, but quickly followed in other arenas (see this volume, Gold), the idea of sameness is crushed and replaced by difference, something that is neither to be hidden nor to be exposed, but rather needs to be celebrated. The second is one that pulls away from the person as the problem and concentrates on the environment: disability is the result of the making of an imperfect environment. Legislation, such as the Americans with Disabilities Act, demands the remaking of our environments, not of people, the making of a new ecology in which disability is present and announced for. Unauthorized parking in a "handicapped" spot will cost you currently $150.00, to give just one example.

It may become clear that in a modernist, machine driven society, disabilities are liabilities, and in the post-modern era a token of diversity, the meaning of disability in an information age will take on new, still unknown dimensions, that may include the potential of more positive qualities than we could have imagined! In an information market, the experience of disability may, at least partly, become an asset because the uniqueness of experience and inherent contradictions drives such a market into further development, overturning common solutions, and exploring alternatives. We should however not be naive and also anticipate that the information age will also develop its own set of classifications and categories, turning a good set of the populations who lack the skills in producing, accessing, and using the information into a functionally disabled status.

In this book we explore the co-existence of sameness and difference as parts of the same emerging picture. In dealing with this complexity, we may regain, perhaps systematically explore for the first time, not to destroy, but to appreciate the wealth and richness of pre-modern views of disability. We do not favor a "return" to pre-modern views or times, but an attention to the ancient questions that guided pre-modern views and that have been only latently present in modern and post-modern discourse. These questions are ultimate questions, those that every person with a disability and his or her family must confront. Those are the questions that have willingly been ignored by service providers and academics because they are not controllable, seemingly idiosyncratic, and beyond the usual ideological and scientific inclinations. To understand that persons with disabilities are human and rightfully belong to the human category, but also deserve a degree of difference that connects them with the outer world, requires a flexibility of thought and method of inquiry that challenges much of what we are currently involved with. Ironically, it is these questions that appear to be dominant in religious or moral models of disability.

The core contribution of disability studies is not in simplifying matters. Rather, its incessant challenge will be to reframe the nature of disability, concretely addressing aspects of human experience but also of policy and service. Adrienne Asch eloquently said "We should strive to find the pieces that are common in human experience and the pieces that are different and say what we have to say about them" (Quoted in Linton, 1994). However, the meaning of human experience can only be addressed in a multi-faceted context that includes history, culture, and ecologies. Scholars who wish to venture into disability studies need the tools that are honest to a phenomenon that in nature makes things more complex. Ideas that direct towards the simple fixing would be dishonest; rather, the attention must be geared to emphasizing the social, cultural and political realities of disability in an attempt to uncover wholeness, historical depth, and cross-cultural comparison. As Ablon (1990) experienced in her work with self-help groups, complexity does not come without ambiguity. The careful unraveling of what she calls the *culture of ambiguity* may make the best yet warranty for good policies and services.

The use of "sameness" and "difference" as analytical concepts requires an explanation. At the heart of our attitudes toward disability Stiker (1999) analyzes a fear at two levels. At the most superficial level, there is an almost visceral reaction because disability evokes a disturbance. It is a disturbance because the world is not ready; the world is organized for "the normal". This fear is further accentuated as we try to confront the consequences of disability: life explodes, project crumble, constituting a disorganization at a second and deeper level, namely of established values. A confrontation with established values puts people in front of their own fears. Longmore (1985) has pointed out "what we fear, we often stigmatize and shun and sometimes seek to destroy". Stiker is more interested in the cultural response to this fear. He continues to explain that it is from the confrontation of people with their own fears that they start to name that for which they are not ready, with an immense amount of terminologies, to show that what is "different". The history of the sciences seems to be an enormous effort to be protected against that "difference". Stiker proposes a simple, quasi-utopian alternative: "Aimons la différence" (Let's love that difference), facing difference and making it part of life.

Stiker's analysis and attitude to disability-as-difference prompts questions to its implementation. If to love is to know, a resurgence of the liberal arts disciplines seems to be needed to strongly infuse the study of disability. Philosophy, history, linguistics, ethnology and other disciplines in the humanistic traditions could contribute to this development. Of pertinent importance is the contribution of these disciplines in documenting the representation of disability-as-fear and the production of stereotypes in oral history, literature, and visual imagery. "To know" also requires activity beyond the intellectual. Weinberg (1988) wrote that "there is a positive relationship between contact and perceived similarity: as contact increases, perceived similarity increases". We should however also be aware that as old differences dissipate, new ones emerge. Classification as a way of making sense of the world cannot be ruled out. Therefore, mindfulness may be a more promising perspective for the study of disability. Langer and Chanowitz (1990:68) argued, "When mindful, one actively constructs categories and draws conclusions. When mindless, one relies on already constructed categories".

…. And the Coming of Age of Disability Studies

About a decade ago, in a special issue of Disability Studies Quarterly, Irving Zola (1994) observed, "By the 1990s, Disability Studies is in the midst of its promulgation and institutionalization phase. Courses abound but not programs. Each of the major supporting disciplines have created a presence of disability studies at their annual conventions and have task forces and standing committees on the topic". Following Zola in supporting these developments, we also travel with him to his early roots and support in this book the development of a cross- and multi-disciplinary area of study. In taking an inclusive view, the relationships between the disciplines and disability studies must be specified. We also must revise older definitions of disability studies as the sole focus on disability as a social phenomenon, its emanation from the civil rights movement, and consequent advocating for self-determination and its shifting away from the prevention, education, and rehabilitation paradigms.

If disability studies is "not a frail weed growing haphazardly, but a strong plant which is beginning to take its place in the fields of academia" (Pfeiffer and Yoshida 1994:489), we must start to address the issues that are derived from its interdisciplinary character and beyond, locate its generating forces. This opportunity comes at a time when the normalization ideologies are beginning to reach their full potential, both in legislation and in practice, and where a need has arisen to effectively deal with the claim of persons with disabilities to give voice to their difference.

The interdisciplinary character of disability studies may yield the most promising in reuniting the breaks and shifts that have occurred, bringing to the forefront the total-person-in-context, bringing various perspectives that emphasize complexity rather than simple and often radical solutions. An analysis of medical practices and an attention to the body cannot be ignored (Barnes, Oliver, and Barton, 2002). Yet, the challenge in including multiple perspectives is in the coordination (for a good example, see Albrecht, Seelman, and Bury, 2001). At the teaching end of this, Pfeiffer and Yoshida (1994) have noted that persons who teach disability studies come from a variety of fields and that they teach in various schools and colleges, in an assortment of departments, and at different levels. In starting to locate some of its generating forces, disability studies must be developed and taught in the community as well as in the university. The input of persons who have direct experience with disability, be it persons with disabilities themselves, practitioners, or parents, is critical. The disability movement, disability communities and cultures, universities, foundations, and the federal government all have potential as major actors in the development of Disability Studies.

In much of its implementation as an interdisciplinary program, the disability community can partly depend on models set by women's, ethnic and cultural studies programs that already have a presence in some universities and in their respective community settings (Seelman, 1994). However, in many ways the implementation of an academic program of disability studies should also differ considerably from these programs because of the history of the status of persons with disabilities in society, the variety of services and legislation, and the responsibilities of the disciplines related to disability. Such issues must be discussed as factors that will enhance or diminish the potential of disability studies.

The necessity of multiple perspectives, the inclusion of the voices of persons with disabilities and those who represent disability, demands the development of a methodological principle that legitimates a unique perspective. Such a principle is found in the positioning of the speaker. There has been much debate in many interdisciplinary programs on the legitimacy of one perspective against another. Common questions, such as "Can men participate in a women's studies program" are replicated by "Can able bodied participate in disability studies"? Such questions are necessary to deepen the nature of programs and the content of study. As "women's studies" evolved into gender studies, a more comprehensive perspective is being developed that includes complementary perspectives, including men's perspectives. We can expect similar developments for disability studies, and perhaps we can anticipate them by clarifying the nature of our unique positions, as they are generated by ability, gender, ethnic and national background, disciplinary background, age, and other characteristics. Such clarification may make the current use of "minority status" oblivious.

Towards a cultural model of disability

Model thinking as pragmatic tools for reflecting are dominant in disability studies. More systematic epistemological reflections on the other hand remain rare (for an example see Skrtic, 1995). Models provide ways of reflecting about a reality, they are the tool of the pragmatist, both the intellectual, professional, and disabled individual use them to make sense and act. Models are simplified presentations of reality because the pure model can hardly be found. Historical shifts, dominations about the definitions, control and interventions, intersperse model thinking. In the worst case, models may be misleading. Nevertheless, it can be assumed that model thinking will remain to be dominant in the near future of disability studies.

Figure 1 provides an overview of important models to disability. Thinking according to a certain model is dependent on particular dimensions that define the roots or origins of disability, localize the phenomenon in entities such as evil, the individual body, the environment, or in representations such as words and images, or more broadly in information. With the dimensions of origins and localization, perceptions of whether or not disability can be thought off as a problem, its solutions, its implications for quality of life, and an overall approach are derived. For example, in religious model thinking, disability is mostly a problem, resulting sometimes from a punishment, but not always as in some cases it could also be seen as a gift. The implications for quality of life are then mostly marginalizing but in certain cases also reason for enhanced quality of life. Where the moral model excels is in its answering of existential questions. A similar coherence can be attributed to other models of thought, while recognizing its particular strengths.

Model Dimensions	Religious Model	Medical Model	Social Model	Cultural Model
Roots	*God(s)*	*Natural World*	*Social structure*	*Human thought*
Localization	Evil force(s)	Individual	Society	Representations
Problem level	Punishment or gift	Measurable defect	Interaction pattern	Identity
Explanation	Cosmology	Natural Sciences	Social Sciences	Humanities
Quality of Life	Marginal, Exceptional	Diminished	Being-in-the-world	Transformational
Approach	Existential ("Why?")	Technical ("How?")	Justice	Critique

Figure 1: Models of disability

Models are dominant for certain periods in history, for certain populations and sub-populations. It is perhaps fair to say that these models are juxtaposed in contemporary society with pockets of moral, medical, social, and some cultural model thinking simultaneously being practiced. Is it a myth of ideological and professional thought that medical model thinking and in turn social model thinking replaced moral model thinking? Today, we may recognize that in globalized and intercultural worlds, all these models are very much present although their expressions may be localized and excluded from certain settings. A first attempt of a cultural model should then perhaps lie in recognizing and integrating the strengths that are present in each of the practiced models and recognize that they are localized. A development of a cultural model therefore should therefore not lie in superseding but rather in integrating ways of thinking. A second challenge lies in an attempt to develop a method of analysis, which can be thought of as "disability critique", a continuous deconstruction, adding on, repairing, and creating of information. "Disability" in such a model then is localized in the ways people could not and cannot conceptualize the phenomenon in all its complexity, i.e., as same and different. All produced words and images take away from its complexity and need to be opened up for further discussion. In such a view, disability is not any more a category of certain populations, but the knowledge that we are all wounded beings (Davis, 2002). More strongly, the interstitial nature of disabled people, and more correctly of all people, can bring into motion the possibility of growth, at the individual level known as disability identity, at the social level as disability identity, and at the transcendent level as disability culture and cosmology. A cultural model therefore emphasizes potentiality and transformation, as it can be reached from the construction and deconstruction of information, emotionality, and spiritual growth.

References cited

Ablon, J. (1990). Ambiguity and difference: families with dwarf children. *Social Science and Medicine, 30,* 879-887.
Albrecht, G.L., Seelman, K.D. Bury, M. (Eds.) (2001). Handbook of Disability Studies. Thousand Oaks, CA: Sage
Armstrong, F. and L. Barton (Eds.) (1999). *Disability, human rights, and education: Cross-cultural perspectives.* Buckingham: Open University Press.
Barnes, C., Oliver, M., Barton, L. (Eds.) (2002). *Disability studies today.* Cambridge: Polity Press.

Davis, L.J. (2002). *Bending over backwards: Disability, dismodernism & other difficult positions.* New York and London: New York University Press.

Devlieger, P. (1999). From Handicap to Disability: Language Use and Cultural Meaning in the United States. *Disability and Rehabilitation,* 21, 7, 346-354.

Frank, G. (1988). Beyond stigma: visibility and self-empowerment of persons with congenital limb deficiencies. *Journal of Social Issues,* 44, 1, 95-115.

Ingstad, B. and Reynolds-Whyte, S. (Eds.) (1995). *Disability and culture.* Berkeley: University of California Press.

Langer, E.J., & Chanowitz, B. (1988). Mindfulness/Mindlessness: A new perspective for the study of disability. In H.E. Yuker (Ed.), *Attitudes toward persons with disabilities.* (Pp. 82-106). New York : Springer.

Linton, S. (1994). Teaching disability studies. *Disability Studies Quarterly,* 14, 44-46.

Linton, S. (1998). *Claiming Disability: Knowledge and Identity.* New York and London: New York University Press.

Longmore, P. (1985). Screening stereotypes: Images of disabled people. *Social Policy,* 16, 31-37.

Pfeiffer, D., & Yoshida, K. (1995). Teaching disability studies in Canada and the USA. *Disability & Society,* 10, 475-500.

Skrtic, T.M. (Ed.) (1995). *Disability and democracy: Reconstructing (special) education for postmodernity.* New York and London: Teachers College Press.

Seelman, K.D. (1994). Future scenarios for disability studies. *Disability Studies Quarterly,* 14, 20-23.

Stiker, H.-J. (1997). *Corps infirmes et sociétés.* Paris:Dunod.

Stiker, H.-J. (1999). The History of Disability. (transl. William Sayers). Ann Arbor: The University of Michigan Press.

Weinberg, N. (1988). Another perspective: attitudes of persons with disabilities. In H. E. Yuker (Ed.), *Attitudes toward persons with disabilities* (pp. 141-153). New York: Springer.

Woodill, G. (1994) The social semiotics of disability. In M. H. Rioux & M. Bach (Eds.), *Disability is not measles: New research paradigms in disability* (pp. 201-226). North York, Ontario: L'Institut Roeher Institute.

Zola, I. (1994). Shaping an interdisciplinary field of disability studies: The perspective of sociology. *Disability Studies Quarterly,* 14, 17-20.

In Memoriam Irving Kenneth Zola (1935-1994)
Disability: From Deviance to Autonomy

Carol S. Goldin

Understanding disability, with perspectives ranging from "deviance" to "advocacy" to "autonomy", was a central focus of the wide range of professional and personal interests of the late Irving Kenneth Zola, Professor of Human Relations at Brandeis University. A description of his intellectual development is a history of the development of the field of disability studies, and his contributions to this field, in his formal roles as well as his personal relationships, significantly shaped its course. An interdisciplinary volume dedicated to an exploration of the tension between "similarity" and "difference" in analyses of disability is a tribute to his legacy.

This brief sketch of Zola's contributions to disability studies focuses on the audience to whom and for whom Zola gave his energies and talents. **By understanding the many voices in which Zola spoke simultaneously, we may gain a greater understanding of the central issue of this volume.** For a far more extensive review of Zola's work, see his own reflections, presented upon the receipt of the Leo G. Reeder Award for Distinguished Scholarship in Sociology in 1990 (Zola, 1991) and the recently published, excellent intellectual biography by Gareth Williams. (Williams, 1996).

The Academic Audience

While still an undergraduate at Harvard University, Zola participated in a classic study of deviance. This study examined data from the Cambridge-Somerville Youth Study, a project begun in the 1930s designed "to prevent delinquency and develop character by means of friendly guidance" (McCord, McCord, & Zola, 1959, vii). Finding no difference in official police and court records for boys who had received "treatment" three years before and those who did not, the researchers concluded that incarceration in reform school is "about as effective in curing delinquency as is whipping a stubborn donkey to make him carry a load" (p. 178). Thus, even in his earliest work Zola combined a keen interest in the role of external social factors on individual behavior and the negative consequences of punishment for deviance control.

In his graduate studies Zola became increasingly interested in medical settings. His Ph.D. thesis, based on fieldwork at Massachusetts General Hospital, explored sociocultural factors in the seeking of medical aid. Years later he wrote that at that time "I conceived of myself and was conceived of as a specialist in deviance" (1983, p.33). As a teaching assistant and research associate he taught criminology courses and did work on aging, gambling, medical care - all "under the general rubric of deviance" (p. 33). Zola turned to the study of physical disease as a form of deviance that is accepted as "real, objective, scientific" (p.33) and he continued to write for an academic audience. **He carried from this early work an appreciation of the**

consequences of deviance labeling, stigma and the setting apart of the "other"- perspectives that would remain at the forefront of his intellectual development.

The Medical Audience

Zola's study at Boston General Hospital on patients' presenting complaints provided evidence for the importance of awareness of ethnic difference in treatment. As a result, he sought to improve communication, treatment, and organization of services. Facing an audience of the medical establishment, he hoped to contribute to a more humane and more effective health care system. As he continued work in the hospital setting, Zola also participated in a number of large-scale health surveys from the mid 1960s to the early 1970s for Kaiser-Permanente Health Plan, the United States Public Health Service, the World Health Organization, and the Netherlands Institute of Preventive Medicine.

Through these studies in academic and nonacademic settings, Zola developed what would become one of his key intellectual interests, the study of the organization of health care. (Zola & McKinlay, 1974). His early recognition that the ancillary "helping professions" serve as power brokers and collectively create an institution of social control is especially noteworthy, "in the health field we must be active in seeking out these sources of power which determine the shape and scope of the so-called "helping" organizations, with which clients interact" (Zola & McKinlay, 1974, p. xii).

Even in his early work on health care delivery, Zola focused on the importance of power relationships and warned of danger of "medicalization", themes he continued to explore for the remainder of his career. Eventually he became less interested in why people "got" problems, and more interested in "...why some 'troubles' were 'problems' and others were not" (Zola, 1983, p. 44).

Today, years after the publication of powerful and compelling theoretical works by Foucault (1973), Dubos (1965), Goffman (1963), Mechanic (1986) and others on medicalization and the control functions of the medical establishment, we may fail to recognize the contributions made by Zola's combination of theoretical and practical actions and his nonsectarian voice. This early critic of overcontrol by the medical professions saw himself as a "practical" sociologist and a teacher, rather than a theoretician *per se*.

The "Other" Audience/ Audiences of Others

The conflicts with the biomedical establishment became increasingly apparent, and by the early 1980s Zola (1983) wrote:

As I look over my sociomedical work, I see how trapped I have been between my liberal and radical leanings. In the 1950s I was a part of the humanist-critical group of medical sociologists that sought to reform medicine. I saw that physicians did not sufficiently listen to their patients, so I gave them voice. I felt that physicians needed to incorporate a social science perspective in their education, so I sought out every opportunity to write in *their* journals and teach in *their* courses. I believed that the structure of their research and practice needed to be humanized, so I accepted every chance to review *their* investigations or advise in the reorganization of *their* services...And yet each of these involvements...has brought with it a set of dilemmas...they failed to see that the medical needs of the populace could never be solved by more physicians on 'frontiers of care,' but rather by a conscious redistribution of services and redelegation of responsibilities not only to less highly trained personnel but to the people themselves. (pp. 299-300)

***

Locating the action in "fixing the problem" among the people most affected became a critically important focus of the remainder of Zola's professional life. **By organizing alternative structures and by giving people opportunity to develop voice, Zola sought to provide persons with disabilities with the space to create experiences that more closely suited their needs and aspirations.**

His ability to integrate the academic and the practical was profoundly shaped by his own unique integration of the personal with the political. Deeply affected by his involvement in the civil rights and anti-war movements in the 1960s, and subsequently by the women's movement, Zola developed fresh perspectives on "relevance" and powerful models for disability rights movements.

But it was his personal struggle and understanding of his own experiences that most deeply affected his work. Beginning with his published work from the early 1980s, he used his own personal narratives to make sense of health care and deviance issues. In academic articles, in popular essays, and in public symposia he described the impact of his early life experiences, especially his chronic disabilities from polio and a serious automobile accident. He offered a great deal more than a sanitized moral tale of triumph over adversity. Using self-deprecating humor, self-reflection, and descriptions of a range of very personal experiences, he conveyed to a very diverse audience what disability meant to his own lived experience. As he noted, his accomplishments are "not *despite* such incidents...I want ...to bring these personal bodily experiences closer to my center-not to claim that they constitute all of who I am, but that they are a central part of my identity; ...they are essential to understanding what I have done" (Zola, 1991, p. 2).

Through an understanding of multidimensional power relationships, disempowerment, and a growing consciousness of a positive role for group self-determination, Zola began devoting more of his efforts outside of academe, and outside of the medical establishment, and towards the creation of grass roots counseling and advocacy organizations, most notably the Boston Self-Help Center. And to provide a forum for practitioners, academics and persons with disabilities to discuss and act on issues relevant to both the academy and advocacy groups, he and others created the Society for Disability Studies.

At about the same time as he was bringing "context" to the larger nonacademic audience, he was increasingly involved with the politically assertive nascent independent living movement:

Independent Living (IL) has been called a social movement, a service paradigm, a research model, a new discipline, a source of hope, and an idea whose time has come...In essence, IL means allowing people with disabilities to live as they choose in their communities rather than confining them in institutions. But this straightforward concept is not simple in its implementation. For the disabled person, it involves exchanging the safety of custodial care for the risk, stress, and effort involved in making the innumerable large and small decisions that shape one's life. It means finding and maintaining the network of support services that are required just to survive and then reaching for the kind of involvement with other people that gives life meaning. (Crewe, Zola, & Associates, 1983, p. ix)

Covering legislative issues, describing IL programs in the U.S. and abroad, describing family support systems and low-cost technology, services, transportation, housing, and communications, this collection of essays is for a different audience for those already in the IL movement, as consumers or providers of services, and those who may join. Zola's grasp of the complexity of deinstitutionalization is evident in the preceding quote, as he stressed the need for ongoing support systems as people take the inevitable risks associated with achieving independence.

In keeping with his growing interest in advocacy Zola published in nonacademic presses, including his 1982 edited volume, *Ordinary Lives,* a collection of first-hand accounts of experience of disability and disease (Zola, 1982a). This volume of prose and some poetry, for a lay audience, introduces "others" to the individual worlds of experience of its authors, and at the same time provides a phenomenological perspective that serves to inform discussions in medical sociology and anthropology.

Ourselves as Audience

By the 1990s, Zola was even more conscious of the role of the individual's experience, as he continued to integrate activism with scholarship (Zola, 1991). Writing in 1991 he noted that until the early 1980s, he had not looked at deviance theory and "applied these insights directly to that minority group of which I am a member - persons with a chronic illness or disability. Clearly it is far easier to identify with others' trouble and pain than with my own" (Zola, 1991, p. 3).

He eventually concluded that the experience of discomfort and exhaustion associated with disability is in no small way socially constructed and maintained. He also became increasingly interested in how language plays a critical role in defining our world, noting, for example, the profound difference between "being confined to" a wheelchair and "using" one.

With these personal insights, Zola challenged taken-for-granted assumptions about research, notably the apparent contrast and even conflict between objective/subjective; public/private; dispassion/affect; political neutrality/political stance; and distance/intimacy. He argued that not only are these false dichotomies, each of these sets is mutually interdependent. Research and practice are enriched by an appreciation of these relationships because the perspective of each informs the understanding of its counterpart. **The intertwining of the personal and the political is empowering in his terms, because of its impact both on advocacy and on scholarship.**

The integration of the personal and the political also provides a basis for understanding Zola's view of the tension between similarity and difference. His scholarly work described and analyzed "difference", first in his studies of deviance, and later in his studies of illness behavior. In contrast, his advocacy work was concerned with "similarity"–primarily, with equal legal rights and with equity and self-determiniation in treatment options. But his advocacy work also addressed issues of uniqueness in his appreciation of the social and psychological power of unique narratives of disability experience, and in his interest in the development of disability culture. Making sense of his own degenerative disease, the cultural anthropologist Robert Murphy wrote of the relationship between the self and the "other", using his illness experience to reassess taken-for-granted notions about culture and human interaction (1990). While Murphy and Zola were both interested in the relationship between personal experiences and larger socio-cultural issues, the former prodded us to use our analysis of disability issues to better understand ourselves and wider issues in culture and society, while the latter emphasized the role of personal experiences in understanding social and cultural institutions. (For a more extensive discussion of Murphy's perspective, see Goldin and Scheer, 1995.)

Zola himself embodied the tensions between sameness and difference as he integrated the many facets of his private and professional lives. By his openness to varying perspectives, he encouraged dialogue among individuals and groups whose differing perspectives may have kept them apart. Noting that disability is an experience all of us can anticipate if we live long enough, he understood the attendant fear and stigma we may experience when first confronting disability in others and the underlying fear we have of our own vulnerabilities. **The autonomy that Zola sought is based on self-understanding and an appreciation of our mutual interdependence.**

To his spirit, his insights, and his profound humanity, we dedicate this multidisciplinary volume on disability issues.

References Cited

Crewe, N.M., Zola, I.K., & Associates. (1983). *Independent living for physically disabled people.* San Francisco: Jossey-Bass.

Dubos, R. (1965). *Man adapting.* New Haven, CT: Yale University Press.

Foucault, M. (1973). *The birth of the clinic: An archaeology of medical perception.* New York: Pantheon.

Goffman, E. (1963). *Stigma: Notes on the management of spoiled identity.* Englewood Cliffs, NJ: Prentice-Hall.

Goldin, C.S., & Scheer, J. (1995, June). *Murphy's contributions to disability studies: an inquiry into ourselves.* Social Science and Medicine, 40(11), 1443-1445.

McCord, W., McCord, J., with Zola, I.K. (1959). *Origins of crime: A new evaluation of the Cambridge-Somerville youth study.* New York: Columbia University Press.

Mechanic, D. (1986). *Illness behavior: An overview.* In S. McHugh & T.M. Vallis (Eds.), Illness behavior: A multidisciplinary model (pp.?). New York: Plenum.

Murphy, R. (1990). The body silent. New York: W. W. Norton.

Williams, G. (1996). Irving Kenneth Zola (1935-1994): *An appreciation.* Sociology of Health and Illness, 18(1), 107-125.

Zola, I.K., & McKinlay, J.B. (Eds.). (1974). *Organizational issues in the delivery of health services:* A selection of articles from the Milbank Memorial Fund Quarterly. New York: Prodist.

Zola, I.K. (Ed.). (1982a). *Ordinary lives: Voices of disease and disability.* Philadelphia: Temple University Press.

Zola, I.K. (1982b). *Missing pieces: A chronicle of living with a disability.* Philadelphia: Temple University Press.

Zola, I.K. (1983). *Socio-medical inquiries: Recollections, reflections and reconsiderations.* Philadelphia: Temple University Press.

Zola, I.K. (1991, March). Bringing our bodies and ourselves back in: Reflections on past, present, and future "medical sociology". *Journal of Health and Social Behavior, 32,* 1-16.

Part 2
Toward Definitions and Conceptual Alignment

The authors in this second part of the volume are very well aware that the understanding of disability does not occur in a vacuum, but rather is defined by the social-political perspectives in our cultures, personal alignments to professional developments, and historical developments of our disciplines and our society. Conceptual developments that tend to singularly characterize individuals with disabilities as "same" – just like anyone else – or as "different" are questioned in this first part.

We first turn to a social-political perspective of disabilities in our culture. Gary Albrecht starts off the five articles that make up Part 2 by pointing out that to understand the place of persons with disabilities in American society – in this discussion, how they are the same or different – it is important to examine three major factors: Our country's value structure and how it pertains to disability; the pervasive power of the media in portraying persons with disabilities; and, finally, the experienced reality of persons with disabilities.

Albrecht concludes that our value system historically has created a discrepancy for people with disabilities by granting them a set of basic rights based on equity but at the same time allowing them to be treated as less than equal; to be marginalized. Indeed, the most prevailing values in the country tend to run counter to what characterizes peoples with disabilities as a group, ranging from ethnocentrism to rugged individualism, competitiveness and an emphasis on productive work as the basis for self-respect, power and justice. While many people with disabilities share these core values, they often find that it impossible to act on their values and achieve their goals, because society has placed insurmountable barriers in their way. Furthermore, there are major value conflicts within the disability community itself, including disagreement on what constitutes "true" disability.

Values are also reflected in the way persons with disabilities are presented in public arenas. Portrayals of individuals with disabilities who have heroically overcome major obstacles continue to be popular, thereby often perpetuating the notion that people with disabilities can achieve anything they wish. While such examples can serve as role models, standards that are too lofty tend to be discouraging for the ordinary individual with disabilities. Instead, what is needed, Albrecht proposes, is an enabling environment; the resources and opportunities to succeed.

Albrecht sees values, representations, and realities as essential conceptual building blocks for the field of disability studies because they provide the assumptions and the context within which the experiences of persons with disabilities can be understood and interpreted.

In the following article of this section, Venta Kabzems illustrates a specific instance of the impact of the social and political arenas on disability by examining how the education of students with disabilities over the years has been affected by the changing demography of disabilities, legislative changes, social policies, educational practices, public expenditures, and a shift in attitude toward disabilities.

In its focus on right to access – inclusive education – the reform movement has failed to provide clear directions for achieving academic learning outcomes in educational settings, causing the curriculum in an inclusive model of education to teeter between two opposing principles: access to curriculum content and academic learning. Kabzems explains this dilemma, in part, by pointing out that values and beliefs are more likely to effect changes in educational policy than is rationally conducted research driven by a need to improve the state of education. Further, historically, value judgments about which educational goals are worth pursuing and which support should be provided for students in schools have not emanated from persons with disabilities. Rather, legislators, families, advocates, and educational institutions have defined the identities, needs, and interests of disabled persons, particularly those with severe needs.

In further exploring the current educational climate for students with disabilities, Kabzems points out that until recently, special education was a growth industry. However, the range and distribution of educational services in an increasingly market-driven society have been affected as schools adopt the language of the marketplace. Thus, successful schools are defined by balanced budgets, cost-effective programs, and above-average examination results. The latter has serious implications for students with disabilities who bring additional funding to a school–a welcome trait–but may be seen as a liability if their achievement results are pooled with those of the whole school. Also, within a consumer-driven marketplace, programs for students with disabilities are likely to be cut or severely limited.

Kabzems takes the stand that advocates for full inclusion who invoke a civil rights model are wrong in assuming that students with disabilities do not have instructionally relevant needs that may require professionals with specialized training, specialized resources to support them in school, and sometimes even selective placement outside regular classes and schools. Public schools have an obligation to try to meet the educational needs of children, rather than just their social needs, or the political decisions of a family or community.

In addition to the needs of students, Kabzems also discusses the increasing demands placed on classroom teachers having to serve students in an inclusive model. These challenges are exacerbated by many teachers' lack of special training (or traditional training based on a deficit-driven model), and frequent less-than-positive attitudes toward their new roles. Kabzems concludes her discussion of the tensions and conflicting values that currently exist at many levels and among many of the stakeholders relative to the schooling of disabled students with a series of questions to which there is no one single or easy answer. What we have learned, however, is that when students with disabilities are treated differently in order to try to make them more like everyone else, separate does not make educational provision equal or equitable. Overemphasis on individual adaptations and planning has distracted attention from other options and new ways of thinking about disability.

Frank Rusch's reflective overview of the evolution that has taken place over the past three decades in our understanding of disabilities aligns personal and professional alignments, culminating in the realization that "We and They are the same people"– that persons with disabilities are more like persons without disabilities than they are different.

Rusch traces the evolution of the emerging concept of "sameness", starting with the 10-year time span 1968-1978. During this period, services to individuals with disabilities began to be influenced by the concepts of normalization, the competency-deviancy hypothesis, "illustrations of competence", and competitive employment. From previously having focused exclusively on what was different between persons with disabilities and persons without disabilities, human service providers began the important move away from the deficit-remediation model to recognizing that expectations held for the general population could also be considered "normal" expectations for persons with mental retardation.

This trend continued in the second of Rusch's three decades, 1978-1984, when social validation was incorporated with widespread use of applied behavior analysis, leading to greater emphasis on desired outcomes for individuals with disabilities in school, at work, and in the community. As a result, professionals began to question the overall effectiveness of traditional training programs on the lives of people with disabilities. The concern about outcomes led to a primary finding during the period 1984-present that indeed, traditional programs were not effective and that separate systems that promote segregation in our high schools and beyond do, in fact, position persons with disabilities for a life of dependency. The consequences of this realization may necessitate a major systems change, as we try to reform special education and adult human services, Rusch speculates.

Summing up the gradual move toward an emphasis on "sameness" for people with and without disabilities, Rusch concludes that using social validation as an empirical basis for investigating the abilities of persons with disabilities has made it increasingly clear that persons with disabilities are more like their peers without disabilities than they are different.

Henri-Jacques Stiker's anthropological analysis of the changing perspectives of disability over the centuries exhausts disability-as-difference as an analytic concept. Starting from the position that difference is inevitable – without difference everything would be merely repetition–Stiker traces disability as "difference" over the centuries. Based on this premise, according to Stiker, the question is not whether there are differences between people with and without disabilities, but rather how these differences are to be thought of, organized, and integrated into a modern democratic society.

Briefly, from antiquity to the classical age and the beginning of modernity, persons with disabilities were cast in a meta-social position, that is, they were viewed as being outside the economy, legislation, and everything else related to everyday living. Variously seen as an evil spell, and therefore totally abandoned, impure, jesters with a mystical connection to both the "great beyond" (God) and the underside of the world-evil-and paupers deserving of charity and alms, people with disabilities during this period prompted the question "What are they a sign of?"

Beginning in the seventeenth century, this question became "What are we to do with the disabled?", as a result of a social and political mindset that required rational explanations and order, not by looking outside itself as in previous times, but by resorting to science for answers. During this time, disability was viewed as madness, outside of reason. As such, individuals with disabled were seen as a threat, as a pretext for social division unless brought back to the standard of "normality". A means of doing that was found in education, beginning in the democratic principles of the eighteenth century and continuing to the present.

As a metaphor for the twentieth-century view of disability, Stiker analyzes the etymology and evolving use of the word "handicap", expanding his discussion to include language itself as a way of giving meaning to disability and the same-different conflict: Language is a system where all the elements are different, but can exist only through the very way they are related to each other. Returning to his fundamental premise, Stiker proposes that instead of sameness and difference, we talk about alterity, "otherness". This, he claims, would help prevent us from getting stuck in a fruitless attempt to reconcile demands, on the one hand, for assimilating the dissimilar other and, on the other hand, asserting difference to such an extent that we can no longer form a well-functioning society.

It is by wanting too badly to compare – in a vision of alterity that is too tightly linked to difference, according to Stiker – that one establishes conflicting relationships. Instead, as long as the Other is an Other, he or she is not entirely comparable. Translated to the current context, this would mean, suggests Stiker, that if we think of democratic integration, persons with disabilities may find a balance between hidden discrimination and an outward show of nondiscrimination.

David Pfeiffer explores our understanding of disability over the last three decades, summarized in what he calls variations of the disability paradigm as it is emerging from the civil rights movement. These variations are 'disability as social construct', 'disability as minority group', and 'disability as denial of equality'. Pfeiffer points to the problem of defining disability in view of these variations. He also points to the implications of the disability paradigm.

Disability Values, Representations and Realities*

Gary L. Albrecht

This chapter discusses the importance of cultural values in understanding and interpreting the place of persons with disabilities in a society where "all men are created equal". First I point out the salient values in American Society, place them in historical context and indicate the relations, tensions and tradeoffs between them. Comparisons will be made between groups in American society who share similar or hold different values. Second, I examine how cultural values undergird social norms, social networks, stratification systems, the division of labor (including gender, age and disability), and the organization of society. Third, the effect of values on the perception and lives of persons with disabilities will be explored. Specifically, values attributed to exclusion/inclusion; dependent/self-determined; physical vs. mental disabilities; visibility/invisibility; acting alone or belonging to the movement; and cultural sensitivity and competence will be examined within the disability and the larger community. Fourth, comparisons and contrasts will be made between the way people with disabilities are portrayed in the culture and the lives they actually experience. Finally, the consequences of living in a society with a certain set of values and tensions and of having a particular type of disability and life style will be explored.

"I lived the all-American dream until I was blind-sided by a drunk running a red light. I didn't know it at the time but my life just changed. I played high school football, graduated from Iowa, had a girl friend and job. I wanted to save some money, chill out, get married– have a house and kids. When I was first hurt, everybody was nice to me, but little by little they faded away. Everybody left me alone. One day I realized we all shared the same dream but I was different. I was in a wheelchair. They wouldn't let me live my dream with them. I had to make a new world for myself or die". (A 29-year-old man with paraplegia talking to other persons with disability in a Chicago focus group about his experiences with disability. June, 1995)

In laying out the fundamental rights of American citizens, the Bill of Rights asserts that "all men are created equal". The United States Constitution further guarantees that citizens will live in a political economic environment that is characterized by a democratic system where the rights of the individual are respected and protected. This emphasis on the individual includes the right to vote, freedom of speech, right to bear arms, representation in government, and freedom of religious belief. These fundamental values are wedded to a capitalist economy that emphasizes and rewards individual effort and theoretically permits persons to acquire education, accumulate personal wealth, and achieve a corresponding rise in social class (Thurow, 1996). Thus, in principle, it is possible for any person to become wealthy or President of the United States. However, in reality, this is often not the case.

Persons with disabilities live within a political economic system that grants them a set of basic rights based on equity but at the same time allows them to be treated as less than equal citizens; to be marginalized or excluded (Albrecht, 1992). This discrepancy points to the gap between the ideal and the lived experience for persons with disabilities. Equity and

---

* Work on this paper was supported by the Award for the Promotion of Human Welfare and the Institute on Disability and Human Development, University of Illinois at Chicago.

equality are not necessarily synonymous. *Equity* refers to the principle of fairness in human relationships whereas *equality* designates having the same rights and opportunities. The Americans with Disabilities Act of 1990, for example, reaffirms that persons with disabilities should be treated fairly in terms of access to education and jobs, yet cities, schools, and workplaces are architecturally constructed so that persons with disabilities cannot easily get to and function in classrooms, libraries or offices (Imrie, 1996). Even with laws in place and considerable money spent on making buildings accessible, persons with disabilities often have to enter lecture halls and offices by the back door or service entrance, if they are to get in at all. Once at the work site or classroom, they frequently confront inhospitable spaces, unrealistic expectations, and discriminatory attitudes from their peers and superiors.

To understand the place of persons with disabilities in society, it is important to examine the value structure of the nation and how it pertains to those with disabilities (Stiker, 1982; this volume). Since the experience of persons with disabilities is forcefully shaped by the media, the manner in which they are presented to others and others' reactions to them, public portrayal is also of enormous consequence to understanding the disability world. Moreover, the experienced reality of persons with disabilities is one of a struggle between dreams and realities and of dealing with the often misfitting representations and irritating hassles of everyday life.

This chapter focuses on the values, representations and realities confronted daily by persons with disabilities. It addresses the ways in which persons with disabilities are similar to and different from other citizens to understand their world more analytically and sensitively. The discussion considers the importance of cultural values in understanding and interpreting the place of persons with disabilities in a society where "all men are created equal" but are not always treated that way. First, I point out the salient values in American society, place them in historical context, and indicate the relations, tensions and trade-offs between them while also comparing them to the values found in major European countries. Second, comparisons and contrasts are made between the values and representations of people with disabilities and those of the larger American society. Finally, I examine the effect of these values and representations on the perceptions and lives of persons with disabilities. The chapter is based on cross-national research literature and on evidence accumulated from a number of different studies conducted by the author over the last five years.[1]

---

1   This paper is based on research and advocacy literature as well as interviews and focus groups conducted by the author over the last five years. These studies used field-work methods including ethnography, indepth interviews and focus groups with persons with disabilities, family members and their friends, and appropriate physicians in emergency departments, general medicine clinics, rehabilitation facilities and private practice. The goal was to ascertain how persons with disabilities sought help, presented their problems, were diagnosed and treated, and felt about their encounters with medical and social service staff. In addition, the author conducted 114 two-and-one-half hour interviews with persons with disabilities in the community to focus on their daily experiences and how best to understand their lives. The author also interviewed 64 key decision makers including senators and congressmen in Washington, D.C., national lobbyists, disability policy analysts, heads of national organizations for people with disabilities, leaders in the Independent Living Movement, disability activists, heath insurance managers, and administrators in rehabilitation services departments of the federal, state and local government. These personal and frequently "off the record" interviews were designed to capture how these leaders conceptualized the disability world, its problems, and solutions; the political pressures they felt; what actions they were taking to improve the quality of life for persons with disabilities; and, why they took the actions that they did. The analysis and discussion in the paper are based on these multiple data sources.

American Values

Values are the reflection of the ideologies that characterize the culture of a society (Aaron, 1994). Ideologies are "shared, relatively coherent interrelated sets of emotionally charged beliefs, values, and norms that bind some people together and help them to make sense of their worlds" (Trice & Beyer, 1993, p. 33). *Values* indicate the perceived worth of possessing a commodity or of having individual rights and responsibilities. Hechter (1992) adds that values are "relatively general and durable internal criteria for evaluation" (p. 217) to emphasize that values are relatively firm, internal to the individual, and persistent (Hechter, 1992, 1994). *Beliefs* are shared perceptions about how things work whereas *norms* are shared rules expressing how people are expected to behave.

While the strength of certain American values have changed over the years, the key values of the culture remain remarkably constant (DiMaggio, Evans, & Bryson, 1996). In studying values from 1946 to 1976, Williams (1970, 1979) identified five sets of American values and identified them as follows:

- Cluster I:
  - Competitive achievement and success
  - Activity and work
  - Efficiency and practicality
  - Science and secular rationality
- Cluster II: Individual personality and value of self
  - Freedom
  - Equality
  - Democracy
- Cluster III:
  - Progress
  - Material comfort
- Cluster IV:
  - Humanitarian customs
  - Moral orientation
- Cluster V:
  - Nationalism
  - Racism and group superiority
  - External conformity

The first value cluster highlights the primacy of individual achievement and work in the competitive American environment. This set of values is buttressed by the underlying Protestant ethic, the survival demands of a capitalist economy, and the fact that the early American population was recruited from the working classes of England, Ireland, and the European continent. Williams' analysis has been consistently supported by more recent research on American values (McClosky & Zaller, 1984; Meyer, 1993).

Kanter (1978) reports in the late 1970s, for example, that Americans view work as a source of self-respect and material success and that productive work is the basis for their belief in the rights of the individual, power, equity, and justice. Over the years, work has taken on a symbolic meaning in society as well. A paid job provides the individual with feelings of self-respect, independence, participation, and freedom (Yankelovich, 1979). In fact, work is such a central value in American society that 88% of people who win the lottery report that they want to continue working even though they do not have an economic need to do so (Harpaz, 1986). Within the work domain, practicality and efficiency are prized. Americans are most comfortable in a "can do", "bottom line"-oriented work environment. Thus, they generally look to short-term outcomes rather than long-term consequences in their work objectives.

The second cluster of values underlines the paramount importance of the individual in American society. In marked contrast to most European and Asian cultures, Americans stand for a "rugged individualism" in which self-reliance and a heightened sense of self dominate their reasons for action. People are expected to be self-sufficient: "I'm going to look out for number one first", and focus on self-fulfillment and growth at work. As a consequence, de Tocqueville noted as early as 1877 that individualism promoted social isolation and withdrawal of Americans from each other. This early development of individualistic cultural values laid the foundations for contemporary social policies dealing with those in need (Lipset, 1991). Thus, over one hundred years after de Tocqueville's analysis, Bellah et al. observed that people's notions of success were almost universally linked to perceptions of individual accomplishments in their work, measured in terms of earned income, job status, and projects completed (Bellah, Madsen, Sullivan, Swidler, & Tipton, 1985).

Work presents problems for many people with disabilities (Yellin, 1992; Yellin & Katz, 1994). Like the general population of working-age adults, the vast majority of persons with disabilities (79%) would like to work (Bristo, 1996). Yet, a 1994 Lou Harris poll indicates that two-thirds of working-age persons with disabilities are not working (Harris & Associates, 1995) and 82% of those who do work have part-time jobs that often do not offer adequate health or retirement benefits (Kraus, Stoddard, & Gilmartin, 1996). In addition, persons with disabilities earn up to 50% less per job than do members of the general population. As a consequence, **persons with disabilities do not have the opportunity to work or to engage in the type of jobs that will give them self-respect and permit them to be independent.** They are structurally prevented from living the work ethic expressed in value cluster I and the independence implied in value cluster II.

The third cluster of salient American values centers on an irrepressible optimism and belief in the improvement of the human condition. From the admonition of Horace Greeley, "Go West young man, go West", to the unwavering conviction of Bill Gates that Microsoft can lead the way into the world's electronic future and improve the lives of billions of people in the process, most Americans are convinced that their country is the "best" in the world and will lead by industrious example. As a result, naysayers are often told, "love it or leave it". "Where else is there to go"? "It may not be perfect, but it's all we've got".

Coupled with this optimism and focused self-confidence is the expression of success through conspicuous consumption and material possessions. A popular adult T-shirt seen on the streets during the last summers reads, "The guy with the most toys wins". Whether one looks at the spaciousness of American houses, the number and types of cars, clothing sales per person, or the purchase of electronic goods, Veblen's (1899) observations about Americans as conspicuous consumers holds today. Individual status and worth are often measured in purchasing patterns and material possessions evaluated both in volume and recognizable brand names.

The fourth cluster of values illustrates an inherent contradiction in the American value system. Whereas the first three clusters emphasize competition and individualism, this fourth cluster expresses a humanitarianism and moral concern for the plight of others. In historical context, this apparent conflict has been resolved by successful individuals first earning significant wealth and social position *and then* giving money to charities for the public good.

Andrew Carnegie, for example, gave money for libraries across the land only after he had amassed an incredible fortune. The Ford, Rockefeller, and Carnegie Foundations are other examples of this behavior pattern.

The value of humanitarianism, which seems to be at odds with the values of material success and individualism, causes considerable conflict and consternation to American citizens. They are not comfortable with the wealthiest nation on earth having major problems with the homeless, neglected children, and elderly persons. Thomas Jefferson, the major architect of the American Constitution, lived daily with a similar quandary. In principle, he did not believe in slavery and indeed wanted to abolish it. At the same time, he realized that he would have to dramatically change his life-style and give up his beloved Monticello, if he gave freedom to his slaves. In the end, he kept his slaves and Monticello but often mentioned his moral dilemma. Today's young entrepreneurs face similar value conflicts. Many have accumulated substantial power and wealth but have not yet demonstrated the *noblesse oblige* of earlier generations. And, like Jefferson, people today also have considerable difficulty in reconciling their actual behavior with their moral pronouncements. Such dilemmas of moral choice are being played out in the current debates over social security and welfare reform.

The fifth value cluster centers on ethnocentrism favoring American culture. On the whole, this is expressed in strong nationalism and patriotic displays on American holidays and at trigger events such as the Gulf War. Except for Australians, Americans report less desire to live in other countries than people from other cultures (Trice & Beyer, 1993). More recently, Americans have questioned their responsibility to contribute to the United Nations and to repeatedly send armed forces abroad to assist in peace-keeping and humanitarian missions. These ethnocentric values can lead to isolationism, limited knowledge and appreciation of other cultures, a narrow view of world events, and unwillingness to remain a world leader in diplomatic and peace keeping initiatives.

Domestically, ethnocentrism is expressed through themes of racism, preference for the Anglo culture, ageism, sexism, and general dominant-group superiority. This is a disturbing tendency because the nation has been a significant melting pot and demographic data indicate that close to 50% of the population and the adult labor force in 2020 will be composed of non-Anglo citizens. To be competitive in a world-wide marketplace and adapt to the changing demographics in the labor force, American companies will have to include more members of minority groups, women, and workers from other countries. For these reasons, many employers have developed training programs to understand and promote multicultural diversity (Cox, 1991). In addition, large international companies headquartered in the United States have established policies to send their managers abroad for experience and to bring managers from other countries to the United States to promote a better understanding of operating in a world-wide marketplace and developing a work-force with the competencies and experience to do so.

In the disability arena, ethnocentrism is expressed in aversion to persons with disabilities, conflict over abortion of defective fetuses, and advocacy of euthanasia for those with severe disability or pain. Disability is an additional burden for women, members of non-white racial/ethnic groups, and the poor who already face considerable discrimination and stigma. Having a disability usually marks individuals and marginalizes them.

Research by Bengston in California between 1971 and 1986 indicates that the fundamental values discussed above are unlikely to change over time or across generations (Bengston, 1989). In his study, the younger generation expressed higher levels of individualism and lower level of humanitarianism than their grandparents, but the remarkable conclusion was that values remain relatively constant within and between groups. This conclusion is supported by considerable survey work on American public opinions over the last 50 years (Campbell, Converse, Miller, & Stokes, 1960; Inglehart, 1977; Page & Shapiro, 1992). While there have been modifications in the expression of these core American values influenced by social and political circumstances over the last two hundred years, the underlying values persist (Varenne, 1986). Lipset notes, for example, that affirmative action was advocated as a compensatory action for previous discrimination to allow minorities into the competitive capitalistic system and second, that America stands out among Western nations in the low level of support it provides for the people who are poor or disabled through welfare and health care policies (Lipset, 1991, 1996). Yet, he concludes that these actions have not basically modified the emphasis on individual success and equality of opportunity. When taken in concert, these studies and data suggest that the American value system is well defined and stable, favors members of the larger group, encourages introspection, is suspicious of outsiders or those with differences, and places emphasis on the individual over the group (DiMaggio, Evan, & Bryson, 1996).

These same general clusters of values and temporal patterns persist when we examine specific items in opinion polls on "hot topics" that operationalize the more general American values. In an analysis of a series of national surveys on public opinion, for example, Shafer and Claggett (1995) discovered through factor-analytic techniques that items measuring opinions on current "hot button" concerns clustered into six groups: (a) cultural values measured by such items as "School boards ought to have the right to fire teachers who are known homosexuals"; (b) social welfare issues indicated by such items as, "It is the responsibility of government to take care of people who can't take care of themselves", and "Our society should do what is necessary to make sure that everyone has an equal opportunity to succeed"; (c) foreign relations pointed to by statements like, "Cutting back federal spending for defense and military strength"; (d) social insurance indicated by questions like, "Spending on social security"; (e) civil rights symbolized by the item, "We have gone too far in pushing equal rights in this country"; and, (f) civil liberties measured by the item, "Freedom of speech should not be extended to groups like the Communist party or the Klu Klux Klan". On careful scrutiny, the six clusters of salient issues identified by Shafer and Claggett closely mirror the sets of dominant values identified earlier by Williams and confirmed by numerous later surveys (Page & Shapiro, 1992; Stimson, 1991; Williams, 1979).

These same clusters and patterns are also apparent in opinion surveys about American health and welfare issues. In a recent study, Fuchs (1996) identified 20 key questions to measure the attitudes of expert health economists, theoretical economists, and practicing physicians about health care delivery and reform. He employed such questions as: "The high cost of health care in the United States makes U.S. firms less competitive in the global economy than others" and "The U.S. should now enact some law that covers the entire population". Respondents were interested in these questions but had major disagreement over what position to take on policy-value questions. Fuchs concluded that the range in opinion over what actions to take was due in large part to differences in values among these groups of people. In summarizing his work, Fuchs suggested that the United States is the only major industrialized nation not to have national health insurance because of a distrust of government, a heterogeneity in the population, and a weak sense of *noblesse oblige.*

Some of these themes are picked up in the work of Angell (1993), Etizioni (1996), and Hay (1988) who point out that although major American values are the same for most citizens, they get expressed differently depending on one's social class, membership in a community, and belief in communitarianism. In general, the privileged, the healthy and the wealthy have more sympathy for values of rugged individualism, each person for himself/herself and a decreased role for government in health and welfare programs. Yet, while there are differences in the expression of values among cultural subgroups and social classes throughout these focused studies, the underlying American values are remarkably stable and persistent over time and across groups. Differences between groups lie in their perceived relative importance and concrete expressions of values in programs and policies.

While the humanitarian aspects of this value system are encouraging and supportive of persons with disabilities, there are many potentially troubling features of the American value system. Ethnocentrism is a particularly disturbing feature for persons with disabilities because they are different from the larger group of American citizens. They have developed their own sets of subcultures that are not fully appreciated or understood by the larger society. People with disabilities are often not in the position of being able to participate in an unrestricted fashion in the labor force. They do not have the same earning potential and status as others, and therefore are at risk for discrimination or being treated as token members of minority groups merely to fulfill government quotas. Furthermore, persons with disabilities often need to rely on others; to belong to groups to maximize their quality of life. Clearly, emphasis on groups over the individual runs against some of the dominant values in American culture.

Contrasts with Europe

By contrast, **European nations, while also espousing democratic values, are more benign to those is need, have more comprehensive and complete health and welfare systems, and manifest less extreme differences in income distribution in society and in services available to those in need such as the unemployed, poor, women, children, and people with disabilities** (Ardigó, 1995). In a comparative study, Evans (1995) examined similarities and differences in public attitudes toward (a) social assistance, (b) full employment, (c) minimum wage legislation, and (d) the general principle of redistribution of income to make inequalities within a country less severe. In comparing Australia, Switzerland, the Netherlands, Great Britain, West Germany, Austria, Italy, and Hungary to the United States on all four issues, he discovered that the United States is exceptional in that respondents in national surveys were generally less committed to redistributive welfare policies than respondents in any of the other nations. While he found some social class differences expressed in self-interest (the lower more so than the higher social classes support income redistribution across all countries), the more important explanation for differences between the United States and other countries in attitudes towards redistribution of income were American beliefs that inequality is necessary for efficiency, that all Americans have an opportunity to get ahead, and that social position and connections are not important ways of getting ahead.

These expressions of underlying values towards the redistribution of income are reflected in actual income distribution within the United States and the major European countries. For example, when comparing earnings dispersion for males over an 18-year period for France, Germany, Italy, Great Britain, Australia, Canada, Sweden and Japan, Nickell and Bell (1995) found that income dispersion across workers is much larger in the United States than for any other country. Thus, attitudes, values, and actual income dispersion show very consistent patterns cross-nationally when comparing the United States with major European countries.

The United States in all instances is more tolerant of inequities. American reformers have focused on these inequalities in calling for the development of a more communitarian approach to social policy (Etzioni, 1996), the cultivation of a moral sense (Wilson, 1993), and developing a new values framework for reconfiguring American health care (Priester, 1992). Regardless of good intentions, however, the actual public opinion and behavior present a formidable challenge to people with disabilities.

Values of Persons with Disabilities

People with disabilities experience a general tension between their personal values and the values of the larger society (Whyte, 1995). Their daily experiences are complicated for, on the one hand, they share the values of other Americans while, on the other hand, they develop their own set of values shaped by their experiences with disability. As a consequence, they often modify their own values in light of experience and are frustrated by the structural strain generated between the values espoused by the larger society and the formidable barriers that prevent them from living out the values of the larger society (Anderson, 1986; Chermak, 1991).

In such instances, the culture itself has the power to disable (McDermott & Varenne, 1995). As one young woman in the United States related, "After my multiple sclerosis was diagnosed, I decided to tell my best friend, Emily. Since high school, we shared all of our secrets. I said, Emily, I'm scared because I just found out that I have M.S., but I feel lucky because I have good friends and I'll be able to keep on working. Emily said, 'I'm so sorry, Jenny. Now you won't be able to come skiing with us any more or get married and have kids.' Her words cut me like a knife. I knew I'd have to make new friends".

In a similar vein, a 31-year-old African-American man with epilepsy exploded: "I'm so pissed off. I'm controlling my epilepsy with medicine. The rehab people sent me to school to learn computer programming, but nobody 'll hire me because they're afraid of me – a black man with epilepsy. None of those fuckers wants to hire me. So I just sit home and rot". His rehab counselor said to me: "James has given up hope. Society says that you only have value if you work. We told him that we would get him a job, if he learned how to use computers. He worked hard in school, became good, but no employer would have him when they found out about the possible insurance risk. What are we supposed to tell him now"?

As in the larger society, persons with disabilities share some core values. At the same time, there is considerable variation in values, outlooks, and perspectives (Westbrook, Legge, & Pennay,1993). Based on the evidence of multiple studies and my ethnographies and interviews, people with disabilities express different sets of values depending on whether or not they are activists in the movement, are participating members of the disability community, acknowledge themselves as having a disability but are not active in the disability community, are isolated from any community, or try to hide their disability and pass as persons without disabilities. Within each of these groups of people with disabilities there are those who are perceived as deviant and those who are accepted into the group.

Many people with disabilities want to have the opportunity to be independent; to work and live a full life. As a young woman with low vision working in a human resources department of a community agency said: "We don't want a handout or to be on the welfare rolls. We just want an opportunity to work; to carry our own weight and take care of ourselves. All we ask for is some help to get started and to be given a fair shot like anybody else". A veteran of the Gulf War with chronic respiratory problems similarly related: "I was proud to serve my country and don't ask for any special favors. I've been treated well and we all owe our country. My boss took me back but my breathing acts up when it gets hot and polluted. The V.A. has been O.K. to me but I get god damned mad when nobody believes that the air wasn't filled with shit that'd about kill ya. Where were they when I was fighting in the desert"?

While most of the people I interviewed shared the larger American values of work, individualism, patriotism, and self-reliancy, a few deviated from this norm. In one rehabilitation facility, I noticed that two people were not improving in physical function as were the others. When I asked them why not, the man is his middle 50s responded: "If I get better, I'll have to go back to my mind-killing job in a sweat shop. If I don't get better, I can go home and collect. I'll get more for not working than for working. Do you think I'm crazy"? The other, a young paraplegic male man said, "I'm not going to go out in the work world and have people laugh at me for peeing in a plastic bottle and rolling around in a wheelchair. No way, I'm going home and live with my parents".

Finding a place in the disability community seems to fill a vacuum for many. As a middle-aged woman with two teenaged children remarked: "I was seriously depressed for over three years but no one took me seriously. My husband kicked me out of the house, divorced me, and kept the kids. I was really down until I found a self-help group for people with chronic depression. They taught me to fight, supported me when I was at rock bottom, and helped me put my life back together. I did the work but they showed me the way. Unless you've been there, you don't know. My old friends didn't have a clue. You can't work or be a mom until you get help with your depression. I had to choose between living and dying. Everything else had to wait". A man with spinal cord injury acquired in a violent automobile accident recounted: "Finding the disability community gave me a whole new purpose and meaning in life. We have to remind the public that they owe us a chance. We have rights and will help each other stick up for them. I couldn't fight by myself but I can with other people who have disabilities. They understand".

Other persons with disabilities avoid the disability community altogether. A recent college graduate said: "I didn't want to be seen with all of those people. When you look at me, I look normal. Nobody knows that I can't hear very well. I can get along without any of their help and I don't want to be like them". People like this man want to pass without being marked as a person with a disability. They try to avoid the label and the stigma of being called disabled by covering their impairment. Others just wanted to be out of the public eye. For example, a woman in her 50s with Parkinson's Disease confided: "If I went out with the people in that bunch, everybody would be staring at us as we demonstrated or pushed for our rights. I'm afraid of crowds and scared of people pointing at me or feeling sorry for me. I don't like people to be mad at me. I just want to stay home and make the best out of my life. My husband and kids take care of me and I don't want to be the screaming advocate I see on TV. I don't want to be on TV. I just want to be left alone where I'm comfortable".

Value conflicts are discovered and are exacerbated when persons with disabilities realize that the public does not treat all persons with disability alike (Albrecht, Walker, & Levy, 1982). **They experience differential acceptance and discrimination depending on their race/ethnicity, type of disability, sex, ability to work, and the subculture of the person they are dealing with** (Anderson, 1986; Longmore, 1987). Australian researchers, for example, asked health practitioners (N=665) in Anglo-Australian, Arabic, Chinese, Italian, German, and Greek communities to rate the attitudes of people in their communities toward

20 disability groups (Westbrook, et al., 1993). While the German community was the most and the Arabic community the least accepting of people with disabilities, the community ratings did not differ much. In all communities, people with AIDS, mental retardation, mental illness, and cerebral palsy were less accepted than those with asthma, diabetes, and heart disease. These findings confirm those discovered earlier in the United States (Albrecht et al., 1982).

People with disabilities are frustrated when they confront such differential evaluations among groups. A young woman in her late 20s lamented: "Why do people treat my friend Susan who has AIDS so much worse than they treat her sister who had an operation for breast cancer. Susan got AIDS from a blood transfusion in the hospital. She didn't ask for it. Neither did her sister ask for breast cancer". Differential discrimination is particularly apparent to those with mental illness. A mother and father complained: "We can't understand our old friends and relatives. When our son, Byron, had a nervous breakdown after his wife died in a terrible accident, they avoided him like the plague. You would think that he had leprosy. Anyone would have been crushed under that grief and being left alone with two young children. We just had to help him on our own". These differences in attitudes and behaviors reflect underlying differences in the evaluations that people make of those with different types of disabilities.

Value conflicts among those in the disability community are also noticeable. People with disabilities sometimes argue among themselves about who has a disability. In a Veteran's Administration (V.A.) Hospital, for example, a Korean War veteran who had lost his right leg and the toes on his left foot due to frost bite in a winter campaign near the Chinese border sneered: "That guy over there is a fake. He's supposed to have some nerve problem but he's not nuts. He just wants to collect his monthly check and not have to work. Look at me. I'm really disabled. I've lost a leg. Anybody can see that".

This evaluation highlights the difference in judgments made about those with visible impairments and those whose impairments are not readily visible. Those with visible impairments have an easier time claiming to be disabled than those who do not. Similarly, people with physical disabilities usually stick together and are rarely found with people with mental illnesses. According to their evaluative framework, a visible, physical impairment gives one a better claim to disability. Furthermore, visible, physical disabilities reduce ambiguity in judgment and do not disrupt social interaction in the way that mental illness or severe communicative disorders do.

Just as judgments are made among persons with disabilities about who has a "true" disability, groups of individuals with specific disabilities often bond together in organizations seeking their own goals without including all disability groups. For years, the disability community was divided into a multitude of associations that usually went their own way. Such groups as the Paralyzed Veterans of America, the National Foundation for the Blind, the National Head Injury Foundation, "Jerry's Kids" (muscular dystrophy), National Easter Seal Society, and the American Heart Association made only temporary liaisons to achieve short-term goals. As one president of a national association confided "off the record", "Until the Americans with Disabilities Act came along, we thought that we could do better by arguing for our own constituency. We did not want to have to include ourselves with all of the other disability groups. We thought that we would lose our identity and ability to raise money. If you concentrate on one disability, you have a clear image and identity to sell. Also, not every disability is popular. We knew that if we joined forces with groups advocating for those with HIV/AIDS and mental illness, we would lose much of our traditional support. Therefore, we stayed focused on our group".

Another executive of a national association for a disability group pointed out: "Not all disabilities are alike. Some are more acceptable to the general public and easier to sell. People want to help children and those who were not responsible for their disability". These remarks suggest that **not all disability groups share the same values and approaches for representing those with disabilities to legislatures, the government, and the public.**

This analysis suggests that people with disabilities share the same fundamental values of the country as other citizens but that these values are frequently shaped by their own experiences and the type of disability they have. Second, people with disabilities often find that it is impossible to act on their values and achieve their goals because society has placed insurmountable barriers in their way. Or, to act on their values and achieve their dreams would require an heroic effort, unrealistic for the typical person with disability who has limited resources. Third, people with disabilities are not a homogeneous lot. They share many values and experiences among themselves and with the general public, but there are considerable differences and variations that are not always appreciated. Fourth, while disability groups seem to share the same values and work towards similar goals, there is a marked self-interest and focus on specific disabilities rather than on *all* persons with disabilities. Finally, persons with disabilities like most other people seek out those with whom they share similar values and with whom they feel the most comfortable.

Representations and Realities

Values are reflected in the ways persons with disabilities present themselves to others and are represented in public arenas. **Given the emphasis on rugged individualism and self-sufficiency in the United States, there is considerable pressure on persons with disabilities to present themselves as "can do" people.** John Kemp, Executive Director of United Cerebral Palsy Associations, is such a person (Fleming, 1995). Kemp was born a congenital, quadruple amputee. His mother died of ovarian cancer when he was 15 months old. John Kemp is an example of a person with disabilities who overcame numerous obstacles to achieve national prominence for his leadership and executive abilities, being photographed with presidents of the United States and leaders of industry and Congress. Kemp was active in athletics as a youngster, graduated from Georgetown University, and completed a law degree in two and one half years. He rose through the ranks of the National Easter Society until he was selected Executive Director of the United Cerebral Palsy Associations in 1990. He was actively involved in the passage of the ADA. Kemp credits much of his success to his father, who reared him after the death of his mother. As he was struggling with little league baseball, "My dad took me aside and stood me up and said, 'You're going to have to face a terrible reality. All the other kids will be bigger, stronger, and throw faster.' I didn't believe it then. I'm just as good, I said. But sure enough, I learned. My dad had to dose me with reality".

The example of John Kemp illustrates the tensions that people with disabilities feel when trying to make their way in a society that demands individual achievement but constructs extraordinary barriers in the way of access to schools and jobs, inaccessible work spaces, unadapted public transportation, and discriminatory attitudes towards people with impairments. While John Kemp is a success story illustrating that people with disabilities can achieve anything they want, not everyone is a John Kemp. Many people with disabilities do not have his talent, determination, or such a father.

Yet the tensions between the value sets and opportunity structures remain. In health care journals and magazines for people with disabilities, advertisements for wheelchairs and prosthetics often show young, beautiful world-class athletes with the equipment suggesting that "You too can look and achieve like this if only you buy and use our equipment". Articles in the press reinforce this image. For example, a piece written on Dennis Oehler, the Gold Medal winner of 100 meter dash in the Paralympics in 1986, reads "Athlete's world-class achievements inspire others to overcome obstacles" (Flanagan, 1995, p. 2).

Such people can be a role model for persons with disabilities, but more often than not these incredibly lofty standards are discouraging for the ordinary individual or do not take into account socially imposed obstacles to success. As a young paraplegic mother lamented: "I feel so inadequate when I read about these people. I get discouraged. I'd like to do more than I do but I'm not Superwoman. Besides how can I raise two girls, have dinner on the table for my husband, and build a promising career at the same time"?

People with disabilities need more than space-age assistive technologies and world-class roles models. They need to have an enabling environment; the resources and opportunities to succeed. To be effective, role models need to be realistic – people with whom the majority can identify and emulate. The ordinary person with disabilities cannot hope to achieve without being enabled; being allowed to achieve and given the resources for doing so.

Finally, there are many who have such serious disabilities that they cannot hope to meet the standards of being completely independent or self-sufficient. Does that mean that they have no value? A 61-year-old grandmother who was severely limited with osteoarthritis said: "I'm worth something because I show my children and husband that life is worth living to the full every day. Living cheerfully without continually complaining is what I can give others".

Also, holding up middle-class, Anglo role models and life paths does little for the inner-city gang member who was cut down by a paralyzing bullet. As a young man mused: "Give me a fucking break. If the white man wouldn't let me make it in his world when I was a 22 years old and healthy. How the hell am I supposed to believe he'll let me in now that I'm in a wheelchair and on welfare and disability"? This man could see through the hype to what he could realistically expect.

At this point, it is useful to return to another level of analysis: cross-national values and the realities of citizens living under different social welfare systems. According to existing stereotypes, in the United States there is an optimism and harsh reality while in Western Europe there is a pessimism and soft reality. Analysis reveals that there is considerable support for these stereotypes but that the European model is becoming increasingly unsustainable. The difficult question then remains, what are nations to do to fulfill their social contracts while maintaining a competitive economy in the world market? This is an intractable problem for Western countries. **American welfare and social security systems reflect the nation's cultural values, which express individual optimism until people discover that their needs are unmet or they fall through the alleged "safety net".** The result is that they are confronted with a harsh reality. The wealthy and the middle class in the United States frequently think that they are protected from such problems. A couple attending a Cancer Survivors meeting in Washington, D.C., provided a poignant case study that indicates otherwise. "Recurrent cancer has changed our lives. Margaret and I were living the American dream. We had raised our children, put them through college and saw them married. We owned two houses, two expensive cars and traveled a lot together. I was executive vice President of.....earning a large salary with generous stock options. Margaret had a good job in the human resource management department of... We were sailing along enjoying life. But our world changed. We lost everything and almost got a divorce. Now we are in business for ourselves, in debt and self-insured. No business will hire either one of us. We can't get health insurance. Margaret discovered that she had breast cancer. After the first recurrence and third operation, she was fired during a reorganization. After a year, she was without insurance and she couldn't get another job with health benefits when employers found out about her medical history. About the same time after her second operation, I found out that I had cancer of the colon and the same damn thing happened to me. I was fired and couldn't get a job with health insurance. No one would hire me when they heard about our cancer. We had to sell everything. We had to deal with medical bills and go into business for ourselves. We have nothing; nobody to rely on and the cancer won't go away. Margaret had two more operations and I have had two. Boy, did we change our views. Everything is great as long as you have no problems. Then, they chew you up and spit you out. We were almost broken".

At the other end of the social spectrum people are less shocked. They live with insecurity every day. An older African-American man in the emergency department of Cook County Hospital said: "You white folks think that the system won't fuck you over until some shit happens to you. Then ya find out they don't want you if you is damaged goods. You'll have to come to here like me".

In Western European countries people with disabilities are more pessimistic than Americans about their futures, but they also experience a more comprehensive and integrated social welfare system that cares for their basic needs. A young man in Paris with paraplegia as the result of an automobile accident reflected: "I get discouraged about ever being able to go back to work or have a girlfriend. My friends are good to me but I don't know what I'm going to do". But, when asked, if he was worried about medical care or having money to live on, he said: "No, I have had everything paid for and I get money to live on from the government".

The problem in the United States is providing a minimum standard universal coverage. This is a key issue in the ongoing debate over health care reform. Indeed, many states and the federal government are enacting strategies to limit social welfare benefits so that these costs and future risk exposures can be limited (National Governor's Association staff, 1995). These moves are taking place in an environment where the United States ranks only 11th among the 18 major European countries and Canada in terms of the average benefit costs expended per worker in the manufacturing sector of the economy (Harris, 1996).While these actions move people off welfare rolls who could in fact work, they also punish many in need, including those with disabilities. As a consequence, citizens are increasingly asking how a great nation like the United States can have no effective "safety net" for those in need.

The problem in Western Europe is different; it is paying for the social welfare benefits that are already in place when world economic pressures are forcing production costs down. In recent surveys of national competitiveness in the world marketplace, only Luxembourg among European Union members made the top 10 in the World Economic Forum's study (Malkin, 1996). This is in part due to high labor costs and generous fringe benefits. For example, when a German company hires a German worker, it must pay benefits that total 85% of salary. This makes labor costs in Germany about $27.00 an hour or almost 50% higher than in the United States (Glassman, 1996). At the same time, European unemployment rates are high: Spain over 20%, Belgium 13.4%, France 11.9%, and Denmark 9.1%. The unemployment benefits in these countries are more generous than those in the United States.

While the scenarios are different for the United States and Europe, the compelling dilemma of how to provide a "safety net" for all citizens under increasingly competitive economic pressures is unavoidable for politicians and the voting public. This is a major tension in modern nations between the democratic values and the pressures of the free market under capitalism. This general problem is a fertile area for research.

Conclusion

The consequences of these values, representations, and realities for persons with disabilities are enormous. There are strong and complex connections between culture, the values of society, and the way that disability is experienced on a personal level. People with disabilities in some ways have more in common with one another across national and cultural boundaries than they do with the able-bodied citizens of their own cultures. On the other hand, persons with disabilities are captured by their own cultures; they live their disabilities within the context of their own culture.

On the individual level, persons with disabilities are similar to others in their general values but they have evolved their own concrete expression of these values depending on their experiences, type of disability, demographic characteristics and available resources. Persons with disabilities are not a homogenous group. Just as there are similarities and differences between persons with disabilities and other citizens so there are marked differences between different persons with disabilities. Therefore, **concluding that persons with disabilities are totally different from others or that all persons with disabilities belong to some homogenous group is erroneous. Programs based on such assumptions are doomed to failure.**

To understand these complexities, Schein (1996) suggests that researchers immerse themselves in fieldwork where they can observe individuals acting within their own and different cultural contexts. The purpose of such contextualized observations is to generate concepts and theory inductively that incorporate the viewpoints and experiences of persons with disabilities into the categorization and interpretation of their behavior. This approach cautions against prematurely applying existing concepts to the complex interplay of individuals in their cultural context. Instead, a grounded theory is developed that is sensitive to the relationships between experienced reality, representations, and culture as viewed by persons with disabilities.

On the national level, we discovered that social welfare systems reflect the underlying values of the country. In the United States, a core value set can be identified that has held together over time. For all of the social change and cultural diversity in the United States, it is remarkable that the fundamental values expressed by the people have remained reasonably constant. These value sets exhibit conflicts between emphasis on rugged individualism and humanitarianism. In this culture, the extremes of capitalism clash with concerns for the needy. In comparing values in the U.S. with those in Western Europe, it is clear that democracy has different operational forms and expressions of values.

The American social welfare system is a patchwork, with numerous holes allowing many citizens with serious health and disability problems to fall to the bottom where they languish without security in a poor quality of life. Universal health coverage would be one mechanism to remedy this situation but that solution has not met with overwhelming support. On the other hand, Western European countries have a different form of democracy that puts more importance on the group and community responsibility. This is seen in the extensive and integrated social welfare programs that are in force. The problem facing European nations today is paying for these programs, and they, like the United States are under intense financial pressures to cut social welfare programs. They must balance their budgets as they anticipate entry into the European Community. They also are concerned with keeping their economies competitive in the world markets.

We have seen that there are similarities and differences between the United States and Western European countries with regard to the ways they treat persons with disabilities. Without exception, a nation's programs for persons with disabilities mirror the values of the country and the way in which they interpret the social contract between government and the people. Therefore, it is unlikely that there will ever be some uniform model that all nations will adopt. Rather, each country will evolve its own policies based on its particular cultural values, economy, and will of the people. Reconciling the conflict between publicly espoused democratic values that suggest equity for all citizens with the persistent experience of inequality remains a critical problem in Western societies. This issue gets played out in the daily lives of persons with disabilities.

Values, representations, and realities are essential conceptual building blocks for the emerging field of disability studies because they provide the assumptions and the context within which the experiences of persons with disabilities can be understood and interpreted (Devlieger, 1995). These concepts are necessary components of any theories modeling the place of people with disabilities in society and generating effective disability policy. This discussion raised numerous questions for research concerning the similarities and differences between Western nations in their treatment of persons with disabilities. Careful analysis of these similarities and differences within and between countries will lead to better theory, research, and practice.

References Cited

Aaron, H.J. (1994). Distinguished lecture on economics in government: Public policy, values and consciousness. *Journal of Economic Perspectives, 8*(2), 3-21.

Albrecht, G.L. (1992). *The disability business; Rehabilitation in America.* Newbury Park, CA: Sage.

Albrecht, G.L., Walker, V.G., & Levy, J.A. (1982). Social distance from the stigmatized: A test of two theories. *Social Science and Medicine, 16*, 1319-1327.

Anderson, J.M. (1986). Ethnicity and illness experience: Ideological structures and the health care delivery system. *Social Science and Medicine, 22*, 1277-1283.

Angell, M. (1993). Privilege and health – What is the connection? *The New England Journal of Medicine, 329*, 126-127.

Ardigó, A. (1995). Public attitudes and changes in health care systems: A confrontation and a puzzle. In O. Borre & E. Scarbrough (Eds.), *The scope of government* (pp. 388-406). Oxford: Oxford University Press.

Bellah, R.N., Madsen, R., Sullivan, W.M., Swidler, A., & Tipton, S.M. (1985). *Habits of the heart.* New York: Harper and Row, Publishers.

Bengston, V.L. (1989). The problem of generations: Age group contrasts, continuities, and social change. In V.L. Bengston & L.W. Schaie (Eds.), *The course of later life: Research and reflections* (pp. 126-141). New York: Springer Publishing.

Bristo, M. (1996). *Achieving independence: The challenge for the 21*st *century*. Washington, DC: The National Council on Disability.

Campbell, A., Converse, P.E., Miller, W.E., & Stokes, D.E. (1960). *The American voter*. New York: Wiley.

Chermak, G.D. (1991). A global perspective on disability: A review of efforts to increase access and advance social integration for disabled persons. *International Disability Studies, 12* 123-127.

Cox, T., Jr. (1991). The multicultural organization. *The Academy of Management Executives, 5* (2), 34-47.

Devlieger, P. (1995). Why disabled? The cultural understanding of physical disability in an African society. In B. Ingstad & S.R. Whyte (Eds.), *Disability and culture* (pp. 94-106). Berkeley: University of California Press.

de Tocqueville, A. (1877). *Democracy in America: Republic of the United States of America and its political institutions*. New York: Barnes.

DiMaggio, P., Evans, J., & Bryson, B. (1996). Have Americans' social attitudes become more polarized? *American Journal of Sociology, 102*, 690-755.

Etzioni, A. (1996). The responsive community: A communitarian perspective. *American Sociological Review, 61*, 1-11.

Evans, G. (1995). Why is America different: Explaining cross-national variation in support for welfare distribution. *Working Paper Series, Centre for Research into Elections and Social Trends, Nuffield College, The University of Oxford, 36*, 1-28.

Flanagan, D.M. (1995). Seeing is Believing: Dennis Oehler. *In Motion, 5*, 12-13.

Fleming, M.B. (1995). In empowering people with disabilities, the direction is UP! *In Motion, 5*, 24-29.

Fuchs, V.R. (1996). Economics, values and health care reform. *American Economic Review, 86* (1), 1-24.

Glassman, J.K. (1996). There's still time to stop the "germanization" of America. *International Herald Tribune, 35224* (May 30), 8.

Harpaz, I. (1986,). *A multinational perspective on the current state of the work ethic*. Paper presented at the Academy of Management, Chicago.

Harris, A. (1996). Why Clinton is enjoying the recovery planned for Bush. *The Times* (June 13), 29.

Harris, L., & Associates. (1995). *The NOD/Harris survey on employment of people with disabilities*. New York: Lou Harris & Associates.

Hay, D.I. (1988). Socioeconomic status and health status. *Social Science and Medicine, 27*, 37-325.

Hechter, M. (1992). Should values be written out of the social scientist's lexicon? *Sociological Theory, 10*, 214-230.

Hechter, M. (1994). The role of values in rational choice theory. *Rationality and Society, 6*, 318-333.

Imrie, R. (1996). *Disability and the city*. New York: St. Martin's Press.

Inglehart, R. (1977). *The silent revolution: Changing values and political styles among Western Publics*. Princeton, NJ: Princeton University Press.

Kanter, R.M. (1978). The long-term trends in work values. *Daedelus, 107*(1), 51-59.

Kraus, L.E., Stoddard, S., & Gilmartin, D. (1996). *Chartbook on disability in the United States, 1996*. Washington, DC: National Institute on Disability and Rehabilitation Research.

Lipset, S.M. (1991). American exceptionalism reaffirmed. In B.E. Shafer (Ed.), *Is America different? A new look at American exceptionalism* (pp. 231-258). Oxford: Clarendon Press.

Lipset, S.M. (1996). *American exceptionalism: A double edged sword*. New York: W.W. Norton and Company.

Longmore, P.K. (1987). Uncovering the hidden history of people with disabilities. *Review of American History, 15*, 355-364.

Malkin, L. (1996). Ranking potential growth: West European competitiveness seen slipping. *International Herald Tribune, 35224* (May, 30), 13.

McClosky, H., & Zaller, J. (1984). *The American ethos: Public attitudes toward capitalism and democracy*. Cambridge, MA: Harvard University Press.

McDermott, R., & Varenne, H. (1995). Culture as disability. *Anthropology and Education Quarterly, 26*, 324-348.

Meyer, W.G. (1993). *The changing American mind: How and why American public opinion changed between 1960 and 1988*. Ann Arbor: The University of Michigan Press.

National Governor's Association Staff . (1995). *Welfare waivers*. Washington, DC: Author.
Nickell, S., & Bell, B. (1995). The collapse in demand for the unskilled and unemployment across the OECD. *Oxford Review of Economic Policy, 11*, 40-62.
Page, B.I., & Shapiro, R.Y. (1992). *The rational public: Fifty years of trends in Americans' policy preferences*. Chicago: University of Chicago Press.
Priester, R. (1992). A values framework for health system reform. *Health Affairs, 11*, 84-107.
Reynolds-Whyte, S. (1995). Disability and culture: An overview. In B. Ingstad & S. Reynolds-Whyte (Eds.), *Disability and culture*. Berkeley: University of California Press.
Shafer, B.E., & Claggett, W.J.M. (1995). *The two majorities: The issue context of modern American politics*. Baltimore: The Johns Hopkins University Press.
Schein, E.H. (1996). Culture: The missing concept in organizational studies. *Administrative Science Quarterly,* 41:229-240.
Stiker, H.-J. (1982). *Corps infirmes et sociétés*. Paris: Aubier Montaigne.
Stimson, J.A. (1991). *Public opinion in America: Moods, cycles and swings*. Boulder, CO: Westview Press.
Thurow, L. (1996). *The future of capitalism: How today's economic forces will shape tomorrow's world*. London: Nicholas Brealey Publishing.
Trice, H.M., & Beyer, J.M. (1993). *The cultures of work organizations*. Englewood Cliffs, NJ: Prentice Hall.
Varenne, H. (1986). Creating America. In H. Varenne (Ed.), *Symbolizing America*. (pp. 3-28). Lincoln: University of Nebraska Press.
Veblen, T. (1899). *The theory of the leisure class*. New York: Macmillan.
Westbrook, M.T., Legge, V., & Pennay, M. (1993). Attitudes towards disabilities in a multicultural society. *Social Science and Medicine, 37*, 615-623.
Williams, R. (1970). *American society*. New York: Knopf.
Williams, R.M., Jr. (1979). Change and stability in values and value systems: a sociological perspective. In M. Rokeach (Ed.), *Understanding human values* (pp.164-179). Free Press.
Wilson, J.Q. (1993). The moral sense. *American Political Science Review, 87*, 1-11.
Yankelovich, D. (1979). Work values and the new breed. In J.M. Yinger & S.J. Cutler (Eds.), *Work values in America* (pp. 324-352). New York: Van Nostrand Reinhold.
Yellin, E. (1992). *Disability and the displaced worker*. New Brunswick, NJ: Rutgers University Press.
Yellin, E. & Katz, P. (1994). Making work more central to work disability policy. *Milbank Quarterly, 72*, 593-619.

Study Questions:

1. What are "cultural values"?
2. What are main social values in society ?
3. Do these values remain relatively constant or do they change considerably over time?
4. What social forces preserve values in society and what forces change values?
5. How are American and European values similar and different?
6. What are the values of persons with disabilities?
7. Are the values of persons with disabilities similar to or different from the values of the larger society?
8. How do these similarities and differences affect incorporation of persons with disabilities into the larger society?
9. How do persons with disabilities call basic societal values into question?
10. How do persons with disabilities express their values in their daily lives and what effect does this have on the larger society?

Labeling in the Name of Equality: Political and Social Realities in the Schooling of Disabled Students

Venta Kabzems

The educational reform initiatives of normalization, integration, mainstreaming and inclusion have drawn heavily from social and political arenas in the Western world. Every child in most democratic societies is currently "legislatively" entitled to a public education. Focus on the human right of access to public education, however, has not provided any clear direction for achieving "academic" learning outcomes in educational settings. Key issues in the minds of educators, namely appropriate curriculum and program design, have assumed secondary importance to social inclusion.

The objectives of this chapter are to show how the effects of the changing demography of disabilities, legislative changes, social policies, educational practices, public expenditure and a shift in attitudes towards disability in Western societies have affected the education of students with disabilities. How have students with disabilities fared when considered "the same as everyone else" or when they have been considered "undeniably different"? How have educational systems, including teaching training institutions, responded to the concept of a disability culture? With respect to funding for education, health and social services, whose interpretation or vision is seen as significant and what are the educational consequences?

This chapter will make reference to changes in the range and distribution of educational services in an increasingly market-driven society, how teachers see their work with students with disabilities in a variety of educational contexts, and how public perception need not be fair or accurate to be important in setting the agenda for public education.

Perspectives

It was my first classroom as a teacher in the early 1970s, 18 students with a variety of disabilities, a teaching partner, a classroom assistant, and lots of financial support in a small, urban elementary school. Our mandate was to integrate these students into the everyday life of the school. As we tried to find teachers who would accept our students as participants in their classrooms, we had weekly visits from the superintendent of schools with touring dignitaries, curious folk from the university, a few parents, and student buddies who came to spend time in our class. Outside our classroom, the educational reform initiatives of normalization and integration were hotly debated in social and political arenas. We "failed" our externally based normalization evaluation (a blow to the jurisdiction), but consoled ourselves with thoughts that our students were simply not "normal", that it was high time the rest of the world realized that interpersonal differences existed, and that we should not waste our time trying to deny these differences. Besides, we had to teach David to read, Darryl to cross the street unassisted, Anne-Marie to respond to her name, Kathy not to scream when she heard loud noises, Arthur to look after his hearing aids, Gerry the rules for floor hockey so he could be more effective on the school team – and we would ask to be reviewed again the next year.

Twenty-five years later, after teaching in a variety of segregated and integrated educational settings as well as holding positions in teacher training institutions, I work with administrators and classroom staff involved in the schooling of about 70 students with disabilities between the ages of 2 and 20. The majority of these students spend most of their day in ordinary classrooms. Today, although students with disabilities are more visible, the issues that surround their inclusion in public school settings have not decreased proportionately.

This chapter draws heavily on 25 years of observation in schools, in circumstances where students with disabilities have been considered to be the same as everyone else and in circumstances when they have been seen as undeniably different. The chapter focuses on how legislative policies, government spending, educational practices, and a shift in public attitudes have affected the schooling of students with disabilities. Can educational funding and service delivery occur on the basis of needed support versus categorization by disability? What happens when attempts are made to minimize differences between individuals in terms of educational programming? How have educational systems, including teacher training institutions, responded to students with disabilities in inclusive settings?

Introduction

Every child in most democratic societies is at present legally entitled to free public education, at least at the primary level. **However, the legislative focus on right to access has not provided clear direction for achieving academic learning outcomes in educational settings.** Basic issues in the minds of educators such as appropriate curriculum and program design have assumed secondary importance to an emphasis on social outcomes, particularly for students with severe disabilities. At the same time, the Deaf community has opposed inclusion, seeing it as a way of ignoring the educational and cultural needs of Deaf students. Without specialized communication and instructional techniques coupled with a corresponding level of training for classroom personnel, Deaf students do not feel they can be successful in public school classrooms (Lane, 1995). Most Deaf students are not interested in access to public schools: they want access to an appropriate curriculum and medium of instruction.

The range and distribution of educational services in an increasingly market-driven society have been affected as schools adopt the language of the marketplace. One expressed belief is that competition in the educational marketplace will lead to improvement at school and district levels and that consumer choice will decide how and which educational services will be provided (Barton, 1993). Successful schools are defined by balanced budgets, cost-effective programs, and above-average examination results. Site-based management, corporate partnerships, school councils composed of community members, and mandatory examinations have contributed to changes in the taxpayers' perceptions of the functions and purposes of public education.

The changing demographics of students with disabilities in schools has had an impact on the provision of service and the disbursement of funds. Governments must be seen as distributing tax revenues in an egalitarian manner, so legislation and government directives are used to define disability based on specific criteria. Eligibility for any additional funding is based on the categorical definition rather than on the educational needs or support required for the student to be able to progress academically (or socially) in a public school.

Historically, specialized educational methods and equipment were reserved for students with obvious sensory or physical disabilities. As the nature and number of students unable to succeed in general education settings grew, specialized educational practices and related support services intended to bolster student achievement were introduced. New instructional methodologies and a wider range of service provision became part of the general educational service. Until recently, special education has been a growth industry, but the situation is changing, particularly in the scramble for funds to support schools.

Students with brain injuries are seen more frequently in ordinary classrooms. The incidence of infectious diseases in children is rising, as is the recognition of fetal alcohol syndrome. These conditions are noteworthy because they do not regularly appear in more traditional classification systems of students with special needs. These "new" disabilities may be less visible from a physical perspective, but they require considerable effort and resources in an educational setting. They reflect deficiencies in health and social welfare systems due to government downloading of responsibilities to regional, local or private sector services. They also reflect chronic learning and behavioral concerns, students whose difficulties are unlikely to ever be resolved, completely.

The number of children surviving today with severe and complex medical and health problems that make their accommodation in ordinary classrooms more complex is increasing. School personnel may be expected to perform tasks such as chest physiotherapy so that a student may be included in a neighborhood school, they must have knowledge of sophisticated augmentative communication devices, they must be alert for signs of mental health concerns, and by the way, there's a new math curriculum this year.

The distinctions between educational, welfare and health supports required to accommodate a student with disabilities in a school program become blurred. The question, "Who pays – health? education? social services?", creates practical and moral dilemmas. Tensions between social and political ideals and their realities in the schooling of students with disabilities are exacerbated.

Legislation, Social Policy, and Service Delivery

Governments influence educational practices through legislation, regulations, policies, and financial support. Human rights legislation was intended to address employment equity, access to public transport and public buildings (including schools), access to housing, and access to social and recreational facilities. Simple physical access, however, does not ensure group membership, active participation in the activities of the group, or, in the case of schools, learning. The right to access does not provide direction for academic outcomes, nor does it necessarily maximize personal and social outcomes for students with disabilities.

Education and human rights legislation affecting the schooling of students with disabilities is rarely the product of considered, empirical research. As Keogh (1990) points out, **values and beliefs are more likely to effect changes in educational policy than is rationally conducted research driven by a need to improve the state of education.** The drive comes from value judgments about what educational goals are worth pursuing and what supports should be provided for students in schools. Historically, these value judgments have not stemmed from persons with disabilities. Rather, legislators, families, advocates, and educational institutions have defined the identities, needs, and interests of disabled persons, particularly those with severe disabilities (Barton, 1993).

A current focus of proponents of school improvement is not instructional practices, but rather the development of educational outcome standards (Carnine, 1994). Student achievement measured by standardized, external measures has become a means of steering school district policies. High levels of student achievement show taxpayers that public education is working. The emphasis is on excellence and cost-effectiveness in both service delivery and educational outcomes: tangibles, the value of which can be measured in economic terms. Per-capita funding is increased if a student can be shown to be eligible for additional funding, a process by which the student has to be made visible (i.e., labeled). Students on a per-capita basis have become the major determinants of school budgets. However, if all students are expected to participate in standardized outcome assessments, these labeled students who bring additional funding to a school are viewed as a liability when their achievement results are pooled with those of the whole school.

The result is both tension and dilemma because the budget of a school depends on the additional funds which accompany disabled students, but the attractiveness of the school to potential consumers is diminished when their examination results lower the school's ranking as parents compare prospective schools' outcomes in the form of examination results (Slee, 1993). A school can be seen as "disability friendly" and attract families with students who cost more than the per-capita allotments for education, which becomes a strain on school resources, particularly with the advent of site-based management.

Practical and moral dilemmas occur because the government funding source requires that all students be treated similarly, which includes taking mandated examinations. Adaptations to assessment procedures are allowed, but often the school must apply for permission to use these adaptations and must also demonstrate that the school has previously been accommodating the students in this manner as part of an Individualized Education Plan (IEP). Many schools are caught, as they do not wish to be perceived as treating students differently and have used this as a rationale for not altering their traditional school assessment practices.

If social policy and legislation continue the move toward a standardization of educational outcomes, assessment becomes an integral part of the curriculum. Assessments will have to be regularly conducted and results will have to be specific about what has been learned, how well it has been mastered and what remains to be learned (Resnick, Nolan & Resnick, 1995). Where does this leave students with disabilities, especially as they are not a homogeneous group? If educational outcomes drive a program or course of studies, what happens to academically competent students who require adaptations to assessment protocols? What happens to those who cannot demonstrate particular knowledge of curriculum content? What about those who place social inclusion above mastery of any curriculum content?

Government policy and shifts in social values affect educational philosophies. For example, the one-curriculum-for-all-students philosophy reflects the intent of equality of access to the same curriculum and, by implication, the content of that curriculum for all students. However, the nature of a student's disability, the developmental or skill variance between many students with disabilities and their classmates, and the educational goals chosen have resulted in curriculum adaptations that reflect more cosmetic value than appropriate skill development. **The appropriateness of a curriculum depends as much on what is being received as what is being delivered; exposure does not equal experience** (Jordan & Powell, 1994).

Government responses to debt management, such as legislating a balanced budget, have had the effect of reducing expenditures on public services. As all levels of government seek to cut spending and to reallocate resources, they have effectively weakened the educational, health, and social services provided by the public sector. Tensions have increased because legislation regarding educational placement of students with disabilities has not been amended to reflect the changes in funding support for the services needed to maintain a student in an educational setting.

In some instances, spending authorities have chosen to allocate the bulk of their resources at the preschool level, a head start model. A high-level, high-cost intervention is delivered to preschoolers in the anticipation that there will be long-term carryover into the school years. The resources required through the school years are then assumed to be fewer, and this is how the savings to "the system" will occur. In practice, this is not what happens, however. We know from follow up studies of American Head start programs that truly long-term effects of early intervention are variable, often depending on the position of the program evaluator, the funding agency, the disability groups represented, the type of program, and the follow up conditions. The students identified early are often those with more severe handicapping conditions that do not disappear on entry to school. These students require ongoing, long-term support, although the combination and intensity of the support will probably vary.

Adoption of a full inclusion model implies that appropriate support for a particular student will be provided in neighborhood schools throughout a student's school career. The first warning sign that rhetoric and practice do not correspond may come with the change in the level of financial support at the preschool level compared with that provided when the child enters a public school, particularly when the family has become accustomed to receiving a high level of direct service. They are distressed when direct health-related support services such as physiotherapy are replaced by an educational consultation service when the child enters the public school system. What was seen as a preschool program of rehabilitation deserving of a high level of financial and resource commitment becomes rationalized as a maintenance program to be carried out by the family members and perhaps a classroom assistant.

Schools are at an advantage if they can pool resources from several labeled students, but services may not then be offered in a full-time inclusive placement – which is what the parents wanted as a result of their preschool experiences. The tension between what a family expects from a school and what the school is capable of providing, given the allocation of funds, may lead to a legal or quasi-legal placement appeal process. The resulting legal precedents designate responsibility for service delivery and access, but they do not address the financial bottom line for a school or district, nor do the judgments necessarily address curriculum issues and anticipated program outcomes.

On the other hand, families who request a segregated program may be ostracized by their disability support network or association because they are seen as having betrayed the ideals of the preschool focus on inclusion. These families may encounter opposition from schools that have been instructed to offer inclusion as the placement of choice and, therefore, may have eliminated all special classes in the district as a demonstration of their commitment to the ideals of inclusive education. Sponsorship to specialized facilities outside a school jurisdiction may be difficult to obtain. The onus may be placed on the family to demonstrate why their request should be honored, as much of the rhetoric surrounding inclusion has focused on the supposed immorality of segregated programs.

The dimension of morality adds to the ethical dilemmas faced by educators. Some parents opt for the inclusive model simply to avoid segregation, rather than because it will provide positive educational outcomes for the student. Families whose child has had a cochlear implant often live in an educational netherworld. By choosing to have the cochlear implant, they are seen by the Deaf community as rejecting Deaf culture and hence are unwelcome. But in schools these students may not hear well enough to function without support and are treated as deaf in inclusive settings. Other families view any time spent away from classroom peers as negative and are in a continual state of tension with educators who perceive that specific instruction or training in particular skills that contribute to the lifelong educational outcomes of the student would be better taught in a setting outside the regular classroom (Baine, 1991).

There is another facet to treating students as if sameness were all that mattered in a classroom. Some of the most widely publicized examples of successful inclusive education have involved students with severe, multiple disabilities. Although it can easily be argued that they are receiving considerably more sensory stimulation than was observed in a previous segregated placement, and that the educational programming focus of sensory stimulation is appropriate, the questions of ethics and respect for diversity emerge. How does the school respond to external measures of educational outcomes when this student is expected to be included in an evaluation process? What is the social message when a student with multiple, severe disabilities is partnered with a classmate for an assignment and receives the same mark as the classmate for the assignment? What is the message when a student who is cortically blind and cortically deaf vocalizes while the class has been told to remain quiet and receives a "time owed" to the teacher?

Educational issues are complex. Proponents of a more consumer-driven education system believe that nongovernmental services are more efficient and effective at resource allocation and that they would be more responsive to consumer need (perhaps because they stand to earn a profit). Corporations may be ready to form school-business partnerships, or to fund a university business school, but corporations are not interested in job creation. Using a business model to treat education as a conglomeration of services to be delivered at the lowest cost to the largest number of consumers may have the veneer of equality, but it is far from equitable.

Should all schools be expected to be capable of providing routinely for the full diversity of children's abilities, disabilities, and attainments (Norwich, 1993)? For proponents of full inclusion this leads to the question of where services are provided, and there is a reluctance to pool resources and consolidate specialized aspects of service delivery, even though it is more expensive and not possible to provide all services in all schools. Sobsey (1991) discussed the search for optimal instructional environments – which are not necessarily school classrooms – for students with disabilities.

With the moves toward inclusion, special educational services provided outside the regular classroom appear to have been replaced by debate about program offerings rather than alternative and improved service to students. Although the debaters persist, governments and funding agencies have been steadily cutting back financial and resource support to schools. Budget cuts have compromised access, quality, and equity in education, health, and social services, all of which may be involved in the support of a student with disabilities in school and in the community.

As some students and their families require access to multiple services, they must also face problems in interagency communication, professional turf wars, and competition for operating funds. Changes to institutional funding have caused a rise in the numbers of part-time employees in education and health systems. Continuity and coordination of services become problematic with reduced working days and the demands on personnel for their services. Staff turnover can be an issue when vacancies are listed as entry-level positions to save on salaries. Communication between different services and with parents is weakened.

Moves to try to provide more community services in public schools, as well as the changes in education funding and related services, have resulted in new staffing patterns. When paraprofessionals, private consultants, or contracted agencies provide services to students with special educational needs in the school setting, the relationships of these service providers to the school are altered (Giangreco, 1995). The school may not be their direct employer, and their commitment to the educational outcomes for the student may vary from that of the persons directly employed by the school.

To compound the issue of service delivery, some teachers' unions are urging their members to resist non-teaching duties in the school. For example, the Alberta Teachers' Association took the position that although the school may serve as the site for delivering noneducational services such as lunches and family counseling, teachers should not be those delivering the services (Committee on Public Education and Professional Practice, 1994). At the same time, a student's existence is not defined solely by school attendance. Social changes affect families and their ability to look after their children. Crowded living conditions promote the spread of infectious diseases; they affect how orthotic and prosthetic devices are stored when the child is at home (sometimes with the resultant irony that teachers keep hearing aids or glasses at school to keep them safe, thus depriving the student of enhanced ability to communicate or to see well outside school hours); they affect sleeping conditions and nutrition for students, as well as a host of other variables that have an impact on the student's ability to function in school.

When considering the idea of educational needs in special education, perhaps it helps to see such needs as supports or accommodations that will help the student. These needs form part of a student's Individualized Education Plan (IEP). However, IEPs, as established in special education circles, may in fact act as a barrier to inclusion. Students who receive additional funds are expected to have an IEP, justifying the additional financial allotment. Because of changes in education funding, more students are being referred for labeling in an attempt to prevent a school from running a deficit. More teachers are asked to do additional paperwork for special needs allotments, leaving proportionately less time for planning for differentiation in instruction for a class of 25 or more students which also contains educationally needy, but unlabeled, students.

Access to Education: Achieving Academic and Social Outcomes

Fifty years ago in North America access to education for students with obvious disabilities was possible in specialized facilities where they were grouped for differential treatment provided by a specialist. The end result was the educational warehousing of students, who did not fit in with mainstream educational practices, into special schools or classes.

In the late 1960s and early 1970s the concepts of normalization, civil rights, and de-institutionalization gained the attention of educators. More local services such as special classes in ordinary schools became available. Special education curricula were developed which focused on categorical skill development.

Next came the model of working toward personal independence using a functional curriculum (Snell, 1983). Attempts were made to teach and practice skills in the environments where students were expected to use the particular skill (Brown et al., 1991). The challenge came in trying to follow through, getting the students into natural environments for teaching and practice (Sobsey, 1991). These natural environments included regular classrooms as places for students with disabilities to learn. Frequently the focus was on the enhancement of interpersonal communication and social skills. Giving all students access to the curriculum in a regular classroom was seen as a means of facilitating social participation and enhancing the visibility and status of students with disabilities. Content mastery was not mentioned.

The curriculum in an inclusive model of education teeters between two opposing principles: access to curriculum content and academic learning outcomes. Giving students with disabilities the same or similar access to the regular curriculum as their classmates, providing the same educational experiences in a classroom, must take into account a student's ability to respond to and gain from those experiences (Jordan & Powell, 1994). Can all schools provide sufficient support to meet the specific and distinct needs of every student, including those with disabilities? The answer is that schools fall short of the ideal for numerous reasons.

For example, assigning worksheets which give the illusion of commonality in a class but take little account of a student's ability to process language at the level used by the teacher during whole-class instruction is a questionable educational practice. Tasks performed by classmates have little meaning for the student who is helped to perform them in class by a peer or a teaching assistant but is unlikely to be able to perform them independently. Should the personnel responsible for developing a student's school program, including parents, be asked to demonstrate the relevance of regular curriculum-based experiences and tasks to the particular needs of the student?

If the starting point for inclusion in an ordinary classroom is an inappropriate curriculum (Ainscow, 1993), then the student is done a disservice. The question of how to adapt curriculum content in specific subject areas for some students becomes increasingly problematic in the higher grades. A more abstract conceptual base, vocabulary, reading, and writing skills are required if a student is truly to have access to the regular curriculum. At this point, one needs to ask about "the disability" for the means of accessing the curriculum for a cognitively normal, visually impaired student will be different from that of a Deaf student, one with a mental disability and so on.

There is a concern with the classroom teacher's acceptance of any curriculum adaptations. **Adaptations need to be grounded in what has been referred to as a *reasonableness factor*. In economic terms, adaptations and the time needed to prepare them need to be viewed from the point of diminishing returns.** Is the effort and time put into curriculum differentiation and materials preparation proportionate to the anticipated educational outcomes? The adaptations and instructional strategies most likely to be accepted and implemented by teachers appear to be those involving relatively minor preparation time and little change to the teacher's current manner of instruction (Norwich, 1994). In addition, it may be a paraprofessional rather than the teacher who delivers the instruction.

Arguments for treating all students similarly in schools are difficult to reconcile with new curricula and subject offerings devised in the competitive, marketable-skills ethos of schools which see themselves as commercial operations rather than public services. Educational outcomes in the form of subject area, content-based, external examinations are presented in tangible form to future consumers and current taxpayers in the form of school rankings or percentage of program graduates employed within a year of graduation. In order to retain students and levels of funding for schools to operate, a multitude of new subject offerings occur at secondary and post-secondary levels, making it possible for mildly disabled students to achieve the requisite number of credits for graduation. More disabled students remain in high school, and for some it has opened the door to post secondary training in community college programs. However, the success of the community college approach lies in a college's ability to change course offerings and diplomas more rapidly than other post secondary institutions such as universities and technical schools. Training received in the college system is not intended for lifelong employment in a single field; rather, the premise is that one will return for regular upgrading in order to remain competitive in the job market. One imagines that this system, while appearing to give individuals greater opportunities in the short term, may not be equitable for the long term, given the financial status of most persons with disabilities and their families. Apparently, equal treatment does not always result in similar outcomes: Persons with disabilities will still get stuck in the educational or employment systems.

Physical placement and simple exposure to the regular curriculum does not equitably meet the educational needs of students who require supportive services in the classroom in order to learn effectively. How do teachers and schools juggle a student's needs for literacy and numeracy with other skills that may be required by that student to live in as independent a manner as possible? Indeed, does personal independence in adulthood continue to be seen as a desirable outcome of schooling for every student with a disability?

An important question in the inclusion movement has concerned the type and form of curriculum that will best facilitate the inclusion process. Can any curriculum meet the educational needs of all students in a classroom? The *one-curriculum-for-all-students* exists in theory, and attempts have been made to put it into practice (Ainscow, 1993). The stumbling blocks in this approach occur because educational outcomes tend to be couched in such broad terms that teachers struggle to decide which practical skills can be drawn from a generic goal statement such as "student will appreciate varied aesthetic experiences".

It is unclear how it can be stated that the goals for education are the same for all students when it appears obvious that some students, particularly those with severe disabilities, may not attain those goals. How does this belief mesh with the perceived push for accountability for educational outcomes–providing consumers of educational services (i.e., students and their families) with knowledge and skill levels guaranteed by a school system?

Advocates for full inclusion who invoke a civil rights model are wrong in assuming that students with disabilities do not have instructionally relevant needs that may require personnel with specialized training, specialized resources to support them in school, and sometimes even selective placement outside regular classes and schools. The medical analogy concerning who provides the level of service needed to maintain reasonable health is classic: A general practitioner with an interest in a medical specialty area can competently treat cases that are slightly unusual. If the situation is more serious, a specialist referral may be required, and if the problem becomes narrowed and more severe, input from a sub-specialist may be requested. In educational situations, classroom teachers with coaching and support are able to manage a wider range of student needs in their classrooms than in the past. However, some students–such as those requiring a teacher to be fluent in signed communication, or programming skills for augmentative communication devices, or sophisticated behavior management strategies–are placed at a disadvantage when all their time is spent in regular school classrooms without ongoing specialist support or the option of direct service to a student from a more highly skilled professional. **Public schools have an obligation to try to meet the educational needs of a student rather than just the social needs or the political desires of a family.**

Students' characteristics must not be used to justify unfair provision of educational services, so gender and skin color are not instructionally relevant variables. A student using a wheelchair may be disabled by attitudes and access to school buildings, but the student's academic instructional needs may not be different from those of others in the class. Deafness, visual impairment, traumatic brain injury, and specific learning disabilities are relevant educational variables that need to be taken into account with respect to instructional methods, social skills development, and outcome measures. Providing a blind student with specialized equipment or instruction in specialized skills (e.g., orientation and mobility, the use of translation software if the student is a braille user) are examples of instructionally relevant variables. Relevant instructional variables may require extraordinary service and support in order for the student with disabilities to achieve the outcomes of which he or she is capable. Extraordinary knowledge on how to provide this support does not reside in most regular classroom teachers, nor has it been any large part of their professional training.

Many teachers feel unsupported and are becoming increasingly open in their resistance to the placement of students with disabilities in their classrooms. The inclusion of students with disabilities has become part of the collective bargaining process for teachers' unions. Parental involvement on school governing councils has led to closer community scrutiny of the financial resources of their neighborhood school. The perception seems to be that, even with additional funding, most students with disabilities are a drain on school funds.

Attitudes in Schools and Other Byproducts of Professional Training

Special education requirements are relative in that as educational and social demands change, so do those characteristics that come to be seen as disabilities (Norwich, 1993). In an international study of attitudes, beliefs, and behaviors toward disabilities, Berry (1994) found that no community presented a profile of beliefs and attitudes toward causes, control, and responsibility for disability and relationships with persons with a disability that was identical to that of any other community. Teachers, who are considered to be representative of the attitudes in a community, also demonstrate that attitudes are not unitary, that they vary by type of disability, and that they differ depending on whether reference is being made to their own classroom or to classrooms in general (Barnartt & Kabzems, 1992).

Teacher training institutions have been relatively slow to change the categorical approach to teacher preparation for students with extraordinary educational needs. When teachers are trained in a deficit model of special needs, the design, selection, and use of specific methods and strategies will be affected by their beliefs about their students and learning. Experience shows that the categorical approach remain influential in most classrooms. For example, intervention strategies may be negated for a student with autism, if they were taken from a book about students with Fragile-x syndrome despite substantial overlap between several developmental disorders in early childhood, including autism and Fragile-x.

The understanding of specific categories or specialist knowledge regarding the education of students with disabilities cannot be avoided. However, the in-depth categorization of disabilities that formed the basis of most teacher education programs is not as useful as it was in the past. Current educational programming tries to avoid a categorical approach as the labels do not provide sufficient relevant information for teaching. There are, of course, exceptions, particularly with respect to specific syndromes. Categorical knowledge is useful for issues related to coding and funding, information that should be a part of initial teacher training.

The attitudes held by a teacher are not only a byproduct of training; rather, teachers' attitudes are often formed before entry into training programs. Teachers are unique in that after having spent thousands of hours in the classroom, they are already socialized into the profession, and not without bias. How many aspiring teachers can say that they have had a teacher with an obvious disability? How many disabled students have had as role models persons with disabilities during their schooling? **Perhaps the time has come for teacher training institutions to attempt to interrupt this professional socialization pattern by presenting course materials from a disability-culture perspective, framing coursework in**

terms of the interests of students with disabilities, and hiring persons with obvious disabilities as faculty members.

It appears that although teachers in general support statements in favor of including students with disabilities in their classrooms, they are less willing to make specific adaptations to accommodate these students on an ongoing basis (Norwich, 1994). Many regular teachers believe they lack the specialized training to teach students with disabilities. Adding to the burden of doubting their professional competence when they encounter these students in their regular classes, they are concerned about accountability should the student not make reasonable gains in their classroom. Secondly, they are taken aback when parents of a student with a severe disability state that they have no interest in progress through the curriculum, they just want their child to have the same experiences as their same-aged peers.

Other attitudes encountered in school settings come from the related service personnel who have been socialized to function independently in their own discipline rather than in collaboration as part of an educational team. Attitudes of "professional knows best" can hamper an integrated approach to educational service delivery. In some instances, minimally trained paraprofessional staff are recruited to work with students with disabilities. A lack of professional orientation and knowledge can affect the direct service to students with disabilities in several crucial ways. For example, the paraprofessional may receive minimal supervision from the teacher (for a number of reasons, including the number of students with disabilities in a class) and so independently makes decisions about the implementation of a child's educational program. Para-professionals trained in early childhood education or as rehabilitation practitioners have a training bias that may conflict with the academic goals for a student to whom they are to provide support in a classroom. For example, the para-professional may focus on the caregiving aspects of the service; or inappropriate early childhood instructional practices may be applied in a secondary school with a developmentally disabled adolescent.

Para-professionals recruited in the current school year have included former parent volunteers in a kindergarten class, a dental hygienist, the parent of a child with attention deficit disorder, an adult group home worker, a retired teacher, a school secretary, and several daycare workers. While there are many para-professionals who are appropriately trained and experienced, many have no special training. **It is ironic that staff members with perhaps the least relevant training are assigned to provide direct instructional and support services to students whose educational needs are extraordinary.**

Families suffer from the attitudes found in schools. These range from thoughtless comments on a child's appearance to outright hostility from school community members who feel that any disabled student costs too much time, money, and attention. The additional resources provided for a disabled student in an attempt to equalize educational outcomes are seen as taking away resources from the programs of other students. As financial and school budget information becomes more readily available to members of a school community, particularly with respect to a site-based budget, more questions are heard about the relationship between spending and student outcomes. Tensions resurface between needing a number of disabled students to help support a school's budget, but not wishing them to be too disabled (or disruptive) because then the revenue is insufficient.

Debate about the question of inclusion continues to catch schools off guard with its ferocity. Just as full inclusionists lobby for full-time placement in regular classes, others lobby for choice along a continuum of service options or service outside the school system. School communities face the dilemma of including students with disabilities because of issues of social justice or attempting to shunt them elsewhere because the current financial allocation is insufficient to cover the costs of their schooling unless disabled students are clustered.

How Teachers See Their Work with Students with Disabilities

Teachers responding to a survey on trends and innovations in education in the province of Alberta stated that the development causing the greatest concern among teachers was *integration* or *inclusive education* (Committee on Public Education and Professional Practice, 1994). Although some respondents expressed absolute support for the placement of students with disabilities in ordinary classrooms in their neighborhood schools, others considered this development to be unworkable when combined with other concurrent changes in education such as new curricula and increased external testing. Support was generally expressed for the principles of inclusion, but critical problems in implementation were identified. The problems listed included: insufficient support with respect to classroom assistants; lack of inservice; poor access to counseling or consultation services; lack of financial support for student programs; planning time needed to set up and monitor what was perceived as a distinctly different program; the impact on the other students in the classroom; and concerns regarding the medical management of some students. For some teachers, particularly at the subject-oriented secondary level, these new responsibilities were akin to changing their job descriptions in mid-contract.

In many jurisdictions, inclusion of students with disabilities has become a bargaining item during collective negotiations. Teachers see that basic shifts in terms of the nature of their work as externally imposed changes to education have created a competitive market atmosphere (Barton, 1993). Teachers are leaving the profession in increasing numbers. In the Canadian province of Nova Scotia, for example, one in 10 teachers is opting for early retirement (Dare, 1996). Employee benefit plans report greater numbers of teachers applying for long-term disability benefits as well as a dramatic increase in spending on prescription drugs (Russell, 1996).

Teachers are socialized, particularly in special education courses, to explain learning difficulties in terms of the characteristics of individual pupils. Educational supports are designed to assist a particular student and are written in a prescriptive, individualized format such as an Individualized Education Plan (IEP). The focus on the individual student implies that the teacher must continually modify and adapt for that student while teaching, in addition to coordinating any services provided by paraprofessionals, consultants, parent volunteers, and student buddies. Fuchs and Fuchs (1995) see this approach to instruction as impractical in a regular class, which is statistically likely to include several students with exceptional learning needs whether funded or not.

One wonders where the empirical proof is that individualized programming has paid off. If specialized programming had not been available, what might the outcomes have been? We know from the past when students dropped out of school or simply did not attend that the situation was unsatisfactory, and remediation was attempted through legislation designed both to keep and allow all students in schools. We also know that classrooms continue to function even without specialized training for teachers (Upton, 1991). Furthermore, what is reasonable with respect to the amount of individualized, specialized instruction a teacher can be expected to provide or to coordinate in regular education classrooms? **Teachers struggle with the dilemma of wanting to provide uniquely tailored programs or supports for students, particularly those with disabilities, and being unable to do so in a professionally** respectable, competent manner given their current resources of time, money, and specialized knowledge.

If one takes the perspective that learning difficulties are the result of an environmental or situational mismatch between a student and the school, then it is reasonable to help students meet the demands of a system by changing the system and extending the range of students who can be accommodated in the class. Curriculum adaptations, alternative materials, or support from a classroom assistant are examples of responses in this perspective (Ainscow, 1993). The tensions emerge for the teachers as they are expected to orchestrate these supports when: textbooks do not provide example of adaptations, alternative resources are not to be found in all schools, classroom assistants may require instruction in specific educational management techniques such as recordkeeping, and requests for consultation or the purchase of resources are resisted at the administrative level because of scarce funds. Many teachers face the problem of how far they must act in the capacity of student advocate in order to obtain educationally relevant services.

The impact of technology on the school has been cited as a critical area of knowledge and competence for all teachers, but perhaps it is the more relevant in the education of students with disabilities. Students' use of augmentive communication devices, a teacher's ability to program software, and knowledge of software resources, as well as a teacher's use of information services and data bases relevant to the instruction of students with disabilities are just some of the challenges that technology poses for educators.

Conclusions

Where do these thoughts and observations on the educational treatment of students as "similar" or "different" leave us? Public pressure for major educational reform has been building. Public funding for education has been reduced. Innovation in schools today is more likely to be a survival mechanism or a byproduct of government restructuring rather than a concerted drive by educators and taxpayers to improve the future of education.

Considering special educational needs as a social construct encourages the belief that any difficulties associated with students with disabilities can be overcome. It places the responsibility on social attitudes and institutions, namely, schools. It implies that the institution, and by extension its employees, are adaptable. There is a reluctance, in this view, to acknowledge that individual student variables can place limitations on what a particular school can accommodate (Norwich, 1993). Difficulties in learning can and do originate from biological and psychological processes and are not limited to social processes. Nonetheless, schools are highly structured social systems and change does not come easily (Keogh, 1990). Attitudinal change among teachers, their unions, medical or other professional groups, families, and school communities does not occur in any synchronous fashion, so anticipated changes are likely to be gradual and uneven among the groups involved in the education of students with disabilities.

With respect to inclusionary practices, government rhetoric and policy may espouse the neighborhood school as the first placement of choice, but government funding patterns reward segregated classrooms. This is due in part to the economies of scale that single schools with site-based management schemes do not receive sufficient allocation for high-needs students. Funding allotments are pooled and students may be clustered in order to receive support from an assistant. Some students who have been eligible for additional funds do not see the funds translated into additional classroom assistance, one implication being that a categorical labeling scheme may not accurately reflect the amount of support required for a particular student.

Have special educators erred in focusing on planning for individuals rather than for the class as a whole? Does a curriculum perspective offer new opportunities to create an environment that will support the learning of all students? Are teachers suffering from "innovation overload" (Ainscow, 1993)? There are promising nuggets in these ideas, but to say that the solution lies in a single facet of educational practice is insufficient. A reacquaintance with the principles of larger group instruction and less singling out of students with disabilities has some merit, but it needs to resist the notion that equal treatment will result in equal educational outcomes. Just because reading instruction occurs in the classroom and most students learn to read by a particular method does not mean that some students in that group should not receive alternative or specialized instruction so that they too can learn to read. The curriculum perspective helps to remind schools of what they do best: teaching curriculum content. For some disabled students this may require different approaches to instruction, some of which can be easily implemented during whole-class instruction by the teacher. Other students with disabilities will be further disadvantaged if their academic capabilities are ignored in favor of social outcomes alone. Some students will benefit from instruction in settings other than regular classrooms, perhaps from specialist teachers.

Professional development is touted as a basic element of change, but it has not lived up to expectations, perhaps because school personnel have underestimated the energy, coordination, and level of skills required as well as the endurance needed to introduce and sustain new classroom practices (Malouf & Schiller, 1995). It is ironic that business, on which education is increasingly modeled, sets timelines for change at three to five years of sustained effort, whereas educators have tended to set long-term goals in terms of a single school year.

Giangreco (1995) suggested that services and supports be provided directly, indirectly, or in combination, using an only-as-special-as-necessary system. This approach was intended to avoid the problems of well-intentioned overservice for students who did not meet the norms of mainstream instruction and that kept students with disabilities tied up with therapies rather than with their peers in the classroom. While attempting to avoid the consideration of students with disabilities as more different than similar, a major drawback to such a seemingly rational system could be the professional background of the person(s) responsible for making the decisions. In a smaller urban system, for example, a nurse from a rehabilitation hospital has been seconded to the school system and put in charge of services for students with disabilities. The professional background and limited school-based experience, to this point, of the person charged with decision-making for educational settings has added to the tensions in the schooling of students with disabilities. For example, a cognitive assessment for a physically disabled student who had made limited academic progress over the course of a school year was requested. From the school's perspective it would be helpful to have an updated assessment on file for funding applications, but the student's poor attendance record provided more valid information regarding possible reasons for the lack of academic progress, or just because a student is legally blind, do they need to learn braille? The professional perspective of the decision-maker in an educational service delivery system can directly affect how students' needs are managed in a public education setting.

Restructuring the delivery of educational support services and moving from a predominantly individualized perspective toward a broader, curricular view requires the redefinition of professional roles in an education setting. The use of specialized strategies, which are familiar to professionals in segregated or clinical settings, stands out in regular classrooms. The procedures may be perceived as intrusive by the wider audience. It will be for school personnel to negotiate through the possible confusion, as not all the necessary specialized interventions should or can take place in the regular classroom. Professionals feel disempowered when it is known that specific clinical or instructional techniques could be effectively applied in a setting outside the classroom, but that they would be viewed as treating the student differently and in a potentially stigmatizing manner. For example, it is frustrating to someone working from a behavioral perspective to try to effect behavioral change only in naturally occurring situations when the student involved can be shown to require hundreds or even thousands of practice trials in order to acquire a specific skill (Sobsey, 1991).

Educational visions are numerous and there is a lack of empirical research to show that certain changes would result in improvements. Yet problems and problematic situations arise between conflicting values and their resolution cannot simply be achieved based on empirical findings. Life in classrooms does not lend itself to rational, technical problem-solving. There seems to be no single, clear, articulated policy that might reconcile all the groups who feel they have a stake and a say in matters of the public education of students with disabilities. Nor is there likely to be such a policy. Shortcomings exist when attempts are made to treat all students equally in that equity tends to be sacrificed. When students with disabilities are treated differently in order to try to make them more like everyone else, we have learned that *separate* does not make educational provision *equal* or *equitable*. Overemphasis on individual adaptations and planning has distracted attention from exploring other options and accommodating new ways of thinking about disability- within a social value system which focuses on the individual, as long as he's not too different from everyone else.

References

Ainscow, M. (1993). Beyond special education: Some ways forward. In J. Visser & G. Upton (Eds.), *Special education in Britain after Warnock* (pp. 166-182). London: Fulton.

Baine, D. (1991). Selecting instructional environments for students having severe multiple handicaps. In D. Baine (Ed.), *Instructional environments for learners having severe handicaps* (pp. 1-14). Edmonton, AB: Vector/Educational Psychology.

Barnartt, S.B., & Kabzems, V. (1992). Zimbabwean teachers' attitudes towards the integration of pupils with disabilities into regular classrooms. *International Journal of Disability, Development and Education, 39,* 135-146.

Barton, L. (1993). Labels, markets and inclusive education. In J. Visser & G. Upton (Eds.), *Special education in Britain after Warnock* (pp. 30-42). London: Fulton.

Berry, J.W. (1994, July). Disability attitudes, beliefs and behaviours: Overview of an international project in community-based rehabilitation. In P. Cook (Chair), *Culture, health and disability.* Symposium conducted at the 12th International Congress of Cross-cultural Psychology, Pamplona, Spain.

Brown, L., Schwarz, P., Udvari-Solner, A., Kampschroer, F.K., Johnson, F., Jorgensen, J., & Gruenewald, L. (1991). How much time should students with severe intellectual disabilities spend in regular education classrooms and elsewhere? *Journal of the Association for Persons with Severe Handicaps, 16,* 39-47.

Carnine, D. (1994). Introduction to the mini-series: Diverse learners and prevailing, emerging, and research-based educational approaches and their tools. *School Psychology Review, 23,* 341-350.

Committee on Public Education and Professional Practice. (1994). *Trying to teach: Necessary conditions.* Edmonton, AB: Alberta Teachers' Association.

Dare, P. (1996, January 7). Where are schools headed? *Edmonton Journal*, pp. E1-2.

Fuchs, D., & Fuchs, L.S. (1995). Inclusive schools movement and the radicalization of special education reform. In J.M. Kauffman & D.P. Hallahan (Eds.), *The illusion of full inclusion: A comprehensive critique of a current special education bandwagon* (pp. 213-242). Austin, TX: PRO-ED.

Giangreco, M.F. (1995). Related services decision-making: A foundational component of effective education for students with disabilities. *Physical and Occupational Therapy in Pediatrics, 15*, 47-67.

Jordan, R.R., & Powell, S.D. (1994). Whose curriculum? Critical notes on integration and entitlement. *European Journal of Special Needs Education, 9*, 27-38.

Keogh, B.K. (1990). Narrowing the gap between policy and practice. *Exceptional Children, 57*, 186-190.

Lane, H. (1995). The education of deaf children: Drowning in the mainstream and the sidestream. In J.M. Kauffman & D.P. Hallahan (Eds.), *The illusion of full inclusion: A comprehensive critique of a current special education bandwagon* (pp. 275-289). Austin, TX: PRO-ED.

Malouf, D.B., & Schiller, E.P. (1995). Practice and research in special education. *Exceptional Children, 61*, 414-414.

Norwich, B. (1993). Has "special educational needs" outlived its usefulness? In J. Visser & G. Upton (Eds.), *Special education in Britain after Warnock* (pp. 43-58). London: Fulton.

Norwich, B. (1994). The relationship between attitudes to the integration of children with special educational needs and wider socio-political views: A US-English comparison. *European Journal of Special Needs Education, 9*, 91-107.

Resnick, L.B., Nolan, K.J., & Resnick, D.P. (1995). Benchmarking educational standards. *Educational Evaluation and Policy Analysis, 17*, 438-461.

Russell, S. (1996, January 30). Drugs for ulcers, depression, migraines top ASEBP prescriptions. *Alberta Teachers' Association News*, p. 3.

Slee, R. (1993). Inclusive learning initiatives: Educational policy lessons from the field. In R. Slee (Ed.), *Is there a desk with my name on it? The politics of integration* (pp. 185-200). London: Falmer.

Snell, M.E. (1983). *Systematic instruction of the moderately and severely handicapped*. Columbus, OH: Merrill.

Sobsey, D. (1991). Searching for the criterion environment: Issues in theory and research. In D. Baine (Ed.), *Instructional environments for learners having severe handicaps* (pp. 34-49). Edmonton, AB: Vector/Educational Psychology.

Upton, G. (1991). Introduction: Issues and trends in staff training. In G. Upton (Ed.), *Staff training and special educational needs* (pp. 1-14). London: Fulton.

Study Questions

1. What are some desirable outcomes of schooling for students with disabilities? Does the disability "label" matter?
2. If a parent refuses special education services within a student's current school placement, what options do educators have in your school jurisdiction?
3. Consider three views of inclusive education (e.g., parent, student, paraprofessional, teacher, administrator, member of the school council or parent advisory commitee) and describe their perceptions of appropriate educational objectives for students with disabilities.
4. What are some of the advantages or drawbacks of employing personnel from outside agencies to provide service to a student with disabilities in a public school?
5. How would you defend or refute the statement "Students with disabilities should spend the whole day in regular classrooms with their same-age peers"?
6. How could more individuals with disabilities be recruited to work as educators?

7. Should all students with disabilities be expected to take the standardized achievement tests mandated by their school district?
8. If a student's day is logged and 17% of the available instructional minutes are spent in academic tasks, 23% in medical management (e.g., physical therapy, administering medication) and 60% in personal care (e.g., feeding, toileting), should this be considered an educational program?
9. Should public funds earmarked for education be spent in situations where a student's educational goals focus on social rather than academic areas?
10. How are equality and equity in education for students with disabilities affected by access to the regular curriculum? (Refer to a specific disability)
11. Who should be involved in decisions concerning the allocation of educational funds for students with disabilities?
12. If access to the regular school curriculum is a form of social validation for students with disabilities, what happens to those who have access but cannot demonstrate "mastery"?

Understanding Disabilities:
The Emergence of Our Understanding of Sameness

Frank R. Rusch

The past three decades are rich with "illustrations of competence" among individuals with disabilities. Early illustrations oftentimes served the dual purpose of exposing a behavioral principle's generality (e.g., illustrating that an antecedent stimulus determines the probability that a particular response will occur) and demonstrating that individuals with disabilities can learn behaviors useful to them (e.g., illustrating that a person labeled "severely retarded" can assemble bicycle brakes). Approximately two decades ago, the behavioral research community clarified the intent of applied behavioral analysis by introducing social validation. *Social validation* refers to methods that are used to identity the focus and the results as promised by the particular intervention utilized. In this Chapter, important developments in the behavioral community's understanding of social validation are reviewed, with one of the more important findings being that "We and They were the same people". Social validation will be defined and examples of its use will be reviewed. The primary intent of the chapter will be to expose our emerging understanding of how similar persons with disabilities actually are to persons without disabilities. Examples will be drawn from my research in the area of employment as well as from others. Finally, recommendations will be made in relation to including persons with disabilities in the world as "We" know it.

This chapter introduces major events that have transpired over three fairly equal periods of time, starting almost 30 years ago. The first period began with the introduction of "normalization" and covers a period of time that saw the emergence of new training techniques that demonstrated the abilities of persons with severe disabilities; the second period is defined by major efforts to clarify goals, utilizing procedures that result in achieving these goals, and evaluating the results. The final period is marked by widespread recognition that persons with disabilities control their own destinies. **Major reform is under way that will forever change the human services landscape from one that was characterized by persons without disabilities controlling resources to one where the resources will follow the desires of those who benefit directly from these resources and how they are allocated.**

Some may question these periods as being somewhat arbitrary; however, significant events actually demarcate the beginning of each period. In many ways, these events are methodological in nature, defining methods that have changed the way we view mental retardation in particular, and disabilities in general. For example, social validation is defined by the very methods that we use to identify goals, methods, and results that are considered socially significant. These events are not unique to marking our understanding of mental retardation and disabilities, however; they have influenced how we think about people in the broadest sense. Historically, social validation included comparisons between persons with and without disabilities, and often these comparisons were very favorable to persons with disabilities.

Because these three periods reference my personal understanding of disabilities, I believe that it is necessary also to present the reader with significant events in my personal life that have shaped my interpretation. Five events, occurring over the past 20 years, continue to influence my studies and my understanding of disabilities. These five events are also inextricably intertwined with major events that define the three periods reviewed in this chapter.

The first of these events was the result of accumulated knowledge, which was decidedly behavioral. In the mid-1960s, the science of human behavior was beginning to gain widespread recognition with the introduction of applied behavior analysis (Baer, Wolf, & Risley, 1967). The term "applied" refers to the interest society places on the behavior being studied, typically in an everyday setting as opposed to the analog settings that defined much of behavioral research conducted up to this time; "behavior" focuses upon quantifiable units of human behavior; finally, "analysis" emphasizes individual rather than group analysis of the behavior under study.

I was introduced to "behavior analysis" during my undergraduate work with Bill Sheppard who had trained under Harlan Lane, one of B. F. Skinner's last students, at the University of Michigan. Working at Sheppard's Educational Environments in Eugene, Oregon, I was able to apply recently learned behavioral principles with preschoolers. Being in an educational setting that valued change was important for me, as I began to appreciate the relationship between behavior and the effects of "contingencies of reinforcement".

Following this introduction to applying behavioral principles, I began my graduate work with Hill Walker, a special educator who was interested in young children with behavior disorders. Walker and his colleagues sought effective classroom management techniques that could be exported to regular education classrooms and utilized by regular educators.

This time, my behavioral principles were tested while teaching a group of boys who were considered to be among the most negative and combative in a local school district. An important addition to my understanding of behavior was Walker's insistence upon using data to evaluate the extent to which we, as "change agents", influenced behavior. As a result, during regularly scheduled meetings, his research team sought to identify which behavioral techniques were most effective. Thus, I learned that as we embark upon change, we are best served by collecting data that assist us in making decisions about how effective our intentions are.

An equally important lesson learned from Walker's research was the realization that behavior is important *in context*, and that context defines the applied nature of behavior analysis. As we studied children who were shy, aggressive, or overactive, we always returned to the importance of comparing the behavior of these students with the behavior of their peers in typical educational settings (i.e., the regular classroom). The value of this learning experience was to gain a broader understanding of behavior in the context of what was thought to be "appropriate".

Looking back to this period of my own professional development, I realize that I was beginning to recognize that we were trying to change behavior in selected students to resemble the behavior of peers, particularly peers who had not attracted negative attention to themselves. The primary problem that we were addressing was the behavior of selected students who were failing to achieve in the classroom. The students in the experimental classroom were comparable to students in the regular classroom along the behavioral dimension that was under study; indeed, these students were more alike their peers than different. However, there were additional "problems of social importance" that Walker and his colleagues thought needed to be addressed, including whether students' academic achievement could be improved as a result of addressing behavioral problems, such as acting out in the classroom (Walker, 1979).

Up to this time, much of my work had been undertaken as teacher, graduate research assistant, and student. In 1974, I was asked to consult with staff in a group home for adults with severe mental retardation. These staff were interested in designing a behavior change program for an older man who would steal others' belongings. After designing a behavioral observation and recording scheme, and subsequently training the staff to observe behavior reliably, we learned that this man, in fact, did not "steal" as much as he "searched". Apparently, this man, who had lived the majority of his life in an institution in Oregon, was so enthralled with all the possessions that he and his co-residents acquired in the group home, compared to the sparse and sterile environment of the institution, that he simply could not contain himself from "checking them out".

Nevertheless, his co-residents and the staff felt that he should stop entering others' bedrooms and taking items that did not belong to him. Consequently, we designed a positive-practice overcorrection procedure that included verbally reprimanding the man when he searched, followed by his (a) returning any stolen items, (b) washing his hands, (c) entering the living room, and (d) either looking at magazines or watching television.

As it turned out, this behavioral program was effective (Rusch, Close, Hops, & Agosta, 1976), but it also presented some significant, unexpected side effects. The man was initially very upset at the loss of his recently acquired freedom. I was unaware of this reaction because I was the designer of the behavior change program; not its implementer. However, one late afternoon as I entered the kitchen to review the data that had been collected that day, I was thrown up against a wall by one of my collaborators and asked how I felt being "manhandled". Up to this point in my brief career as a behavior analyst, I had not considered behavior change from the "subject's" perspective. Although my ego was a bit bruised, the lesson learned has remained with me to this day. Thus, this second event clearly centered my attention on the importance of behavior change goals and the nature of the procedures implemented to achieve those goals. This eye-opening event was reinforced 15 years later when Don Baer (1988), in a foreword to one of my books (Rusch, Rose, & Greenwood, 1988), captured my emerging understanding of "professional, personal, and social ethics" (p. x) by writing that **"one of our best values is to recognize that We and They are the same people"** (p. x).

The third event did not have an immediate impact on my research, but it has had an incredible effect on my career. After completing my doctoral work at the University of Washington, another early bastion of behavior analysis, I moved to Urbana, Illinois, where I assumed a position as an assistant professor of special education at the University of Illinois. It was here that I became a "closet" behavior analyst.

Up to this time, I had received an incredible amount of praise from my students and the behavior analytic research community. However, my zeal for applied behavior analysis was not shared by the majority of my colleagues at the University of Illinois. In fact, most of my new colleagues were students of very different schools of thought. These views, and the less than enthusiastic support I received for my perspective, resulted in my beginning to question procedures that I had utilized up to this time and that had previously so completely captured my attention. For example, my early research, which focused upon external mediation of behavior (cf. Rusch & Schutz, 1981), was greatly influenced by Meichenbaum and Goodman (1971) and Israel (1978), who introduced the possibility that persons with mental retardation could implement strategies that controlled one's behavior. This possibility resulted in my long-term interest in utilizing cognitive strategies research (Rusch, Hughes, & Wilson, 1995). This shift in who controls behavior, from external mediation to self-mediation, was an important addition to my understanding of who persons with mental retardation are. Thus, understanding and recognition of the similarities between persons with mental retardation controlling their own behavior and persons without disabilities continued to grow.

The fourth and fifth events in the shaping of my understanding of disabilities involved a series of related events that allowed me to study employment integration and to become a system's analyst, both of which led to a better understanding of the interrelatedness between varying levels of influence on behavioral, programmatic, community, and institutional performance and values. Applied behavior analysis had introduced the professional community to the importance of "examining behaviors which are socially important, rather than convenient for study" (Baer et al., 1967, p. 98), demanding that a given behavior be addressed in the setting in which it is important or valued. For example, utilizing an applied behavior-analytic perspective, teachers would address the behavior of students who misbehaved in the classroom where the misbehavior occurred, as apposed to an analog or experimental setting where the teacher could carefully control environmental or setting events that reduced or eliminated the behavior altogether, but did little to promote acceptable behavior in the regular classroom, academic achievement (Walker, 1979), and better social relations with peers in the mainstream classroom (Strain, Guralnick, & Walker, 1986). Thus, the principal objective was not only to identify procedures that were effective in the classroom where the target behavior occurred, but to address broader goals that included acquiring a better understanding of the relationship between the students' target behaviors (e.g., behavioral and academic) and between the target student and his or her peers.

Around the time that I arrived at Illinois, much attention was focused upon Bronfenbrenner's (1977) seminal article on the importance of "examining the multiperson systems of interaction not limited to a single setting...[which] take into account aspects of the environment beyond the immediate situation containing the subject" (Bronfenbrenner, 1977, p. 514). Bronfenbrenner introduced a conceptual framework that suggested the interrelatedness of behavior, and the effects that varying levels of influence have upon behavior. These varying levels included, but were not limited to, individuals influencing other individuals' behavior, groups of individuals influencing an individual's behavior, and so on. Bronfenbrenner's framework for understanding "behavioral interdependencies" broadened our understanding of behavior. He also challenged developmental psychology's science of [studying] the strange behavior of children in strange situations with strange adults for the briefest possible periods of time (p. 514). I felt at the time that his criticism of developmental psychology was also a harbinger of similar criticism of special education. Special education has also been criticized because it has tended to segregate an entire group of students, rather than teach these students in the settings where their differences exist.

Beyond this fourth event, Bronfrenbrenner (1977) has had a lasting impact on my life's work. Almost 20 years ago he defined social contexts that affect and are affected by individuals as they grow and progress through the life cycle. Introducing the notion that one's perspective changes over time, he also suggested that our relations change throughout the lifespan as a result of cumulated experiences. Thus, the fifth and final event in the evolution of my personal understanding of disabilities can only be truly understood by those who have entered, are in the process of, or have passed through mid-life. Bronfenbrenner's term "life cycle" takes on new meaning when viewed as a process or journey form birth to death, with distinct periods that ultimately define life. Experiencing these periods or "seasons" (Levinson, Darrow, Klein, Levinson, & McKee, 1978) changes one's view of life to being one that consists of periods or seasons and transitions. According to this perspective, then, the transitions are as important as the periods they bridge.

My personal experience with mid-life and its accompanying transition, for example, has enriched my understanding of life and the obvious transitions that define it. Over the past 10 years I have been studying the transition of youth from school to adult life (Rusch, DeStefano, Chadsey-Rusch, Phelps, & Szymanski, 1992). This work has included Bronfenbrenner's belief that each of us enter and pass through different cycles throughout our life time and that these passages and bridges are just as worthy of understanding as the periods that most of us recognize (i.e., early childhood, childhood, adolescence, young adulthood, middle adulthood, and so on). This view continued to shape my view of persons with mental retardation who also must travel similar courses.

A. *Summary.* The significant events that have transpired over the past 20 years in my personal and professional life closely parallel each of the three major periods that I define in this chapter, and some of the primary events that I believe characterize these three periods. Specifically, the empirical nature of my life's work, appreciating the perspective of participants who have been willing and not-so-willing subjects in my research, questions about the value of my research, broadening my perspective from the individual to include systems that vary in size and their influence upon the individual, and recognizing that perspective changes over the course of one's life define personal events that relate to each of the three periods discussed below.

In the first period, "illustrations of competence" among persons with mental retardation, including those with severe mental retardation, are discussed along with a new look at "normalization". These two concepts relate to my empirical work and to my initial understanding of others' perspectives, respectively. Similarly, the questions that resulted from the value of my research being questioned by my colleagues at Illinois and my learning about "systems" relate to the concept of social validation and to our identifying better methods to define goals, the procedures that we use to reach these goals, and the methods we use to evaluate our overall effectiveness. The final period that I will be discussing introduces the importance of a much broader conceptualization of human behavior, and thereby directly relates to personal transitions and subsequent changing perspectives. Each of these periods, and the importance that each has played in the emergence of our understanding of sameness, is also discussed.

B. More important than the personal events was my growing understanding of "We and They are the same people". Behavior analysis can be alarmingly impersonal; the systematic application of behavior principles almost assuredly results in change and the impression that the problem has been fixed. However, as Baer (1988) pointed out, **behavior that behavior analysts view as important to change** (e.g., talking to a peer during a math assignment) **is behavior that may not differ significantly from behavior that is valued** (e.g., requesting help from a peer tutor during math). Further, behavior is contextual, and my better understanding of the effects of setting (Bronfenbrenner, 1977) and seasons (Levinson et al., 1978) has led to increased recognition of how similar persons with mental retardation are to persons without mental retardation. In the next section I underscore several specific events over the past 30 years that reinforce the concept that "We and They are the same person" and our emerging understanding of sameness – the thesis being that persons with mental retardation are more like persons without mental retardation than they are different.

1968-1978: Normalization, Competency-Deviancy Hypothesis, "Illustrations of *Competence*"*, and the Emergence of Competitive Employment*

During this period, a number of events are worthy of note, including the introduction of normalization (Wolfensberger, 1972), the competence-deviance hypothesis (Gold, 1975), "illustrations of competence", and the advent of competitive employment. This first period was an exciting one in the human services. During this period there was tremendous financial growth among the many disciplines associated with mental retardation. During this "Growth Period" in special education (Rusch et al., 1988), several national initiatives that greatly influenced mental retardation and service delivery came about, including the authorization of the Maternal and Child Health and Mental Retardation Planning Amendment (P.L. 88-156) and the Mental Retardation Facilities and Community Mental Health Centers Construction Act (P.L. 88-164). In fact, many programs that are well known today are the result of these two federal initiatives, including, for example, all Office of Special Education Programs, U.S. Department of Education (i.e., the Divisions of Assistance to States, Educational Services, Innovation and Development, Personnel Preparation, and Program Planning and Analysis).

Normalization. Broad acceptance of individual differences may have been the result of our recognition that rather than changing people to fit narrow conceptions of what is "normal", we should adjust our conception of what is normal, recognizing that "being normal" has many different meanings. Thus, "normalization" led service providers, researchers, and persons with disabilities toward a new way of thinking about what is "normal". First used by Bengt Nirje in Sweden (Nirje, 1969), the term "normalization" became popular when introduced by Wolf Wolfensberger (1972) in the United States. Nirje defined "normalization" as "making available to all [people with disabilities] patterns of life and conditions of everyday living which are as close as possible to the regular circumstances of society" (Nirje, 1969, p. 173).

Over time, "normalization" has been used as an arbiter of whether persons with disabilities have achieved a life-style that is as close as possible to "normal;" **most recently**, rather than being interpreted as implying that people with disabilities should do what everyone else is doing, **normalization is regarded more as an effort to rethink human services so as to ensure that persons with disabilities have opportunities to experience the life-style of their choosing, expectations that most people take for granted.**

Competence-deviance hypothesis. Shortly after the introduction of normalization, Marc Gold (1975) presented the "competence-deviance hypothesis", according to which the "more competence an individual has, the more deviance will be tolerated in him by others" (p. 172). Gold challenged the disability field's "overwhelming emphasis on the elimination of deviance, rather than the development of competence" (p. 173), commenting that the field seemed satisfied with trying to eliminate deviance (i.e., aspects of a person's behavior that cause negative attention) in an effort to bring the person up to zero along a scale that would find poles marked negative and positive, respectively. Instead, he urged, individuals should be taught to acquire new skills that would result in them having more skills than deficits.

With his "competence-deviance hypothesis", Gold (1975) reinforced the concept of normalization by stressing that normalization meant "competence as well as the elimination of deviance" (p. 173). This acknowledgment of competence was particularly important to a better understanding of sameness. A great amount of research was focused upon eliminating behavior. Therefore, the implicit message that was being sent to the public was that persons with mental retardation are distinguished by how different they are from persons without disabilities. Gold challenged this perception.

"*Illustrations of competence*". Almost simultaneously with the introduction of normalization and the competence-deviance hypothesis, "illustrations of competence" in sheltered workshop settings emerged. This phrase, introduced by Bellamy, Peterson, and Close (1975), referred to the abilities of adults with severe mental retardation based on a study in which two adults were reported to have learned to assemble a 19-piece cam switch actuator. The primary aim of Bellamy et al.'s early research was to "focus professional attention on the possibility of providing vocational opportunities to [persons with severe mental retardation], to raise expectations regarding the vocational abilities of this group" (Bellamy et al., 1975, p. 175).

These "illustrations" exemplified a growing literature (cf. Crosson, 1969; Gold, 1974) maintaining that persons with mental retardation who resided in daycare facilities could and should be taught to acquire skills that were useful to them and to society. These "illustrations" also resulted in the introduction of behavioral-analytic methodologies that had been used to advance the study of mental retardation, questioning the applied value of the skills being taught, including identifying and implementing effective training procedures, and utilizing observation, recording, and other scientific procedures. These methodologies defined applied, behavioral, and technological characteristics of applied behavior analysis.

Competitive employment. In 1975, my colleagues at the University of Washington and I began teaching persons with mental retardation to work in the food service industry in the greater Seattle area, which marked a dramatic departure from the efforts of Marc Gold and Tom Bellamy and their colleagues in sheltered work settings. To my knowledge, our research and demonstration efforts focused upon training persons with mental retardation for eventual placement in competitive employment were the first such effort in the United States (Rusch, Connis, & Sowers, 1978; Rusch & Mithaug, 1980). All prior efforts in this area had been aimed at determining whether we could "raise expectations regarding the vocational abilities" of persons with mental retardation (Rusch & Schutz, 1981).

We utilized a technical framework to place adults with mental retardation who had resided in a state institution into competitive employment in the Seattle area between 1975 and 1977, and an equivalent number between 1978 and 1981 in Champaign, Illinois (the Champaign project also included some individuals who had resided in state institutions). The framework began with "identifying a placement" and "conducting a job analysis survey", which resulted in identification of "social/vocational survival skills". After placing the individual, we outlined "follow-up" procedures, which incorporated "working through a placement committee" that assisted in "developing a total service plan" consisting of "long-term goals and short-term objectives". One of the most important outcomes of our research was our fledgling understanding of "descriptive validation" and "comparative validation" assessments. Thus, we began to ask important questions, including: (a) What behavior is important to the individual, coworkers, and employers? (b) What procedures are acceptable to coworkers to promote new behavioral repertoires in work settings? and (c) Whose voice is essential in identifying skills that are valued in the workplace and the range of what is acceptable?

Summary. **The late sixties and early- to mid-seventies mark an important period in the emergence of our understanding of "sameness".** Prior to this time, practices in the human services had focused almost exclusively on defining what was different between persons with mental retardation and persons without disabilities. This focus was forever changed with the introduction of "normalization", which directed our attention toward new goals that questioned the status quo. Human service providers began to question what persons with mental retardation should be doing, looking at the general population to find the answers. With the introduction of the competence-deviance hypothesis, Marc Gold sent a stern message to the field to stop thinking of persons with mental retardation as individuals who only possessed "deviancies" that required remediation. Indeed, we were told to teach new skills, just as teachers are expected to do in our high schools, community colleges, and trade schools. Gold also sent an early message of empowerment to the field by suggesting that persons are seen in a different light, depending on the value our society perceives them to possess.

During this period, Crosson (1969), Gold (1980), and Bellamy (Bellamy, Horner, & Inman, 1979) also made important methodological contributions to the field by introducing and refining new training techniques as well as observation and recording procedures. Further, they directed their attention toward persons with severe mental retardation, who, at the time, were not thought to be capable of benefitting from training. Thus, their "illustrations of competence" were remarkable because the general population's approach to persons with mental retardation was then to protect them from society by placing them in institutional settings (Braddock, Hemp, Fujiura, Bachelder, & Mitchell 1990).

As mentioned, after moving to Seattle to begin my doctoral studies in mental retardation in 1975, I assumed the position of coordinator of a vocational training program that sought to place persons with mental retardation into competitive employment. Prior to taking this position, I had been introduced to applied behavior analysis, which is a problem-solving approach to "problems of social importance". Applied to the context of competitive employment, applied behavior analysis directed our attention to the demands of competitive work settings, including delineating goals and objectives as a result of gaining a better understanding of what the job demands were. My research group focused upon teaching competence and extending behavioral approaches to competitive employment. Further, we introduced the concept of "supported employment" by identifying the support that employees needed to remain employed, including the active participation of the employee, coworkers, supervisors, job coaches, advocates, and friends. Our "supported employment" model has since been verified empirically. It includes job restructuring, co-worker involvement, and employee competence as key components to providing structured long-term follow-up support (Hughes, Rusch, & Curl 1990).

Employment integration and the emergence of competitive employment was an important move away from the deficit-remediation model, by recognizing that general population expectations could also be "normal" expectations for persons with mental retardation. In the following period, refinement of these expectations resulted in new expectations that continue to open up new opportunities for persons with mental retardation. I would argue that competitive employment and its sister program, supported employment, began to challenge the broader fields of rehabilitation and education to consider integration as a fundamental goal for all persons with mental retardation, as well as all persons with disabilities. Further, an important dimension of our early work in competitive employment and that of our colleagues at other universities was our growing understanding of social validation and its methodology.

1978-1984: The Emergence of Social Validation

Few people had anticipated the enormous impact that the use of Skinnerian principles of operant conditioning would have on the everyday lives of persons with mental retardation. Numerous accounts of improved classroom behavior, better parent interactions, and the acquisition of useful community-related skills, for example, were published in the professional literature, including in the *Journal of Applied Behavior Analysis* (1968-present). Although "applied behavior analysis" found widespread application in our classrooms, our homes, and throughout the community, exaggerated accounts of behavior modification also emerged in the more popular press with the publication of *Brave New World* by Aldous Huxley and *A Clockwork Orange* by Anthony Burgess. These accounts were important reminders to all of us in the human services that the goals we were selecting, and the procedures used to reach those goals, should not be stipulatively set.

Toward the end of the 1960s, important new clinical models began to surface that provided researchers with a better understanding of the term "social importance", which was discussed by Baer and his colleagues in their landmark article in the *Journal of Applied Behavior Analysis* in 1967. Baer and his colleagues viewed applied behavior analysis as constrained to examining behaviors that are socially important. Essentially, Baer et al. believed that "if the application of behavioral techniques does not produce large enough effects for practical value, then application has failed" (p. 96). Baer and his colleagues also recommended that people who have a vested interest in the anticipated and promised changes should be the judges of that change. For example, these researchers wrote "ward personnel may be able to say that a [person taught] to use 10 verbal labels is not better off in the self-help skills than before, but that one with 50 such labels is a great deal more effective" (p. 96), suggesting that the "opinions of the ward aides may be more relevant than the opinions of psycholinguists" (p. 96). In applied behavior analysis, people who have a vested interest in the focus and the outcome behavior of an educational program, and who are uniquely qualified because of their training, are referred to as "significant others". Over the past 20 years we have continued to wrestle with just who these "significant others" are.

Social validation. **Social validation promoted our understanding of sameness by examining the relationships between the goals that were beginning to surface in formal plans being developed for persons with mental retardation in schools, at work, and in the community, and the procedures that were used to achieve those goals.** Up to this time, the majority of traditional approaches to vocational training, for example, had been insulated from the community because the adults who were being trained were often taught skills that were put to use in sheltered, segregated work settings (e.g., assembling cam switch actuators, cable harnesses, and bicycle brakes). Thus, the primary limitation of this approach was its insulation from the broader needs and concerns of, for example, employers. In fact, goals typically associated with sheltered workshops, including much of the research that focused upon these goals, appeared to be arbitrarily or stipulatively described (Rusch & Schutz, 1981). By contrast, social validation almost always included an evaluation of whether the changes that resulted from implementing certain procedures led to the desired outcomes.

"Social validation" refers to the procedures that are used to identify intervention goals and procedures, as well as evaluation procedures used to examine the effectiveness of a planned intervention by "examining behavior change in light of the performance of peers or in comparison to that of [peers without disabilities]" (White, 1986, p. 199). Two methodological procedures have been used, including social comparison and subjective evaluation. Social comparison typically utilizes objective methods to compare the behavior of an individual with mental retardation to the lower and upper limits of what may be considered acceptable performance, and adjusting any behavior that falls outside this range so that it falls within the acceptable range (the goal of treatment).

Figure 1 displays the procedures that typically are used when incorporating social comparison and subjective evaluation. An important distinction between social comparison and subjective evaluation is that subjective evaluation approaches typically involve the opinions of "significant others", or those who are in a unique position to set goals, select training procedures, or evaluate the results of training. These individuals quite often hold roles like employer, friend, teacher, or parent. Indeed, in many instances, these individuals are the persons for whom the programs are designed. Social validation has promoted a better understanding of sameness by shifting the responsibility for evaluating effectiveness to those individuals whose behavior is affected by treatment.

	Goals	Procedures	Results
Social Comparison	Identify range of acceptable performance by observing valued performance	Identify procedures that are typically used in the target setting	Compare the individual's performance before and after training to determine whether it falls within the acceptable range
Subjective Evaluation	Solicit opinions of others who are capable of making meaningful decisions as a result of their expertise	Solicit opinions whenever possible, as to the acceptability of certain procedures over others	Ask significant others whether the promised changes are important

Figure 1: Overview of social comparison and subjectve evaluation procedures when considering goals, procedures, and results.

Figure 2 presents the efforts of me and my colleagues to teach employees to use self-instructional strategies in a kitchen setting. Two women with mental retardation were competitively employed to wipe counters and to check and restock supplies during the lunch and dinner service. Utilizing social validation procedures, specifically, subjective evaluation to solicit the opinions of significant others, Rusch, Morgan, Martin, Riva, and Agran (1985) learned that these two women did not perform up to the expectations of the kitchen supervisor. The solid horizontal line in Figure 2 represents co-worker performance obtained through the use of social comparison methods, which included directly observing co-workers who were performing exactly the same tasks. This study demonstrated the effectiveness of a self-instructional procedure when applied to the problem of increasing the work performance of the two employees with mental retardation. Additionally, it incorporated social validation in the selection of specific goals by soliciting the opinions of supervisors to identify skill deficiencies in the work setting (subjective evaluation goal setting) and evaluate the results of the treatment against objective data that were obtained by directly observing the performance of co-workers.

This study is representative of numerous investigations that have increased our understanding of how similar employees with mental retardation are to their co-workers without mental retardation. For example, Figure 2 reveals that almost 40% of Beth's baseline performance exceeded the performance of her co-workers. Thus, not only were dramatic gains associated with the introduction of the self-instructional procedures, but claims can also be made that Beth's work behavior was within the range of her coworkers before treatment was implemented. Essentially, therefore, Beth was more alike her co-workers than different.

Summary. Wolf's (1978) formal introduction of social validation marked the beginning of a better understanding of normalization because "social validation" referred to specific methodological procedures that could be used to better identify education and rehabilitation goals that were beginning to be challenged at the time. Introduction of social validation and associated methodology did not only affect research reported in mainstream professional journals. Major changes were also beginning to surface in mainstream textbooks, many of which became devoted to a better understanding of disabilities and "exceptional children and

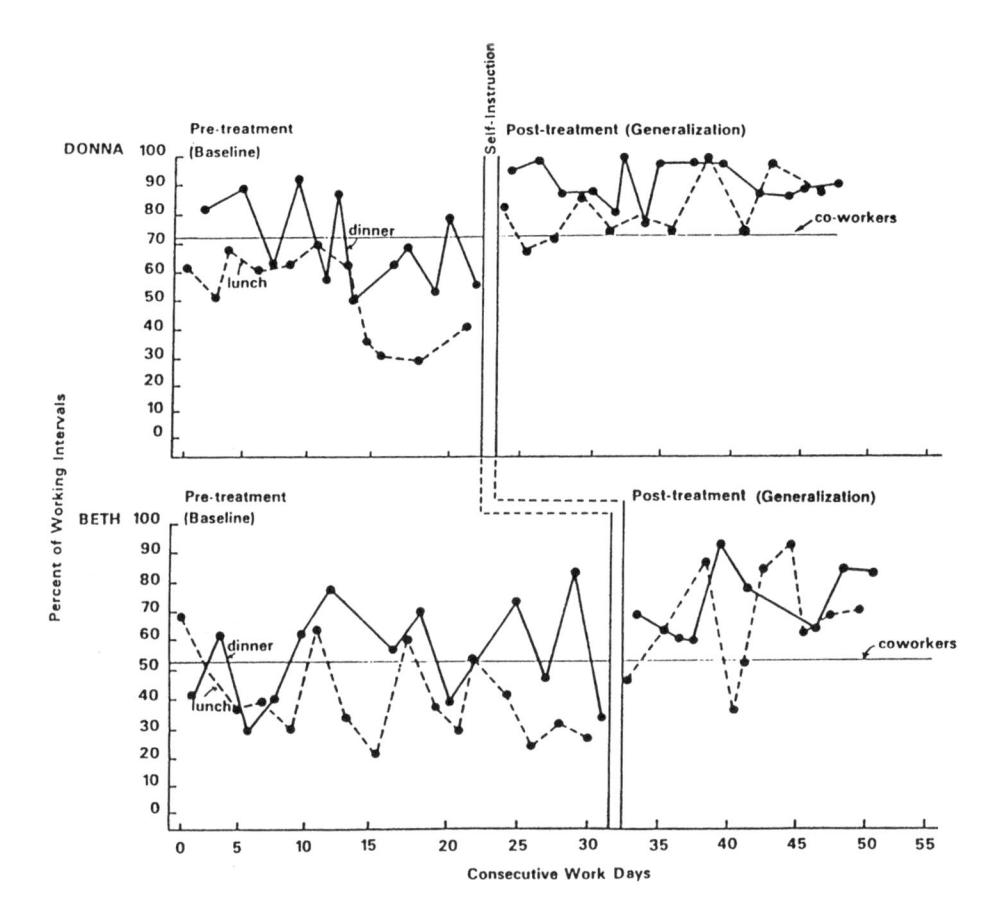

Figure 2: An illustration of how social validation has been utilized to evaluate the effectiveness of a self-instructional training strategy. The solid line in the upper and lower panel denotes coworker performance, which is an example of social comparison.

youth" (Cruickshank, 1980). Prior to 1980, the vast majority of texts in special education were categorical in their treatment of disabilities, with the discussion focusing on perceived differences and competing theories (cf. Haring & Schiefelbush, 1967). Even the most popular text on mental retardation during this period focused on etiology, "symptom groupings", and psychological development, rather than the everyday lives of persons with mental retardation (Robinson & Robinson, 1976, p. vii).

However, new texts introduced social validation methods as part of an overall effort to identify goals for persons with disabilities, including persons with severe mental retardation (cf. Wehman, 1979). Belmore and Brown (1978), for example, introduced a job-skills inventory strategy for use in a public school vocational training program that helped identify what students should be learning based upon what they would be expected to do after they left high schools. These expectations included the demands associated with competitive employment. Further, in the second edition of Martha Snell's text on systematic instruction for persons with severe and profound disabilities (Snell, 1983), I introduced the notion of "seeking validation from significant others" (Rusch, 1983, p. 516) in what may have been one of the first mentions of social validation in the disability literature. Curiously, I used the terms "descriptive validation" and "comparative validation" rather than subjective evaluation and social comparison, respectively (Rusch, 1983, pp. 516-517), probably a reflection of my sophomoric understanding of social validation at the time.

This period ended with new questions about what outcomes are important to individuals and with a beginning focus upon what supports are needed to live and work in the community. Most importantly, professionals began to experiment with identifying rather specific goals and procedures to reach these goals and to question the overall effectiveness of traditional training efforts on the lives of individuals with disabilities.

1984-Present: Outcome Indicators and the Emergence of Self-Determination

The third and final period to be discussed here began roughly in 1984. It was marked by the recognition that the outcomes of existing, institutionalized programs for persons with disabilities were not equitable compared to the outcomes that appeared to be associated with the general population. For example, the difficulties experienced by youth with disabilities who leave our nation's secondary special education programs were exposed by then Assistant Secretary of Education Will (1984), who pointed out that these programs were ineffective for preparing youth for tomorrow's challenges. Her report, as well as those published by Hasazi, Gordon, and Roe (1985), Mithaug, Horiuchi, and Fanning (1985), and Wehman, Kregel, and Seyfarth (1985), noted that youth unemployment among persons with disabilities exceeded 50%.

Further evidence of outcomes that question the overall effectiveness of secondary special education programs has been published in each annual report to Congress since the *Tenth Annual Report to Congress* in 1990 (U. S. Department of Education, 1990). Briefly, these reports showed that 20% of youth with disabilities are never employed, another 20% are unemployed and looking for a job, whereas 6% continue to enter sheltered workshops every year out of high school. Only 1 in 10 youth with disabilities live independently two years after they depart high school, compared with 6 out of 10 youth in the general population.

Importantly, in the 1983 Amendments to the Individuals with Disabilities Act of 1973 (EHA P.L. 98-199), Congress sought to address the major educational and employment transition difficulties encountered by youth with disabilities. Thus, Section 626 of P. L. 98-199, the "Secondary Education and Transitional Services for [youth with disabilities]", authorized the Office of Special Education and Rehabilitative Services, U. S. Department of Education to spend $6.6 million annually in grants to strengthen and coordinate education, training, and related services, thereby assisting these youths in their transition to postsecondary education, competitive employment, and adult living. To date, over 500 model programs have been funded in virtually every state to address these objectives.

These new models launched an era of intense clarification of the outcomes of existing alternative programs, including sheltered employment and secondary special education. Clearly, programs that have historically been associated with disabilities (i.e., sheltered workshops, secondary special education, and most alternative living arrangements) have failed in their promise to provide an education or training that results in a desired life-style s– a life that is full of choices, alternatives, and independence. For example, sheltered workshops were developed to provide opportunities for persons with disabilities to "realize the benefits of work" (DeFazio & Flexer, 1983, p.161). However, Bellamy, Rhodes, Bourbeau, and Mank (1986) reported that fewer than 5% of sheltered employees leave sheltered employment for competitive employment. Even to this day, the chances of leaving a sheltered workshop after being admitted are extremely slim.

Self-determination. The approach taken by the federal government prior to 1990 to stem the tide of failed dreams among youth with disabilities was mainly paternalistic with professionals primarily participating in the decision-making process about the delivery of disabilities-related services. Kennedy (1995) described the problem facing persons with disabilities as being "that the agencies have most of the control. If you need a service, even if you know what your needs are, the agency will develop services that they think you need rather than coming to you to find out what your needs are and what it would take to support you" (p. 44).

This recognition coupled with federal support for student involvement in planning and decisions-making (Ward & Kohler, in press) has led to what Bersani (1995) referred to as the third wave of the disability movement. According to Bersani (1995), the first wave was marked by professionals exclusively making decisions, with the second wave being distinguished by parents demanding that they be included in the decision-making process. A very recent focus is the promotion of self-determination among youth with disabilities, with a systemwide goal being to help persons with disabilities have more influence in the decisions that affect their lives.

Summary. In recent years, increasing attention has been paid to the effectiveness of programs that have principally served persons with disabilities. A primary finding was that these programs were not very effective, neither around the time when much critical attention was originally paid to them, nor during the time when the Individuals with Disabilities Education Act was being reauthorized in 1983 and again in 1990. To date, these programs continue to draw attention to themselves as being fairly ineffective, even after substantial federal investment. Some critics believe that systems change is needed and that persons with disabilities should be positioned to make decisions about resources and programs that control their lives. For example, identifying "waves" of attention in the disabilities field, Bersani (1995) referred to the current wave as being characterized by persons with disabilities gaining power over the major decisions that influence them.

This final period may be the most challenging, both to persons with and without disabilities. The questions that are being posed address a separate system that promotes segregation in our high schools and beyond, a system that positions persons with disabilities toward a life of certain dependency. **In the current period, we find ourselves asking how best to reform special education and adult human services, and the answer may be to scrap the entire system as we know it.** As professionals, parents, and individuals with disabilities grapple with these challenges, an important consideration may be whether further role clarification will result in significant corrections in the system that eventually will lead to desired and equitable goals and outcomes – a system that recognizes that persons with mental retardation can benefit far greater from gaining more control over their lives and the resources that are allocated to improving human conditions and ensuring that the dreams of persons with mental retardation are realized.

Conclusion

As a result of major concepts introduced in the 1960s and the findings of experimental research that reached its zenith in the mid-1980s, the perspectives and viewpoints of persons with disabilities are now better understood by professionals and others without disabilities. In this chapter I argue that normalization, the competency-deviancy hypothesis, and the emergence of behavior analysis set the stage for entirely new challenges to the human services of the 1960s and 1970s, which were principally sheltered services set up to protect persons with mental retardation. With boundless aspirations and armed with a behavioral technology that appeared to be omnipotent, new directions in human services were forged, including competitive employment of persons with severe mental retardation. This new stage (i.e., integrated work settings) promoted entirely new expectations for the reorganization of resources for persons with mental retardation. With these new expectations also came a broadened understanding of normalization. Most important to our emerging understanding of "sameness" was our early focus upon what was considered socially important and relevant. **With social validation methodology as an empirical basis for investigating the abilities of persons with disabilities, therefore, we increasingly found that persons with disabilities were more like their peers without disabilities than they were different.** Quite often the focus of training programs was on behavioral characteristics shared by persons with and without disabilities (e.g., on social and vocational skills necessary for employment survival). Over the course of approximately 20 years, social validation methods have proven influential in promoting whose voice should be considered when considering educational, employment, or quality of life issues. Just as readers of this chapter expect their voices to important in directing their lives, similar expectations now exist promoting the voices persons with disabilities.

References

Baer, D. (1988). Foreword. In Rusch, F.R., Rose, I., & Greenwood, C. (1988) (Eds.), *Introduction to special education and behavior analysis* (pp. ix-xi). Englewood Cliffs, NJ: Prentice-Hall.

Baer, D., Wolf, M.M., & Risley, T. (1967). Some current dimensions of applied behavior analysis. *Journal of Applied Behavior Analysis, 1,* 91-97.

Bellamy, T., Horner, R., & Inman, D. (1979). *Vocational habilitation of severely retarded adults: A direct services technology.* Baltimore: University Park Press.

Bellamy, G.T., Peterson, L., & Close, D. (1975). Habilitation of the severely and profoundly retarded. Illustrations of competence. *Education and Training of the Mentally Retarded, 10,* 174-186.

Bellamy, G.T., Rhodes, L.E., Bourbeau, P.E., & Mank, P.M. (1986). Mental retardation services in sheltered workshops and day activity programs: Consumer benefits and policy alternatives. In F.R. Rusch (Ed.) *Competitive employment issues and strategies* (pp. 257-271). Baltimore: Paul H. Brookes.

Belmore, K., & Brown, L. (1978). Job skills inventory strategy for use in a public school vocational training program for severely handicapped potential workers. In N. Haring & D. Bricker (Eds.), *Teaching the severely handicapped* (Vol. 3). Seattle: American Association for the education of the Severely/Profoundly Handicapped.

Bersani, H. (1995). Leadership: Where we've been, where we are, where we are going. *Institute on Community Integration IMPACT, 8,* 2-3.

Braddock, D., Hemp, R., Fujiura, G., Bachelder, L., & Mitchell, D. (1990). *The state of the states in developmental disabilities.* Baltimore: Paul H. Brookes.

Bronfenbrenner, U. (1977). Toward an experimental ecology of human development. *American Psychologist, 32,* 513-531.

Crosson, J.E. (1969). A technique for programming sheltered workshop environments for training severely retarded workers. *American Journal of Mental Deficiency, 73,* 814-818.

Cruikshank, W.M. (1980). *Psychology of exceptional children and youth.* Englewood Cliffs, NJ: Prentice-Hall Inc.

DeFazio, N., & Flexer, R.W. (1983). Organizational barriers to productivity, wages, and normalized work opportunity for mentally retarded persons. *Mental Retardation, 21,* 157-163.

Gold, M. (1974). Redundant cue removal in skill training for the retarded. *Education and Training of the Mentally Retarded, 9,* 5-8.

Gold, M. (1975).Vocational training. In J. Wortis (Ed.), *Mental retardation and developmental disabilities: An annual review, Vol. 7.* New York: Brunnel/Mazel.

Gold, M. (1980). *Did I say that?: Articles and commentaries on the Tray Another Wat system.* Champaign, IL: Research Press.

Haring, N., & Schiefelbush, R. (1967). *Methods in special education.* New York: McGraw-Hill.

Hasazi, S.B., Gordon, L.R., & Roe, C. A. (1985). Factors associated with the employment status of handicapped youth exiting high school from 1979 to 1983. *Exceptional Children, 51,* 455-469.

Hughes, C., Rusch, F.R., & Curl, R. (1990). Extending individual competence, developing natural support, and promoting social acceptance. In F.Rusch (Ed.), *Supported employment: Models, methods, and issues* (pp. 181-198). Sycamore, IL: Sycamore Publishing.

Israel, A.C. (1978). Some thoughts on correspondence between saying and doing. *Journal of Applied Behavior Analysis, 11,* 271-276.

Kennedy, M.J. (1995). Self-determination and trust: My experiences and thoughts. In D. Sands & M. Wehmeyer (Eds.), *Self-determination across the life span: Independence and choice for people with disabilities* (pp. 35-47). Baltimore: Paul H. Brookes.

Levinson, D.J., Darrow, C.N., Klein, E.B., Levinson, M.H., & McKee, B. (1978). *The seasons of a man's life.* New York: Ballantine Books.

Meichenbaum, D., & Goodman, J. (1971). Training impulsive children to talk to themselves: A means of developing self-control. *Journal of Abnormal Psychology, 77,* 116-126.

Mithaug, D.E., Horiuchi, C.N., & Fanning, P.N. (1985). A report on the Colorado statewide follow-up survey of special education students. *Exceptional Children, 51,* 397-404.

Nirje, B. (1969). The normalization principle and its human management implications. In R. Kugel & W. Wolfensberger (Eds.), *Changing patterns in residential services for the mentally retarded* (pp. 179-195). Washington, DC: President's Committee on Mental Retardation.

Robinson, N., & Robinson, H. (1976). *The mentally retarded child.* New York: McGraw-Hill.

Rusch, F.R. (1983). Competitive vocational training. In M.E. Snell (Ed.), *Systematic instruction of the moderately and severely handicapped* (pp. 503-523). Columbus, OH: Charles E. Merrill Publishing Co.

Rusch, F.R., Close, D., Hops, H., & Agosta, J. (1976). Overcorrection: Generalization and maintenance. *Journal of Applied Behavior Analysis, 9,* 498.

Rusch, F.R., Connis, R.T., & Sowers, J. (1978). The modification and maintenance of time spent attending to task using social reinforcement, token reinforcement and response cost in an applied restaurant setting. *Journal of Special Education Technology, 2,* 18-26.

Rusch, F.R., DeStefano, L., Chadsey-Rusch, J., Phelps, L.A., & Szymanski, E. (1992). *Transition from school to adult life: Models, linkages, and issues.* Sycamore, IL: Sycamore Publishing.

Rusch, F.R., Hughes, C., & Wilson, P.G. (1995). Utilizing cognitive strategies in the acquisition of employment skills. In W. O'Donohue & L. Krasner (Eds.), *Handbook of psychological skills training: Clinical techniques and applications* (pp. 363-382). New York: Pergamon Press.

Rusch, F.R., & Mithaug, D.E.. (1980). *Vocational training for mentally retarded adults: A behavior analytic approach.* Champaign, IL: Research Press.

Rusch, F.R., Morgan, T.K., Martin, J.E., Riva, M., & Agran, M. (1985). Competitive employment: Teaching mentally retarded employees' self-instructional strategies. *Applied research in Mental Retardation, 6,* 389-407.

Rusch, F.R., Rose, I., & Greenwood, C. (1988). *Introduction to special education and behavior analysis.* Englewood Cliffs, NJ: Prentice-Hall.

Rusch, F.R., & Schutz, R.P. (1981). Work behavior: An evaluative review. In J.L. Matson & J.R. McCartney (Eds.), *Handbook of behavior modification with the mentally retarded* (pp. 247-280). New York: Plenum Press.

Snell, M. (Ed.). (1983). *Systematic instruction of the severely and profoundly handicapped.* Columbus, OH: Charles E. Merrill Publishing Company.

Strain, P., Guralnick, M., & Walker, H.M. (Eds.). (1986). *Children's* social behavior: Development, assessment, and modification. New York: Academic Press.

Ward, M.J., & Kohler, P.D. (1996). Teaching self-determination: Content and process. In L. Power, G.H.S. Singer, & J. Sowers (Eds.), *On the road to autonomy* (pp. 275-290). Baltimore: P.H. Brooks Publishing Co.

Walker, H. (1979). The acting-out child: Coping with classroom disruption. Boston: Allyn and Bacon, Inc.

Wehman, P. (1979). *Curriculum design for the severely and profoundly handicapped.* New York: Human Sciences Press.

Wehman, P. Kregel, J., & Seyfarth, J. (1985). Transition from school to work for individuals with severe handicaps: A follow-up study. *Journal of the Association for Persons with Severe Handicaps, 10,* 132-139.

White, D.M. (1986). Social validation. In F.R. Rusch (Ed.), *Competitive employment issues and strategies* (pp. 199-213). Baltimore: Paul Brookes Publishing.

Will, M. (1984). *OSERS programming for the transition of youth with disabilities: Bridges from school to working life.* Washington, DC: U. S. Department of Education, Offices of Special Education and Rehabilitative Services.

Wolf, M.M. (1978). Social validity: The case for subjective measurement or how applied behavior analysis is finding its heart. *Journal of Applied Behavior Analysis, 11,* 203-214.

Wolfensberger, W. (1972). *Normalization: The principle of normalization in human services.* Toronto, Canada: National Institute on Mental Retardation.

Can Disability Be Conceptualized in Terms of "Difference"?

Henri-Jacques Stiker

Translated by Tammy Gravenhorst, Indiana University

A philosophical approach to handicap as a "difference" needs a historical inquiry into symbolization of disability, as philosophy and anthropology are highly interrelated.

First, one has to be aware of anthropological variations throughout the history of societies: disability as an evil spell, a cult prohibition, a fool playing, a figure of poverty, a disorder, an abnormality, a social gap, and as a handicap. Can these variations be thought through the concept of difference? By looking at specific areas (sexual, cultural, racial, age, and so on) that raise the questions of difference, this chapter will show that all differences are not of the same nature and that it is difficult to have a single concept. What kind of differences sets disability apart? While from a historical point of view, outlooks of the difference of disabled persons seem to vary, there is a common level from which the issue arises: this is a difference in the order of life. It allows us to understand the feeling of permanent discomfort in which individual fantasies and social pictures answer each other as systems for readjustment or integration.

These systems have created a double contradiction. Through the will of social similarity (the right to be alike), stemming from an industrial, commercial, spectacular civilization, which is based on competition and feat, background areas are created where people are kept away. I call this a discriminatory assimilation. Further, through a slack and sometimes perverse view of difference, we end in protective and segregative systems that pretend to be integrative. I call this the by-pass without exit.

Under these conditions, it is no wonder that "handicap" appears impossible to dealt with. If, on the one hand, we approach it through the concept of Otherness or alterity rather than difference and if, on the other hand, we think of the conditions for democratic integration, then the "handicapped person" may find a balance between hidden discrimination and an outward show of non-discrimination.

Preliminary Remarks

As a matter of course, we differentiate. Between species, objects, individuals, sexes, historical periods, ethnic groups, and so on, we discern differences. Without them, the world would be completely uniform: each person, each object identical to the next, a series of repetitions. This is not at all the world we live in!

Therefore, the question is not whether differences exist, or whether persons with disabilities are different from able-bodied persons. Instead, we must examine how we think about difference, how we organize it, make sense of it, and according to what principles – questions like: difference between what? Two objects? Two people? At what level?

Before I offer my own thoughts on these issues and the way I hope to integrate them into a democratic society, I am going to survey anthropological history, and ways in which these notions have structured previous periods.

What Do We Mean by "Difference"?

The concept of difference has many meanings – a logical meaning, a linguistic meaning and a sociological meaning. Therefore, the first step in such a survey is to determine which of these is at work in these cultural systems. There is a difference, and then there is difference!

The notion of difference is tricky, and we must work carefully to develop a dialectic between similarity and difference by relying – paradoxically – on the concept of "Otherness"[1]

In fact, even by dealing simply with the paired concepts of "similarity: and "difference", we run the risk of being cornered by a dead-end logic of binarisms, unless we can reconceptualize difference to overcome two trends which define modern times: assimilating the dissimilar-other, or, conversely, asserting difference to such an extent that we no longer from a society.

Thinking about disability: a historical overview

From Antiquity to The Break in The Classical Age

The many centuries which separate Ancient Greece and the end of the Renaissance are obviously not homogenous as far as our subject is concerned. Nonetheless, a fundamental feature remains constant across the cultural shifts which occurred: the predominant discourse centers around the meaning of disability. As an aspect of the human condition, what does a misshapen body, deformed from birth or through injury, signify to people? Definitions are many and varied depending on time period and cultural context, but until the seventeenth century, the cripple[2] occupies what I would call a meta-social position. This position conferred status, or even functional roles upon the cripple of either a social or symbolic nature–beyond the economy, the legal system, or any aspect of everyday life. In other words, disability plays many roles within society, but these are articulated as pure meaning. Nevertheless, by the dawn of science and of the modern state, the question becomes one of social praxis: what to do with these groups of people, rather than, what do the bodies of these people symbolize in terms of human notions of destiny and our relationship to the divine?

In Ancient Greece, disability war regarded as an evil spell. The birth of a deformed child was a divine portent from angered gods to a group which had acted against their wishes. The signifier, the deformed newborn child, must be sent back to the gods as a sign that the message was received. The Greeks then put these babies on exhibit, a spectacle which was called apothesis (as opposed to ekthesis, whereby children born out of wedlock were placed on

---

1 Translated from the French "alterité."
2 The rigor of the historian requires to use only the vocabulary of the studied eras. Otherwise, we fall into anachronism. However, where in the contemporary French vocabulary "handicapped person" (personne handicapée) is the most accepted expression, it is translated in this text as "person with a disability."

exhibit). On order from the city's representatives, children with abnormalities (palmed fingers, various limb deformations, etc.) were taking into wastelands, left in ditches or in water, where they died; not exactly killed, but left to the will of the gods. At least in the social imaginary, those who survived were very special, and were over-endowed with meaning, unless they fell into the hands of merchants or pimps.

Oedipus is a case in point. According to Marie Delcourt (1938, p. 44), a historian specializing in Ancient Greece, Oedipus represents the destiny of those who deviate, an extreme from of "difference" which haunts the Greek mentality. But he is doomed to repetition and mimesis, since he marries his mother, kills his father, and watches his children tear each other apart. The birth of a deformed child si evil and at the same time, it suggests the impossible acceptance of these "others". The human race must be preserved exactly as it is so as to protect itself from the anger of the gods.

Otherness is central to this Latin and Greek notion of disability. A deformed newborn embodies fear of the alteration of the human race and divine curse: that is, being exiled by the gods.

In the Hebrew culture, disability is still articulated at the level of signification, and incarnates impurity. Any disability bears the burden of underscoring the difference between that which is human and that which is divine. Indeed, in the Book of Leviticus, the crippled sons of priest are banned from the cult of priesthood and are not permitted to present the offertory; those who approach the All-Other must be without fault or stain. Contrary to Greek and Roman Gods, the Hebrew God is completely transcendent and does not walk among men. Still, he is present at certain times and in certain places, so Hebrew thought establishes conditions for receiving and "meeting" him. Religious interdiction is strong, but limited, and doesn't imply any hasty practices. Indeed, Hebrew thought recommends kindness towards the poor and the crippled, but has yet to devote an institution to them. Disability is a mark, among others, of that which is sacred, and does not exclude a person from society. There are two sides to Hebrew thought: on the one hand, disabled otherness is quite different from God's otherness. At the same time, it is without measure. God's otherness is perfection itself, while disabled otherness is impure. In society, on the other hand, the latter is a simple difference, a natural consequence of the notion that all men are sons of God.

During the Middle Ages, two main representations of disability emerge. The first of these I call the jester schema, which includes the overvaluation of both the mystic and the court jester. In the latter case, the cripple (primarily the midget, the lame, the misshapen, and the feebleminded) is ascribed a derisive function. Disability always indicates fragility, asserting human arbitrariness over order and establishment. Disability beckons the world's underbelly, and grants one the privilege of saying what no one else can say, especially to those in power. As such, the jester before the king and the leper before St. Francis of Assisi serve the same function, lifting the veil of appearances to reveal the unspeakable, the "meta-worldly". Disability jesting plays a mediator role between two worlds while questioning the very foundations of society the Middle Ages, though tough for the disabled, also demonstrated some tolerance.

Some historians consider all forms of madness to be forms of demonic possession. This may be true in some cases.[3] Even when the cripple is considered as bearing the mark of demonic possession, it is still because his is considered to be part of another world that he is rejected.

In my opinion, the jesting figure, like the evil figure in Antiquity, is more a matter of Otherness than of difference. Crippled jesters speak from another vantage point which makes them capable of judging the present – another world which is also different.

Another figure emerges in the Middle Ages: the cripple as a representation of poverty. The disabled person is my fellow man, for in him we see the face of Christ. The medieval beggar is Christ brought into sharper focus. Since we are all brothers in Christ, the beggar must be welcomed and given alms. The gifts, handled by special foundations run by wealthy laymen, princes, and bishops, guaranteed salvation.

This "noble"brand of charity didn't in the least change the status of the beggars among which most cripples were found; the fact that almsgiving was compulsory meant that it did little to change the attitudes towards suffering and inequality. Indeed, the world itself was the work of a diving hand and wisdom, we humans are not privy to God's purpose. In the end, medieval society never actively seeks to discriminate against cripples. On the other hand, it did nothing to confront or discourage it.

Nonetheless, the notion of Otherness does not apply to the cripple-beggar. Equal in dignity, he constitutes a different and inevitable social category, and exemplifies one of the definitions of difference: alike but forever apart – and one might even add "forever inferior".

The Classical Era and the Beginning of Modernity

Later, both the mental universe–man's relationship to nature and his relationship to men – and the social universe–the theory of politics and the government of public matters, topple. Without developing a chronology or referring to specific events, it is fair to say that the emergence of modern reason radically separates reason from madness, making sense of the latter through what is termed new insanity. Moreover, political and social autonomy were asserted. Gauchet (1985) points out that the concepts of political power and social organization held by the absolute monarchy were neither based on nor depended upon something external, from "elsewhere".

First, the absolute monarch and later, citizens, expressed common will through the vote, proclaiming the source of power as inherent. At the same time, a society best incarnated by the social contract no longer seeks meaning outside of itself: solutions must be sought from within. As such, it is no surprise that disability too is uniquely subject to society, and no longer dependent upon the projection of meaning "elsewhere". Eventually, man himself becomes the subject of scientific inquiry, and thereafter is subject to social praxis and treatment. The birth of the human sciences, which can be tranced to Montesquieu, brings about actions against men and the forces which more or less determine them.

---

3   Muriel Le Larie (1991) has supported the thesis of madness as completely demoniac. On the other hand, Jean-Marie Fritz (1991) has shown the large diversity of conceptions of madness in the Middle Ages.

In the Classical period, disability represents the irrational – that which cannot be assimilated to a norm without undermining it. Centuries of upheaval create a need for order: the state needs strength and undisputed power. Anyone who was marginalized – rogues, criminals, beggars, the insane, or people with deformities – formed an undesirable group which had to be contained to places tailored to their needs. The King's Edict Pertaining to the Establishment of a General Hospital for Locking Up Beggars From the City and Suburbs of Paris", issued in 1657, specified that such a group included persons with disabilities, beggars, and madmen. As Foucault writes in 1972, "deprived the rights of glory and stripped of glory, madness, along with poverty and idleness, appear from this point on quite clearly in the dominant dialectic of the State".[4]

Descartes famous, "I think, therefore, I am" at the same time implies, "I think, therefore, I am not mad".[5] Sanity and madness no longer mix, and for the benefit of society, order must remain distinct from disorder. Over the course of the Classical period developed a true passion for categorical separation of that which si normal and pathological, that which can be assimilated and that which must be marginalized. These basic categories then expanded to include workers and persons unfit to work, non-productive and productive person, etc. Along with other persons rejected by society, the disabled constitute an enemy in the ranks, a pretext for social division, a potential threat to society which must be neutralized and integrated. Thus, at least as far as insanity is concerned, seventeenth-century thought returns to a notions of otherness: a madman is radically and fundamentally, incurably different; he simply cannot be assimilated to Reason.

Enlightenment though was based upon the notion of standardization, but abandoned the notion of the social average for a much grander notion of social equality. Such a notion necessitates that education found the notion of disability. One of the precepts of democracy is the equality of human rights which designates equal education as the basis of genuine citizenship. At the same time, it also applies a degree of heterogeneity in other arenas. It is no coincidence that he eighteenth century was that of Rousseau and Pestalozzi – a passion for education was the mark of both the encyclopedist and the philanthropist. Diderot wrote his famous "Lettre sur les aveugles a l'intention de ceux qui voient" ["Letter On the Blind Intended for the Sighted"] one of the objectives of which was to demonstrate that given adequate teaching and education, all minds are equal. This principle served to mediate the inferiority attached to disability. Those who were "below average" by a standard measuring stick or locked up for reasons of insanity were esteemed worthy of rehabilitation by dint of effort and appropriate means, and eventually, reintegrated into society. Obviously, this is the context in which we are to understand Valentin Hauy's education of the blind, and the development of Braille, which became the standard in Europe. In the same way, the Abbé de l' Epée developed sign language and the education of the deaf, the insane were considered curable and subject to treatment, and Philippe Pinel invented psychiatry.

The nineteenth century brought with it attempts to educate those society referred to as idiots or imbeciles. Itard tried, unsuccessfully, to educate a "wild child", Victor of Aveyron. It

---

[4] "Deprived from the rights of misery and stripped of glory, madness along with poverty and idleness appear, from now on, quite drily in states' immanent dialectic".
[5] "I think, therefore I am". "I think, therefore I am not mad".

was Edouard de Seguin who developed a systematic educational method which will be taken up and redeveloped by Maria Montessori. Seguin's work is taken up again later at the end of the century by Bourneville, who unites the fields of medicine and education. The latter's involvement in politics led to the legislation of special education. Eventually, orthopedic clinics were born and the first physically disabled persons were put to work.

The Dawn of the Notion of a Handicap

At the end of the nineteenth century, industrially disabled persons were a major problem, the result of the exploitation of manpower and a lack of regulation sin the workplace. A considerable proportion of workers were injured on the job. The idea of social responsibility emerges of that eventually these workers ware entitled to recognition and compensation for the injuries incurred at work. Industrially disabled workers are no longer dependent on individual managers, but on the entire nation: after their accidents, they are granted a place in society.

World War I also played a significant role in the development of the modern notion of a "handicap". Certainly the war had greater impact upon Europe, but it was not without its effects on North America as well, which handled its share of world conflicts. Nations were confronted with vast numbers of men injured in the name of patriotism. Liability took the shape of a collective sense of guilt and a sense of economic responsibility. To meet the needs of a population which demanded reparation and compensation for these sacrifices, professional rehabilitation services were created; the recovery of the former status of these citizens became a social imperative.

Another population which emerged during this period was that of tubercular patients. Tuberculosis was contagious, and soon enough, the number of people suffering from it was quite high. It became an issue with ramifications beyond the domain of public health. Impacting the economy as well, it came to be known as a social curse. After their release from sanitoria, tubercular patients demanded the job or schooling that their illness had forced them to abandon.

Finally, I wish to address the consequences of compulsory education. Although special education is the direct result of idiot children released rom hospitals, and not of difficult children in school, the fact remains that the progressive standardization of education based on Simon and Binet's metric scale of intelligence singles out individuals who for one reason or another, did not adapt to standardized schooling. Here again, reintegration becomes increasingly important.

As such, a new social movement developed: the will to integrate all those who had previously been marginalized. In the twenties, a lexical reversal occurred: while "defective" words such as in-firm, im-potent, in-capable, in-valid, im-becile, etc. do not disappear, they are to some degree replaced by re-turn words such as re-habilitation, re-adjustment, re-instatement, re-insertion, re-education, etc. Likewise, a new range of institutions appeared in response to the demands of people seeking a place IN society, as full members. This will to reintegrate the sick and the disabled is quite remarkable. Nonetheless, a gap still remained between what people demanded and what society was able to provide because of very real economic constraints. But efficiency is not the most important aspect of the brief historical and sociological analysis I am developing here. More important is the social representation, the recognition these groups were finally granted.

Keeping this context I mind we now turn to the analysis of vocabulary related to the notion of a handicap. For although it is no longer in common use today in North America, it was for several decades. As everyone knows, the word "handicap" was originally coined in the worlds of sports, first in reference to horse racing. A handicap refers to the manner in which competitors of unequal ability are measured against one another. Once competitors have been compared, the handicap mediates this difference, such that at the starting gate all competitors have an equal chance at victory. In horse racing, either weight or distance is increased and imposed on stronger horses. It is important to understand that a handicap does not imply either advantage or disadvantage, but is rather a question of equalizing condition to isolate and measure the factors of talent and effort. This makes for a more exciting race: without handicapping, it would be much too easy to predict the winner. As one author says, "Whatever the race, the dream of the handicapper is to see all the competitors cross the finish line together" (Hauthuille, p. 63) or, "The programs list the criteria each competitor must meet. These are chose so as to best manage the horses, giving the same chance to all of them, regardless of their breed (p. 61).

Particularly in horse racing, the etymological root of the word "handicap" – hand-in-cap, plays not part; the game to which the term originally referred was used to settle bets at racetracks. Every dictionary of Occidental languages notes a shift in meaning, from sports to a medico-social context. How did the term come to designate the disabled?

Dictionaries concur that until the 1920's, the term was used exclusively in reference to horse racing. Afterwards, it was given a "figurative" meaning synonymous to "obstacle" or inferiority": a country whose industry grows at a slower rate than that of another might be called "handicapped" for example. The medial connotation only appeared in France in the fifties, much more recently than in the United States, where it appeared in newspapers in the early part of the twentieth century, used to refer to people in a difficult social or professional position as well as to those suffering all sorts of abnormalities. The explosion of the term's use seems to coincide with a new social commitment to disability, seen in efforts to equalize the chances of the disabled population to succeed among the able-bodied, to "normalize"them, ultimately giving them the chance to get ahead.

The Handicapped Model

Gradually, the metaphor evolves in the field of human health to designate a treatment model for persons with disabilities. A specific population is isolated and extracted from the population as a whole, just as racehorse might be isolated and withdrawn from the he whole population of horses. Once it has been isolated, it is classified. Just as there are thoroughbreds, and trotters, etc. there are physically, mentally, and sensory disabled persons. A very specialized series of treatments, ranging from special education, rehabilitation, and remedial training courses are available to persons in each of these categories. Eventually, people are evaluated and placed in such a way that ensures equality in competition.

Wittgenstein asserts that a range of language is closely linked to its lifestyle. As such, in our society, the language of handicap reflects the importance of performance. Horse racing, sports in general, and the enthusiasm they generate summarily characterizes contemporary Western society as being industrial, commercial, image-oriented, and ostentatious. To be successful, one must be efficient, competitive, and able to garner the admiration of others. Connecting disability to horse racing allows our culture to integrate disability into ideology, so that it can no longer circumvent the norms that apply to us all. Thus we have mediated the margins that had cordoned off this out-of-the-ordinary population. Disabled people have been designated as handicapped and are seen as citizens to be per-formed. Disabled people are proposed as subjects which, at least theoretically, can and must succeed. The metaphor of handicap is simply a way to articulate and mold nonconformity in the context of our production and technology based reason (Stiker, 1991).

Patterns of "Difference"

The historical trajectory traced so far may only be broadened into several models of difference, as even these are shaped by dominant ideology. Pure difference can really only exist beyond its limits. Indeed, thought itself, regardless of how "free" or original it may seem, is always shaped by historical structures which found it.

The Hierarchical Mode

For complex cultural reasons, this model is much more prevalent in Europe than in North America. Within this model, differences are acknowledged, accepted, and even indispensable. According to the logic of genus and species, the genus of humanity, common to all, includes a range of categories corresponding to at least one specific feature: sex – male and female, man and woman; and biological conformity – the distinction between the able-bodied and the disabled. However, these categories are ranked; they are not equal, and the people within them do not all enjoy the same rights or social status. They exist on a hierarchical scale which also indicates how much each is "valued". This model of integrating – of grouping difference into a coherent network of social representation – is a way to justify ideology: being a man or a woman are two different conceptions of "being human". Yet in our culture, this distinction carries with it the assumption that man's natural role is to dominate woman, since he supposedly possesses more dignity, and importance int he family and the political arena, and in terms of production, education, and authority.

Another such example may be seen in the catholic / ecclesiastical hierarchy. The Christian people is a genus within which their exist tow over-arching species: clerics and laymen. Clerics constitute a category quite distinct from laymen and enjoy a superior status over the latter. The hierarchy is easy enough to establish: at the top exist male clerics, then pious males followed by pious females followed by laymen, and eventually laywomen.

Disability-poverty systems, as well as today's handicap system follow a similar, hierarchical model. Crippled beggars were certainly part of medieval society, part of the great medley of the natural and social world created by God. But they could be part of it on one condition: that they stayed where they belonged. Beggars were always beggars, and their role was to prompt almsgiving, and by extension, salvation. They were accorded a role in society, but at the bottom of the social scale. Likewise, today's disabled poor are assume to be included in society. Although accommodations made for them are hardly adequate, they have the theoretical right to do as they pleas; they are encouraged and motivated to get jobs and to participate in everyday life. Allowance systems exist in many countries to facilitate this integration. Yet as one rebellious disabled person said, "It's the system which designates you, either at birth or after your accident, as a slave. You must have an attitude of submission and gratitude, and can never really express yourself. You'll always have a tendency to be a wallflower, to apologize for your existence. You've got to be grateful for your survival" (E. Aubacher, 1982)

The hierarchical model allows us to erase difference, thanks to acceptance of a modicum of similarity which is relegated to a specific status and strictly circumscribed so that they are assimilated to a preexisting "different" group: cripples have long been excluded from the workplace for centuries while able-bodied beggars have been accused of idleness. Allowing cripples an exception based on their weakness groups cripples with the subjugated persons, useless in their own right.

The Juxtaposition Model. The Juxtaposition model might also be called the Tolerance Model, although it has nothing to do with the respect and acceptance that the name implies. Rather, ti is based upon "putting up" with the disabled for a lack of acting otherwise, due to a complete lack of values in this regard. In other words, "They are other, we are other. Such is their culture and such is ours". In this model, differences are fully recognized but the function of society is founded upon separating, upon drastic culturalizing. Each group is recognized as having its own, distinct organization, feelings, and history.

The model can play itself out in different ways. The first parallels a nationalist ideology which can crescendo into fascism: people who are seen as different pose a risk and must "stay home", in separate places. This model can be articulated in terms of the first: each group has its own place, so that, for example, Whites are superior to Blacks, and anti-establishmentarians. Obviously, it is not longer possible to speak of integration in this case. Such a reactionary stance is intended to create pure spaces untainted by otherness, considered as mutations. Differences are set aside in uncompromising ostracism. Current extreme right-wing thought is more subtle: on the one hand, segregation seems to go with the subordination of certain categories, and on the other hand, it's all done in the name of a national or world order. Thus, such opinions are called "fanaticist", a term which implies extreme integration in a dictatorial ideology.

Another way of implementing a juxtaposition model which is more democratic intends for those who are different to be grouped together, ensuring all rights to everyone without claiming that they will be integrated through some sort of osmosis. Quite similar to the multi-cultural model, this version of the juxtaposition model is based on constituencies asserting authority at a local rather than a centralized level, re-evaluating and reaffirming the identities of historical minorities. Taken to an extreme, assertion of group identities poses a threat to society as a whole, by undermining the universals intended as social cohesivenes. One of the risks is what René Girard (1972, 1978) calls a "mimetic crisis", whereby each group rivals with the others, desiring to have what other groups appear to have. The only way to resolve such a crisis is to sacrifice a scapegoat. Generally weak, the scapegoat falls victim to the violence expressed by other groups in their search for sameness. Juxtaposing differences without a series of universals to encourage integration at some level can lead to violence for its own sake. As mentioned above, the cripple has at various times serves as the scapegoat, as in Antiquity, for example, when deformed children were put on display; those who risk undermining the social order were sacrificed.

Juxtaposition can be regulated at a federal level, but radical federalism is difficult to manage if a common social space cannot be established. There will always be a rejected or marginalized group; the disabled are likely to always be one of these groups, unless they inhabit the equivalent of Indian reservations in our developed societies.

In order to make themselves seem different, the strongest and most successful of these end up fossilizing initial differences imposing adherence to the norms which they themselves pursue. This fits the pattern developed earlier: "Wherever groups exist in sharp opposition, the values and mores of each are juxtaposed. Out of group opposition there arises an intense opposition of values, which come to be projected through the social order and serves to solidify social structuration" (Copeland, 1959, p. 152).

Management of Differences as a Normalizing Model. As soon as one challenges this juxtaposition, restrictive conformity in the form of common objectives and collective values is imposed. These lie at the heart of a democracy. We have used rights, duties, and entitlements to delimit a public space into which all citizens are intended to be integrated. The system of government imposed by the Constitution – election by majority, the power of the state, and the complex system of limitations imposed upon it – are intended to facilitate integration. Political and social structures of this nature limit over-diversification or violence resulting from difference, which could conceivably degenerate into anarchy. Its counterpart is normalization through an imposed mean that eradicates specificity. Western society seems to be heading in this direction: with the intention of being just and egalitarian, they are gradually over-institutionalizing.

Along with a number of other sociologists, Erving Goffman (1963) demonstrates that standardization is an inevitable component of integration. For example, a handicapped person may be invited to participate in able-bodied life and encouraged to contribute to the economy by meands of any number of aids and accommodations. This person is nonetheless expected to adhere to a series of norms ranging from productivity to health and physical appearance. Most of these clash with the characteristics of a handicapped person. When this is the case, it is up to the handicapped person to make the effort, enduring the constraints and challenging himself to meet these norms as best as possible.

This notion underlies the rehabilitation system which has evolved over the last several decades, one which seeks to restore physical and mental functioning to a person through a range of practices including physiotherapy, ergonomic therapy, reeducation, etc. We live in an orthopedic, or even better, a prosthetic society which seeks to model our bodies and minds, to straighten limbs and order our minds, substituting artificial devices for that which is missing or deemed deficient.

It goes without saying that rehabilitation often succeeds in rehabilitating our bodies, in teaching us to cope with limitations, and often enough, in saving lives. Although the rehabilitation movement targets above all the individual, it also reinforces dominant norms, imposing the social average. As such, these efforts nonetheless represent attempts to minimize the difference and failure. Such minimizing is tantamount to effacing as much as possible, rather than diminishing, difference. It is not so far-fetched to assert that our society seeks to delete imperfection in the pursuit of a perfect world. We go so far as to interpret this collective willingness to improve as denial.

Denial is a constant process in the psyche: we deny our class origins, our limitations, the lives we have created for ourselves, our own mortality, etc. Similarly, there exists a collective denial which permits us to justify inequality in the name of wealth and power, poverty and unemployment in the name of competition and modes of production. As constant as these aspects of society may seem, they are not integral to it; social exclusion is due to the central dynamics that ensure our way of life, and industrial and commercial development.

Acknowledging this denial, however would constitute wholesale surrender, jeopardizing general interests and prosperity, and threatening the foundations of government. The marginalized are assisted, anyway – see what we have done fore the handicapped?

Considering These Models

As I have suggested, the challenge lies in linking undeniable differences with the social body in a coherent and just, if not egalitarian, way; grouping specificities in such a way that no one would be or seem to be either relegated to a position of inferiority, forgotten, or denied. By the same token, groups should take free reign at the expense of universal solidarity, which leads to either isolation or violence. Where to find a model which forges middle ground between these two models? A short tangent into linguistic theory might be helpful.

Language makes us human; it shapes and articulates meaning, and event the world we live in. Each element of language, whether a phoneme, morpheme, or unit of discourse, is differentiated from others by at least one specific feature, which may be either sonorous or semantic. And yet language itself would not exist were these elements not linked according to certain rules. Elements are distinct without being separate. They exist only insofar as they are different from other elements; contrasting relations alone constitute each element. This is what Saussure means when he states that in language there is only difference.

Language is instructive in another way, as well: while it is a "closed" system of differences, the number of speech acts one might forge out of it are infinite. No other systems is as propitious in inventing and producing meaning as language; the combinations are endless, poetry literally knows no bounds. Far from being locked inside a series of fixed combinations, we as speakers can manipulate language as it suits us.

Finally, although each language constitutes a system unto itself, it finds its equivalent in other languages; they can be translated. Thus, the specificity which defines language as a system, and indeed, characterizes each language, does not exclude other specificities. Of course, a translation is never as authentic as the text rendered in the language in which it was written. Still, there is not such thing as in communicability between two languages. Despite the "ipseitas" of each language, they are translatable. The language model juggles notions of similarity (social uniformity)and being oneself (pure identity).

This last consideration allows us to return to the notion of otherness: languages are always "foreign" in relation to other languages, as we realize when we learn a foreign language. Complete bilingualism is quite rare, and a child who lacks a firm grasp in a first language has a difficult time forming and asserting an identity. The notion of difference suffices within a specific language, but once they are grouped together, each language is radically "other" from others.

What are we to do with such a lengthy series of apparent abstractions? Social question such as these are not a matter of linguistics, so at best we are dealing with a series of somewhat vague analogies rather than strictly transferable models. As Max Black (1962) demonstrates, there are several kinds of models: the mathematical model, (which doesn't apply to the human sciences), the small-scale model, which is a reduced representation of an object of limited scope, and finally, the hermeneutic model, which allows for interpretation and plays an important role in the social sciences. Language fits into this third model, as it is a means to understand and transform social reality. Such a model provides us with three options: to establish relationships which posit and respect certain terms, to invent various combinations, or to consider the notion of otherness.

Let's begin with the third of these. To speak of difference is to speak from within a system of connections and similarity; even as we diverge from our discussion on language, we must acknowledge the relationship between similarity and difference: men and women are different only because they are similar – members of the same species. The same may be said of skin color, or class, and of able or disabled persons. Consequently, the more we are similar, the more each difference stands out against the uniformity, the less each difference is tolerated. The more the handicapped resemble us, the more frightening they are.

As one handicapped person said, "We have a lot in common with foreigners as far as integration is concerned. The conflicts born of their presence and difference are resolved straightforwardly, through aggression and racist behavior. Too many examples prove this to be true. As for our own difference, there exists no pressure valve of this kind; not because of the tenacious moral or religious notions which have been used against us in the past, but simply because we look like them. We have been like them – ambulatory – and we represent what they could quite plausibly become" (Simon, 1989).

This is the mirror phenomenon, common currency in clinical experiments and psychotherapy: that which resembles us and begins to change poses a threat to our own identity. We are afraid and must not jeopardize our sense of ourselves. Likewise, the proximity of difference is unbearable in society insofar as it is also similar. Recognizing difference can breed rather large conflicts. Once more, Girard's analysis proves helpful. We mus acknowledge the notion of otherness, for recognizing what makes us different – what cannot be minimized or assimilated – probably makes it easier for us to approach others. That which cannot be minimized is the distance which separates myself from another, man from woman, or one ethnic group from another – a trace of otherness which cannot be denied. Naturally, none of these entities are entirely other, but bear more than one difference. For example, male / female relationships would be easier to negotiate if we accepted that, apart from the bisexual nature that humans share, men and women do not share all the same attributes; the latter possess some qualities that are lacking in the former, and vice versa. Just as certain aspects of language are non-translatable, certain things are non-transferable. Handicapped persons have their own bodies and minds, marked uniquely by their experiences. In addition, abnormalities imply a set of characteristics which are different from those implied by physical or social ills, such as poverty and unemployment. There is no use denying it. But who can say that one language is better than another?

The fact that I am my self, rather than another does not at all imply my own superiority. It would be ridiculous and depersonalizing for me to want t the same as anyone else. The history of the deaf community is quite instructive here: deaf persons do not hear, and most of them probably never will. The fact that the hearing and non-hearing must find ways to communicate does little to change the fact that forcing the latter to learn an oral language of which hearing is a component is absurd. They speak their own language and therefore have their own culture. The will to make someone hear is tantamount to alienating them from themselves, unless of course they want and are able to do it. A person wanting to change sexes, cultures, or languages is not shocking. But as long as an other is "other" on some level, there is not grounds for comparison. It is the strong compulsion to compare – in a conception of otherness that relies upon difference – that establishes conflictual relationships which then must be contained within a hierarchy, organized, and normalized. The other is neither absolutely, radically other, nor is he simply different. From an anthropologist's point of view, there are anthropological varieties. This is what Leslie Fielder, a person with a disability, asserts at the end of a talk on images of the crippled in popular art and literature: "In light of all that comes before, it is clear that traditional images of the crippled in popular art and literature contribute very little towards an attitude which would recognize handicapped persons not as some kind of radical and unbearable other but as one extreme among others in a human reality, a world in which differences of perceptions and mobility would mark the distance between individuals, but also between one stage of life and another: from an infant's total dependence to the infirmity of old age. On a psychological level, even the most debilitating disabilities would no longer be perceived as aberrations, but as variations in the infinite diversity of human norms. We would then be able to face pain and even death with sadness or joy, but without embarrassment, terror, or denied through pity".

Considering things on a more academic level, I turn to the work of Levy Bruhl (1922), an ethnologist who simply goes too far when he asserts that societies in history shared a "primitive mentality", absolutely foreign to rational thought. Yet his theory reveals one important point: that anthropological trends and ethnological "choices" do exist. For example, Levi-Strauss demonstrated that symbolic though obeys universal logic, even as he accepts the characteristics of otherness as they shape traditional ethnic groups, in Western culture and amongst themselves.

To argue in favor of recognizing the fundamental difference which marks both individuals and groups is the easiest way to return to the question of the acknowledgment and articulation of specificity and universality. David Cooper offers the notion of being-oneself-with-others, a simple idea with important implications. European society is already working towards creating a balance for the individual: beginning with the Declaration of Human Rights, social rights, such as welfare, social security, education, etc. along with rights specifically targeting the disabled, were granted to citizens. However, such an elaborate network of rights fails of recognize that society is composed of much more that individuals, that the rights of groups and communities within societies must also be ensured. The State's role is not simply to protect the rights of its citizens' it must seek to ensure participation in society, a task which demands more reflection on the balance and interaction of the universal and the specific.

The United States may be evolving towards such a balance, but won't achieve it until it resolves some of the ridiculous consequences of political correctness, which has gone so far that it contradicts the principle of equality, favoring individuals before the law on the pretext of compensating past injustices. This is leading to a very dangerous dispersal of authority and a self-regulating sense of identity.

In his latest book, Paul Ricoeur (1995) asks, "What defines us? What social and civic structures delimit the spaces in which we are recognized? How can we achieve political representation from these structures? Would we be able to restructure political institutions, beginning with the intermediary authorities we are closest to, even while these remain a means of recognition"?

The word "recognition" seems more pertinent than that of "identity", around which the multi cultural debate is centered, since the latter connotes only likeness. "Recognition", on the other hand, connotes both likeness and otherness – a dialectic between the two. Wile identity implies violence against others, recognition implies reciprocity. The key lies in being able to contextualize universals at a regulatory level. According to Kant, society functions according to a logic of conflict, or what he terms, "unsociable sociability". Using this notion of "unsociable sociability", we must conceptualize the recognition of "mine" and "yours".

The flip side of the coin consists of a communal model, like that proposed by Walzer, who suggests that the understanding shared by communities leave the problem unsolved. To found a principle of justice based on reorganized social and political space considered from a legitimate distance, there must be a regulating mechanism. Rather than allying myself clearly with the one model or another, I am interested in this dialectic, the continual back-and-forth between communalism and universality beginning with the fundamental failings of each. This seems most fruitful to me. (Walzer, 1988, p. 95, p. 98)

Conclusion

To summarize the long history of cripples and the situation of "persons with disabilities", I return to the following points:

1. This discussion suggests that we must work towards a judicial system which acknowledges and promotes a well-balanced dialectic between the rights of the individual and the rights of groups – a dialectic between likeness and otherness. In France, this means that specific legislation must be implemented to consistently acknowledge the perspective of all handicapped persons, including the deaf, the blind, the chronically and mentally ill, etc.
   In terms of institutional changes, this would mean abandoning segregated specialization (i.e. in the form of sheltered work programs or special education schools) in favor of special accommodations in an integrated, "ordinary" environment. In this way, the handicapped would be integrated into common social spaces, even while they are respected for their specificity; the individual would be both treated like everyone else and respected as an individual. Accomplishing this means being willing to transform the institutional spaces to which the disabled have been relegated especially as these spaces delimit and shape the workplace. In the workplace, we continue to focus on productivity levels and profit margins rather than assuming our civic responsibility to promote inclusion. Such changes demonstrate the important practical ramifications of elaborating and recognizing a viable dialectic.

2. The anthropological nature of our contribution seems to have been neglected in favor of the philosophical and sociological perspectives. Our main objective was to develop the notion of "anthropological variations" and in so doing, to analyze the continuous tension between generalities and irreducible specificities. The historico-anthropological slant of this discussion allows us to avoid passing judgment upon historical periods wherein otherness alone prevailed, even though the least inclination to return to such a model would be criminal. It is not our intention here to either glorify or vilify societies which wrangle with the ideological notion of difference, but rather to extrapolate and examine the possibilities historical analysis offers us, in order to restore integrity to those who are "out of the ordinary" and ensure the means to fully participate in public space. The creation of this space should not be left to anthropologists alone, but should include the expertise of jurists, philosophers, sociologists, educators, and decision-makers.

Obviously, no decree will do away with fear, embarrassment, mirroring, and psychological trauma that confronting a different body produces in others. But the implementation of public spaces, fair institutions, and respectful regulations may contribute to the development of what we might informally term "mentalities", or systems or representation and social symbolization.

Literature Cited

Auerbacher, E. (1982). *Babette, "handicapée méchante".* Paris: Stock.
Black, M. (1962). *Models and metaphors.* Ithaca: Cornell University Press.
Cooper, D. (1967). *Psychiatry and anti-psychiatry.* London: Tavistock.
Cooper, D. (1971). *The death of the family.* New York: Pantheon.
Copeland, L. (1959). The negro as a contrast conception. In W. Thompson (Ed.), *Race relations and race problem.* (p. 152). Durham, NC: Duke University Press.
Delcourt, M. (1938). *Sterilité mystérieuse et naissance maléfique dans l'Antiquite Classique,* Liège: Ed. Droz, Paris, 1937, Ed. Les Belles Lettres, Paris, 1986.
Delcourt, M. (1944). *Oedipe ou la légende du conquérant.* Liège, Ed. Les Belles Lettres, Paris, 1981.
D'Hauthuille, A. (1982). *Les courses de chevaux.* Paris: Presses Universitaires de France.
Fielder, L. (1982). La pitié et la peur: Images de l'infirme dans la littérature et l'art populaire. *Salmagundi, 57,* New-York: International Center for the Disabled.
Foucault, M. (1972). *Histoire de la folie à l'âge classique.* Paris: Gallimard.
Fritz, J.-M. (1991). *Les discours du fou au Moyen-Age.* Paris: Presses Universitaire de France.
Gauchet, M. (1985). *Le désanchantement du monde, une histoire politique de la religion.* Paris: Gallimard.
Girard, R. (1972). *La violence et le sacré.* Paris: Grasset.
Girard, R. (1978). *Des choses cachées depuis le commencement du monde.* Paris: Grasset.
Goffman, E. (1963). *Stigma: Notes on the management of spoiled identity.* Englewood Cliffs, N.J.: Prentice-Hall.
Le Larie, M. (1991). *Histoire de la folie au Moyen Age, XI-XIII siècles.* Toulouse: Le Rameau d'Or.
Lever, M. (1983). *Le sceptre et la marotte, histoire des fous de cour.* Paris: Fayard.
Lévy-Bruhl, L. (1922). *La mentalité primitive.* Paris: Presses Universitaires de France.
Mollat, M. (1978). *Les pauvres du Moyen Age, étude sociale.* Paris: Hachette.
Ricoeur, P. (1995). *La critique et la conviction.* Paris: Calmann-Lévy.
Saussure, F. de (1969) [1916]. *Cours de linguistique générale.* Paris: Payot.
Simon, J.-L. (1989). *Vivre après l'accident.* Lyon: Chronique sociale.
Stiker, H.-J. (1982). *Corps infirmes et sociétés.* Paris: Aubier.
Stiker, H.-J. (1991). De la métaphone au modele : l'anthropologie du handicap. *Cahiers Ethnologiques, Université de Bordeaux, 13,* 13-37.
Walzer, M. (1988). *La révolution des saints: Ethique protestante et radicalisme politique.* Paris: Belin.
Wittgenstein, L. (1953). *Philosophical investigations.* New York: Macmillan.

Study Questions

1. Does the distinction between the concepts of "Otherness" and "difference" have a historical base?
2. Does this distinction have a philosophical base?
3. At what level does one have to conceive otherness in our developed western societies?
4. Why is it important to think in terms of models?
5. How can "public spaces" be created which justify to difference and also to Otherness?
6. The Nord-American and European cultures have different characteristics, but aren't there also reciprocal influences possible and
7. How can the excess of each be tempered by the other?
8. How to establish a link between different levels of analysis: historical, psycho-analytic, sociological?

9. How can the *International classification of impairments, disabilities and handicaps* be used?
10. Does the concept of "disability" really address the issues?

The Disability Studies Paradigm

David Pfeiffer

Over the last four decades a revolution occurred in the understanding of disability in the U.S. and in the world. This revolution was part of the disability rights movement, which produced new levels of social participation by people with disabilities and achieved many goals in terms of civil rights.

According to popular understanding, disability is sin or the result of sin. People with disabilities are seen as objects of pity or examples of strength and courage. This view is widespread and the new paradigm of disability may never totally replace it.

The new disability paradigm rejects two major professional views of disability – the medical model and the rehabilitation model – even though they are still present in academic circles. It is hoped that the disability paradigm will eventually replace them.

In addition to the disability paradigm, there are varying definitions of a disability, including the lack of the ability to carry out a function, the use of an auxiliary aid, an unusual physique, atypical behavior, being unemployed, and having a history of one or more of them. These definitions interact with the disability paradigm in varying ways, but no single definition is found in the disability paradigm. The proper definition remains an unresolved question.

There are definite implications of the disability paradigm and varying disability definitions for service providers, policy makers, and academics studying disability. These implications are elaborated in this chapter. They must be studied by persons involved in and concerned about disability, human services, and the managing of human service agencies, including those agencies providing services to people with disabilities.

Over the last four decades in the United States and in other English speaking countries, a revolution occurred in the way people view disabilities and people with disabilities. This revolution was part of the disability rights movement, which produced new levels of social participation by people with disabilities and achieved many goals in terms of civil rights. Although some would say that the popular view of disability as sin and of people with disabilities as objects of pity will never disappear, profound change occurred for professionals and researchers who deal with disabilities and in the disability community itself.

This change began to build immediately after World War II when disabled veterans would not accept a passive, dependent role. Instead, they pointed out that although they were different because they had certain limitations, they were still people, could still engage in a normal life, and in this sense were the same as other people. By the 1970s even this view was challenged, in the sense that people with disabilities argued that they were no more limited than other people in society and that the concept of normality was flawed.

Early Activities

Parents, siblings, other family members, and friends of people with disabilities as early as the 1920s were creating organizations to assist them. Among the earliest were parent organizations that insisted that children could not be excluded from public school just because they were labeled as disabled. Other organizations appeared too often with the purpose of raising funds to help the poor, pitiful cripples, but increasingly to assist newly disabled people learn the skills necessary to live independently. It was the World War II veterans, however, who gave the disability movement the push necessary for it to develop as it did. (Pfeiffer, 2003)

One of the first policy outcomes occurred in 1968 when the Architectural Barriers Act (42 USC 4151) was passed. It requires all buildings constructed with federal funds to be physically accessible. This act was the product of public education by the Paralyzed Veterans of America, internal government initiative by such pioneers as Mary Switzer, general activity by persons in the area of vocational rehabilitation, and pressure by disability advocates.

The momentum built up by these activities resulted in more federal legislation during the 1970s such as the Rehabilitation Act of 1973 (29 USC 790), the Education of All Handicapped Children Act (20 USC 1401), now known as the Individuals with Disabilities Education Act (IDEA), the Developmental Disabilities Assistance and Bill of Rights Act of 1975 (42 USC 6001), and other statutes. All of these statutes were based on the concept that although people with disabilities may seem to be different from other people, there is a sameness about all people with regard to rights.

The Rehabilitation Act of 1973 – the first to drop the prefix "vocational" – contained Section 504 which became known as the first civil rights act for people with disabilities. A number of subsequent statutes were promulgated including the best known, the Americans with Disabilities Act (ADA) in 1990. It was called the most significant civil rights statute since the Civil Rights Act of 1964.

At the same time, local and statewide activity resulted in organizations that were founded and controlled by people with disabilities. For example, chapters of Disabled in Action appeared in Philadelphia and New Jersey. The California Association of the Physically Disabled and the Massachusetts Coalition of Citizens with Disabilities emerged. Nationally, the American Coalition of Citizens with Disabilities (ACCD) was created through the activities of many persons from these local and statewide organizations. The ACCD helped Jimmy Carter win the 1976 presidential election and received a strong boost from the Carter administration.

In 1974 legislation was passed that created the White House Conference on Handicapped Individuals (WHCHI). The concept of different, but same, was the basis for this legislation. In it Congress made a finding that: "It is of critical importance to this nation that equality of opportunity, equal access to all aspects of society and equal rights guaranteed by the Constitution of the United States be provided to all individuals with handicaps" (U.S. Congress, 1974:2). The finding presages the ADA 16 years later, but at the time it went almost unnoticed. The WHCHI, however, did not go unnoticed.

From 1974 to 1976 disability advocates pressed the administration of President Jerry Ford to issue the regulations implementing Section 504. Various reasons were given for the delay, resulting in a law suit in the summer of 1976. Just as Ford's last Secretary of Health, Education, and Welfare was about to be found in contempt of court for not issuing them, he argued that in 10 days a new administration (Jimmy Carter's) would be taking office and they should issue them. The court agreed with him. By saving himself from a contempt citation, he set the stage for a major confrontation between the federal government and people with disabilities.

When the regulations still had not been issued by April of 1977, groups of people with disabilities demonstrated and expressed their outrage in every major city containing regional offices of the federal government. In Boston, after confrontation with the General Service Administration police who tried to restrict admittance to Congressional offices by persons in wheelchairs, the demonstrators held a press conference and left. The same thing occurred in most other cities.

In San Francisco, however, the demonstrators occupied the regional office of the U.S. Department of Health, Education, and Welfare. In Washington, D.C., the demonstrators occupied the office of Joseph Califano, the Secretary of Health, Education, and Welfare. After three weeks during which the demonstrators showed no sign of leaving, the Secretary capitulated and agreed to sign and issue the Section 504 regulations.

One reason why he did was that the WHCHI was convening in Washington, D.C., in May. Over 3,000 people with disabilities and their supporters were converging on the capital, and they would quickly have occupied the entire HEW building if he had not issued the regulations. When Secretary Califano addressed the WHCHI, the American sign language interpreters used the sign name that had been given to him. The name, to phrase it politely, was the sign for bull dung.

At the WHCHI advocates, researchers, teachers, providers, and others (over half of whom had visible disabilities) met and began to network. Out of the WHCHI came the impetus that eventually resulted in considerable federal and state legislation, including the ADA, which embodied the revolutionary view that although people with disabilities had a difference, they also had a sameness with all other persons.

In the early 1980s, a number of persons who were both academics and disabled began to write and present papers at professional conferences. One of the first to welcome these papers was the newly organized association of persons that ran centers offering services to students with disabilities in colleges and universities. Today it is known as the Association on Higher Education and Disability (AHEAD).

Another was the Section on Chronic Illness and Disability of the Western Social Science Association. Out of this section grew the Society for Disability Studies (SDS), which today meets annually offering academic presentations across the broad spectrum of disability studies.

One of the founders of SDS was the late Irving Kenneth Zola, who, in addition, was the founding editor of what is now known as the *Disability Studies Quarterly* (DSQ). The DSQ is viewed by many as the journal of disability studies and the disability movement. Other journals include the *Journal of Disability Policy Studies* (founded and first edited by Kay Schriner at the University of Arkansas) and *Disability & Society* (founded and still edited by Len Barton then of the University of Sheffield and now of the University of London). Other journals such as the *Policy Studies Journal*, the *American Behavioral Scientist*, and the *Journal of Health and Human Services Administration* published symposiums on disability studies topics.

The field of disability studies is firmly established in academia today. As such, is the product of the revolution in the perspective on disability and the disability movement. Its fundamental paradigm must be understood in order to grasp the implications of disability studies and to utilize the knowledge produced by it. But first, the popular view of disability as well as the medical model and the rehabilitation model of disability need to be reviewed. In a sense, it is necessary to know what the disability paradigm is not before one can say what it is.

Popular Perspective

The two governing institutions in the U.S. over most of its history were religion and law. In the twentieth century, medicine appeared as the third institution to exert social control. Today medicine is, in a real sense, nudging out the other two institutions, but it is through religion that one can best understand the popular perspective on disability.

Because of what can be called an "innate pragmatism" or a streak of practicality among many persons in the U.S. over the last three centuries, there is a popular need to find an explanation for what happens in the world: Americans need to know why something happened. This intense curiosity is beneficial to technological and scientific advances, but it also leads to a demand for a causal explanation where none exists that will satisfy the seeker. When that happens, Americans often turn to a religious explanation. The search for an explanation of what is different and feared then becomes the need to find blame for what happened.

The explanation for why one person becomes disabled and another one does not is too often found in the concept of sin.

It is sinful behavior, according to far too many people, that produces the activities spreading HIV leading to AIDS. On a milder basis, it is failure to stop smoking or engaging in other harmful activities that leads to cancer and heart disease. When no particular behavior can be pointed to, then it is just generalized sinful behavior — either by the person with a disability or by that person's parents. **The popular view is that disability comes from sinful activity because God would not allow such a terrible thing to happen to good people.**

Many persons reject this popular view of people with disabilities as sinners. Instead, they experience other reactions to disability. They fear that they will become disabled, different in a way they do not like. They cannot understand how we, persons with disabilities, can possibly, bear our lives because they are so repugnant to them. People with disabilities are seen as objects of pity and many organizations raise considerable monies picturing us in that way.

Some people reject this pitiful approach, especially when confronted by people with disabilities who in no way can be viewed in this light. Instead, we become examples of strength. They admire our courage and are inspired by us. However, this view is contaminated by the intense desire in the U.S. today to attain celebrity status or at least to have it rub off by close proximity. In an almost paradoxical way, successful people with disabilities become celebrities.

None of these popular views of people with disabilities as sinners, objects of pity, examples of strength, courage, and inspiration is an adequate explanation of disability. Most of these views have their beginnings in the fear of disability, but disability is a part of human life. Everyone, if he or she does not now identify as a person with a disability, will become disabled before death. Maybe it will happen for only a short time before dying of a heart attack or in a car wreck, but most people will spend a considerable length of time as a person with a disability and so will someone they dearly love.

The popular view of disability is not confined to the newspapers and pulp fiction. It is found in all institutions of society, including academia. In the governmental realm it was strongly ensconced in the Reagan administration's policies. Perhaps the best example was expressed by Eileen Gardner, who worked for a short while in the Office of Educational Philosophy and Practice of the U.S. Department of Education. Gardner opposed funds for special education because it is "counterproductive." According to Gardner, people with disabilities are responsible for whatever happens to them because a "person's external circumstances do fit his level of inner spiritual development." She describes "normal" and "handicapped" persons as "higher" and "lower" individuals, respectively.

Her full views are contained in the report "The Federal Role of Education," published by the Heritage Foundation in 1983. In this report Ms. Gardner wrote:

> ...those of the handicapped constituency who seek to have others bear their burdens and eliminate their challenges are seeking to avoid the central issues of their lives. . . . [Disabled people]...falsely assume that the lottery of life has penalized them at random. (Gardner, 1983, p. 22)

Lowell Weicker (the parent of a child with a disability and then U.S. Senator) publicized Ms. Gardner's views in a Senate subcommittee hearing. Many persons were astounded that such views could be found at the highest level of government.

U.S. Secretary of Education William Bennett attacked Senator Weicker for, as he phrased it, "ridiculing...[Gardner's] beliefs and trying to embarrass her." Bennett's remarks indicate that Ms. Gardner's views were known and accepted at least at the Cabinet level, and maybe at a higher level, in the Reagan administration. It can still be found today in popular discussion of disability.

The Medical Model of Disability

The second model to be considered is the medical model, which dominated much of the academic discussion of disability in the past and still is widely used. **Firmly rooted in the history of the twentieth century, it is a view that focuses on the difference (the deficit) and forgets the sameness.**

The institution of medicine in the early part of the twentieth century started to become the center piece of community life. The kindly family physician made famous by the Norman Rockwell painting struck a comfortable chord in people. The gradual remake of medicine into scientific medicine (excluding homeopathic, chiropractic, herbal, and other types of traditional medicine) gave these kindly physicians powerful authority. They knew why things happened, what could be done to alleviate the distress, and they wanted to help people. It was not sin, but disease or injury that caused disability. Cure the disease and remedy the injury and all will be fine!

The sociologist Talcott Parsons described the role the physician came to hold in society. The physician is the professional who commands the knowledge, the right, and the responsibility to heal the sick and the injured. The physician is licensed by the state to make life and death decisions. It is the physician who truly knows good and bad, right and wrong, normal and abnormal. The physician is the one to trust. It is the physician who can change the difference into sameness (Parsons, 1957: 146-50; Parsons, 1975; Bickenbach, 1993: 61-92).

The patient assumes the sick role (whether ill or injured) and turns to the physician for help in all areas of life (Parsons, 1951: 285). A person with a disability is viewed by the medical model as a patient in the sick role. When someone is in the sick role he or she must obey the physician in order to get well.

The physician can prescribe otherwise prohibited substances (like antibiotics or narcotics) in order to help the person become well. The physician can make all sorts of decisions about the life of the patient such as being confined to a hospital or other institution, being forced to take medicine either physically or by social pressure, whether the person can go to work and when, what work the person can undertake, and even with whom the person can associate.

The person in the sick role receives privileges from being a good patient. The major one is "getting well." During the time in the sick role, however, the person is exempt from social obligations. He or she can be excused from school or work with a doctor's note. If someone comes to work with a cold, co-workers will tolerate work habits not otherwise seen as acceptable. That is, the person is excused from social responsibilities.

The other side to this absolution from all usual social responsibilities is that the person gives up his or her rights. Fulfilling obligations and responsibilities entitles a person to rights. No responsibilities means no rights. The sick person can be told what to do, when to do it, and how to do it by the physician or a surrogate.

There is a problem with the medical model of disability. A person with a disability - such as a wheelchair user who is a polio survivor - will never get well in the sense of not having to use the wheelchair. That person will never cease being different and thus become the same as other people. As a result, the physician will view such a person as a failure and as an example of inadequacy. Such inadequacies are embarrassing and threatening to physicians. For many years, the physician's reaction to disability was simply institutionalization.

One of the extreme examples of the medicalization of disability is the International Classification of Impairments, Disabilities, and Handicaps (ICIDH) created by the World Health Organization. The ICIDH mentions the sick role explicitly: "...the sick person is unable to sustain his accustomed social role and cannot maintain his customary relationships with others" (Wood, 1980, p.10). In other words, the sick person is different in an undesirable way.

The ICIDH is presented as relevant "to the mitigation of environmental and society barriers" and was used for the "assessment for work" (Wood, 1980, p. 2). "At the community level, it [the ICIDH] has helped in identifying the needs of people with disabilities and handicaps, identifying handicapping situations in the social and physical environment, and formulating the policy decisions necessary for improvements in everyday life, including modifications of the physical and social environment" (Wood, 1980, p. 3). These problems are not medical problems, but economic, social, and political problems. The ICIDH easily becomes a tool of eugenics and a threat to people with disabilities everywhere.

The ICIDH was revised due to criticism most vocally from the disability community. (Pfeiffer, 1998) Its successor, the International Classification of Functioning, Disability, and Health (ICF) is not considered to be much of an improvement. It was adopted by the World Health Assembly of the World Health Organization in May 2001.

Recognizing that institutionalization was not a satisfactory solution for every person with a disability, an entire field grew up as an alternative. Rehabilitation or rehabilitation counseling (to distinguish it from medical rehabilitation involving surgery, medicine, physical therapy, occupational therapy, and other things) appeared in the 1920s. It has grown into a major industry today.

The Rehabilitation Model of Disability

The rehabilitation model is an offshoot of the medical model. In a sense, when physicians have gone as far they can go, the rehabilitation counselor takes over. The basic thrust of the rehabilitation model is to change or hide the difference so the person with a disability can pass as being the same as other people.

At one time the model viewed a person with a disability in terms of employment. The person with a disability has a problem (a deficit), which makes him or her unemployed. The rehabilitation counselor determines what the deficit is. For example, it might be a lack of training or lack of tools, or something that requires ongoing medical intervention. Whatever it is, the rehabilitation counselor acts as the case manager coordinating and obtaining the needed services.

Until the last decade rehabilitation counselors were told that they were the professionals and, therefore, could determine what the person with a disability needed. The person with a disability, in turn, had to accept the situation or otherwise would be seen as "not adjusted" or "not accepting" the disability. The independent living movement has convinced rehabilitation counselors that the person with a disability must be folded into the decision making process. Not all of the rehabilitation counselors are convinced, but they often see that it is the easiest way to obtain the now needed consent to the rehabilitation plan.

The problem with the rehabilitation model is twofold. By viewing the person with a disability as a worker and nothing else, it warps its own thinking. A person is not just a cog in the machine of production. There are other aspects of life for a worker and there are other roles that can be fulfilling in society besides being a worker. In order to avoid this problem, the independent living movement had written into law that market place employment is not the only goal of rehabilitation.

The second problem with the rehabilitation model is that it actually blames the victim for what happens. If the person with a disability cannot find a job because the transportation systems, the buildings, and the schools are not accessible in physical, sensory, and cognitive terms, the solution is not for the individual to be molded to fit society, but for society to be changed to be accessible to all people.

The Disability Paradigm

As the disability movement arose and eventually became established in academia, the disability paradigm came to be formalized. The earliest version was elaborated by Irving Zola, who viewed disability as a social construct. Others saw people with disabilities as an oppressed group and put forth the minority model. More recently, disability is seen as existing only in specific acts of discrimination for which there are political, legal, and economic recourse.

Irv Zola probably exerted more of an influence on the disability movement and the development of the disability paradigm in academia than any other person. His incredible ability to weave the personal (which he came to see is also political) with the sociological knowledge that he was developing ranks him as a major thinker of the social sciences (Williams, 1996).

For Zola disability was something that was constructed by other people. Using the concept of stigma (Goffman, 1963; Zola, 1982), he elaborated how people with disabilities were discriminated against by being invisible to "normal" people who largely avoided them and segregated them. Being a sociologist, Zola focused on the social processes by which this happens. The medicalization of disability was one of the primary ways in which disability was socially constructed (Zola, 1972, 1983).

Others, especially disability advocates, were more concerned with the political processes by which people with disabilities are oppressed. For example, people with disabilities are similar to other oppressed people – we are rejected, receive a reduced share of social resources, are ridiculed, segregated, and persecuted. We internalize these actions and feel that they must be correct. We then feel guilty and begin to act in ways that encourage our oppression. The only way to break out of this killing cycle is to organize and demand a share of the resources of society and an end to discrimination.

There is nothing inherently wrong with either the social construction model or the minority model of disability. For many persons, they are adequate explanatory frameworks. For many others, however, they are not. To people not trained as sociologists, social processes sometimes appear to be wishful thinking – something happens and it becomes a social process. For people not trained as political scientists, oppression of minorities and rebellion appear to be extreme interpretations of events. They say that such a view does not foster problem solving. Never denying that people with disabilities suffer discrimination and oppression, another view is slowly emerging, encouraged by the legal bent of U.S. society. It is one that recognizes the differences of people with disabilities while at the same time emphasizing the sameness.

This model or version of the paradigm perceives disability to exist during and as the result of discrimination. If there is no discrimination, there is no disability. Normal behavior is a statistical artifact that encourages people with power and resources to label people without power and resources as abnormal. Being seen as different, people with disabilities can then be denied their sameness. (Pfeiffer, 2000, 2001)

While resembling and not contradicting the social construction and minority group models, the legal model of disability provides remedies that can be used to fight discrimination. Some of these remedies are legal ones, which can be used in courts such as the Americans with Disabilities Act. Other remedies are individual and group demonstrations, which educate people and sometimes force them to face the fact of discrimination. Education is a remedy, as is the use of body language, voice, and other types of behavior.

This emerging model of disability is closely tied to the rejection of modernity and its categories. It is existentialist in the sense that it denies objective reality to disability. People with disabilities are not different from other people in any basic, essential way. To assume that disability has an essential existence is to give it objective reality, as do the social construction and minority group models. To assume that there are people with disabilities and people without disabilities is to surrender to the discrimination. To assume this dualism is to consent to the "us and them" distinction and "we" are always better than "they" are.

There are common elements in all three versions of the disability paradigm. In the disability paradigm, the person with the disability is the decision maker. The slogan "nothing about me without me" sums up this principle. Professionals are the source of expert advice only and are not the decision makers. Providers of services must treat the person with a disability as a customer in the traditional sense. If the service is of poor quality, is delivered in a discriminatory manner, or is overpriced, then the person with a disability must have the option of going elsewhere.

Another common element of the three versions of the disability paradigm is that barriers (attitudinal, sensory, cognitive, architectural) are to be changed, not the people with disabilities. Instead of surgical operations to make us able to walk up stairs, ramps and elevators must be provided. It is society and policy that needs to be reformed, not the people with disabilities.

A question is raised by a number of researchers and advocates with disabilities: Should a person without a disability be allowed to carry out disability research? Feminists, African-Americans, Hispanics, Asian-Americans, Native Americans, and other groups all protest that unless the researcher partakes of their particular view, then she or he cannot understand it. Any results are bound to be bogus, they say. Perhaps because disability is so ubiquitous (anyone at any time can become disabled), the disability paradigm implies something else. The disability paradigm, and not the person using it, determines the quality of the research. Anyone using the disability paradigm to do research is doing disability research.

The disability paradigm is not without its problems. One is the lack of extensive understanding of it by other academics. Another is the existence of strong proponents of the medical and rehabilitation models. A third problem is the difficulty of defining disability.

Definitions of Disability

There is no generally accepted definition of disability. None of the models found in the disability paradigm clearly defines disability. According to the legal model, if there are no social and political acts producing discrimination based upon a disability, then there is no disability. The social construction and minority group models insist that the discrimination is real and ongoing. It is an epistemological problem that has yet to be solved.

However, six definitions of disability are in common use. They emphasize the difference and are based on (a) functional abilities, (b) the use of an auxiliary aid, (c) physical appearance, (d) behavior, (e) unemployment, and (f) the perception of a disability.

The first defines disability as the lack of an ability to carry out a normal function such as the activities of daily living. That is, if people are unable to walk up a flight of stairs, they lack the ability to perform normally. The problem with this definition is that there is no normal way to carry out activities of daily living. What is the normal way of going a mile? Take a taxi? Drive your own car? Rollerblade? Use a wheelchair? Go by subway? Walk? There are many ways in which people are mobile.

What is the normal way to make a living? Academics certainly have unusual daily lives, earning a living in strange ways such as writing chapters in books and attending conferences. Other persons have extremely odd ways of making a living – there is no normal way to make a living.

What is the normal way of making love? This question can be answered in many different ways. There is no normal way to make love.

A second definition comes out of the suggested solution to the problem of normality and daily functioning. The question is asked if the function is done with the use of an auxiliary aid. If so, then the person must be disabled. Again, this definition suffers from the fact that many persons use auxiliary aids such as bicycles, cars, taxis, and buses in order to be mobile. It simply shifts the focus from the activity to the aid and gains little in the process.

Another suggested definition involves unusual physical appearances and atypical behavior. Again, both of these definitions involve cultural views of appearance and behavior. What is normal in one part of the country may not be normal in another. Both of these definitions fall before the question of what is normal appearance and behavior.

It is understandable why vocational rehabilitation used its definition of disability as being unemployed due to some deficiency that can be corrected. But to tell an employed person with a disability that he or she is no longer disabled because of being employed is ludicrous. If unemployment were the essence of disability, then there would be no need for the Americans with Disabilities Act and other legislation. Yet, their need is amply demonstrated and destroys this definition of disability.

It is also suggested that disability can be defined as having a history of one or more of the various defining situations. If the definitions themselves are not adequate, then having such a history fails. But this leads us to a possible definition.

Disability can be defined as being regarded as being disabled. If being regarded as being disabled is seen as beautiful, then that is a good situation. If being regarded as being disabled is seen in a neutral light, then that is also a good result. But being regarded as being disabled leads to exclusion, segregation, persecution, discrimination, and even death, then the situation is bad.

If the differences that people with disabilities have are seen as being bad, then discrimination occurs. This definition is the one that the legal version of the disability paradigm puts forth. It is the one that will produce more beneficial outcomes in the future. It is the one that carries out the intention and the principles of the disability paradigm.

Implications of the Disability Paradigm

What are the implications of disability paradigm? There are four major implications involving professionals, social change, research, and differences.

It is clear that in the disability paradigm professionals are not the decision makers. Physicians, rehabilitation counselors, service providers, parents, spouses, friends, social workers, teachers, policy makers, and researchers must acknowledge that they do not have the right to make decisions for the person with a disability. It is the person with a disability who makes the decision. Although she or he may consult with others and may invite different, conflicting opinions, the decision is to be made by the person who best knows the situation: the person with the disability. Extenuating conditions such as age or lack of consciousness may force the decision to be made by someone else, but the existence of a disability – no matter how severe – can never be the reason why someone else decides.

A second implication involves all of society. Change must occur in the policies and the conditions within which people with disabilities live. Barriers of all descriptions must be eliminated. Discrimination must cease. Educational opportunities must be provided. Employment decisions must be made on the basis of ability and not the perception of a disability.

The irony is that all of these requirements now exist in federal law and in different versions in every set of state laws. In addition to these legal requirements, persons with disabilities must be accepted as people and not treated as subhuman. People with disabilities are not the ones who must change. People without disabilities are the ones who must change.

A third implication is that acceptable research on disability and about people with disabilities must be based upon the disability paradigm. While another model might be appropriate in some circumstances, it is the disability paradigm that distinguishes disability studies from all other areas of knowledge. Only its use will produce more and better knowledge in the field.

The final implication of the disability paradigm is that our differences are to be preserved, not submerged. People with a disability have the right to be different and the right to be treated equally with all other people. Admittedly, social, political, and economic forces are imperfect and people with greater resources will always have an edge, but discrimination against people with disabilities because of the perception of a disability must and will cease.

References

Bickenbach, Jerome E. (1993). *Physical disability and social policy.* Toronto: University of Toronto Press.
Gardner, Eileen. (1983). *The federal role of education.* Washington, D.C.: Heritage Foundation.
Goffman, Erving. (1963). *Stigma.* Englewood Cliffs, N.J.: Prentice-Hall.
Parsons, Talcott. (1951). *The social system.* Glencoe: The Free Press.
Parsons, Talcott. (1957). Illness and the role of the physician: A sociological perspective. *American Journal of Orthopsychiatry*, 2: 452-60; reprinted in Peter Hamilton (editor), (1985) *Readings from Talcott Parsons*, New York: Tavistock Publications, Reading 11, pages 145-55.
Parsons, Talcott. (1975). The sick role and the role of the physician reconsidered. *Health and Society*, 53: 257-78.
Pfeiffer, David. (1998). The ICIDH and the need for its revision. *Disability and Society*, 13(4): 503-23.
Pfeiffer, David. (2000). The disability paradigm. *Disability policy: Issues and implications for the new millennium – A report on the 21st Mary E. Switzer memorial seminar, held September 1999*, edited by L. Robert McConnell and Carl E. Hansen, Alexandria, VA: National Rehabilitation Association, pages 81-82.
Pfeiffer, David. (2001). The conceptualization of disability. *Exploring theories and expanding methodologies: Where we are and where we need to go. Research in Social Science and Disability*, volume 2. Edited by Barbara M. Altman and Sharon N. Barnartt. Oxford: Elsevier Science, pages 29-52.
Pfeiffer, David. (2003). The disability movement: Ubiquitous but unknown. *Teamsters and Turtles? U.S. Progressive Political Movements in the 21st Century* edited by John C. Berg, Lanham, MD: Rowman and Littlefield, chapter 8, pages 159-83.
U.S., Congress. (1974). PL 93-516, Rehabilitation Act Amendments of 1974.
Williams, Garreth. (1996). Irving Kenneth Zola (1935-1994): An appreciation. *Sociology of Health & Illness*, 18(1): 107-25.
Wood, Philip. (1980). *International classification of impairments, disabilities, and handicaps: A manual of classification relating to the consequences of disease.* Geneva: World Health Organization.
Zola, Irving K. (1972). Medicine as an institution of social control. *Sociological Review*, 20, 487-504.
Zola, Irving K. (1982). *Missing pieces: A chronicle of living with a disability.* Philadelphia: Temple University Press.
Zola, Irving K. (1983). *Socio-medical inquiries: Recollections, reflections and reconsiderations.* Philadelphia: Temple University Press.

Study Questions

1. Name some of the local and state organizations created by people with disabilities in the 1970's to fight for their rights.
2. What role did the 1977 White Conference on Handicapped Individuals play in the development of the Disability movement?
3. What was the origin of the Society for Disability Studies?
4. What is the common, popular view of disability and what is its origin?

5. What is the medical model of disability and what is its origin?
6. What are the main problems with the medical model of disability?
7. How are the medical model and the rehabilitation model of disability related?
8. What is similar and what is different in the three versions of the disability paradigm?
9. Discuss why it is difficult to arrive at a definition of disability which is accepted by everyone.
10. What are the implications of the disability paradigm regarding professionals, social change, research, and differences between people?

Part 3
Emerging Disability Communities

The study of community has been a central focus for social scientists, yet it has rarely been explored in relation to disability. In the following chapters, the authors challenge any fixed understanding of community, and ultimately of culture. The fit between disability and community is clearly an unsettled one that invites further work. The authors bring perspectives based on the commonality of impairment, family dynamics, political agenda formation, and terminologies as part of larger discourses, and new information technologies, as the basis of social realities that question and redefine the possibility of community.

As the greater disability community increasingly defines itself as having a unique culture, many culturally Deaf people have historically distanced themselves from such efforts. In the first article in this section, Susan Foster examines how deafness fits within the broad disability studies paradigm.

Despite major areas of convergence between deafness and disability, including a shared history of definition and experience and a similar vocabulary and metaphors, controversy surrounding non-disabled/hearing people in leadership, activism and other roles and a view of deafness/disability as handicap only under certain social conditions, in several important ways deafness has been defined as different from disability. Major among these is the notion that culturally Deaf persons constitute a linguistic minority rather than a disability group, a proposition that has far-reaching implications, especially for education and preferred "ways of naming". Thus, a sense of pride encourages the primary role assigned to being deaf (e.g., deaf person rather than person who is deaf) and the call for separate education as ways to develop and preserve Deaf identity and culture. In terms of advocacy, many deaf people also differ from the larger disability community by traditionally focusing on social interaction and fellowship rather than political action. Thus, deaf culture and deaf communities long predated the deaf rights movement. Finally, many deaf people feel as isolated in the disabled community as among nondisabled people and, therefore, see no difference between hearing people and disabled people – they are all part of the hearing world to them.

As Foster points out, these major areas of divergence primarily represent the views of the culturally Deaf community, however, which constitutes only approximately 10% of the 20 million Americans with a hearing loss of some kind. Thus, the larger community of deaf and heard-of-hearing persons may identify with the perspectives of persons with disabilities. In addition, some deaf persons incorporate both Deaf culture and disability culture within their identity. Indeed, based on the finding of a recent study of deaf minority students that identity is fluid, responding to the demands of a given situation, Foster proposes the notion of a multidimensional identity as a useful way to think of deafness, disability, and the question of "same or different". For these reasons, she concludes by recommending that deafness be acknowledged and incorporated in disability studies curricula as both "same and different".

Philip Ferguson suggests that it is in talking about the culture *of* disability, rather than talking about culture and disability, that the tension between "same" and "different" most clearly emerges. In his chapter, he explores what it might mean to speak of a culture of mental retardation, using the Independent Living Movement (ILM) and the Community Inclusion Movement (CIM) as reference points, along with events from the life of his adult son who has multiple disabilities.

Within the present context of culture, Ferguson concludes that when we encounter somebody with so-called profound mental retardation, we don't see any culture. And without a cultural context, people with significant cognitive disabilities are neither the same as, nor different from, the non-disabled population due to a lack of comparative context to make such a judgment. Further, for individuals with severe cognitive disabilities, Ferguson points out, there is no alternative or subculture available to replace the absent culture of dominant society, unlike other disabilities such as deafness. As a result, there may be little use in trying to speak of a true mental retardation culture as opposed to a professional or bureaucratic subculture that often surrounds people with mental retardation.

Ferguson examines the cultural implications embedded within the ILM and the CIM as examples of the different cultural histories of cognitive and physical disability and concludes that, however unintended, the logic behind these two movements tends to legitimize the continued ghettoization of individuals with cognitive disabilities to margins of both the disability community and mainstream culture. Thus, according to Ferguson, the risk in the cultural essentialism of some versions of inclusion is that its implicit denial of essential differences from the dominant culture can also deny people with cognitive disabilities access to the alternative cultures and traditions that the larger disability community is beginning to celebrate. To avoid the traditional "difference dilemma", Ferguson advocates for a "social relations" approach whereby we approach disability as relational, not essential. Rather than diminishing disability or discredit its centrality to our lives, Ferguson claims, a relational approach to disability merely shows us where to look; not what we should see.

Madelyn Iris broadens the discussion by examining how public policy has affected self-concept as well as social definitions of aging and disability and how these, in turn, have provided a framework for alignment or disparity. Whereas the elderly as a group are evolving into being seen as having special status, persons with disabilities are increasingly viewed as a legal, protected minority in accordance with the emerging paradigm discussed by Pfeiffer. Indeed, the position as a legally recognized minority population may be the biggest barrier to a common consensus or a common agenda through coalition building by the two groups, according to Iris. Despite differences in how disability and aging symbolize the natural processes of life, at some point, the world of the elderly and that of the disabled intersect: People with disabilities grow old along with their non-disabled peers, and many elderly become functionally and/or cognitively disabled. For these reasons, as well as others discussed in detail by Iris, the two groups are gradually being pushed toward a common agenda. Nevertheless, as illustrated in the case study of Mary Henderson, a 62-year-old woman with multiple sclerosis who wants to be considered neither old, nor disabled, understanding the totality of individual identity as a function of a single characteristic such as chronological age or a particular impairment is fraught with problems. This partly explains why historically there has been few attempts to develop even a unified posture of support for programs that otherwise clearly benefit both groups.

However, despite numerous differences within and between the two groups, Iris reminds us of the "powerful glue" that could hold them together: the common threat from the outside, as increasingly manifested in the 1990s in cuts in benefit programs, greater restrictions on eligibility criteria, and a more general conservatism that argues against public support for any minority or group of individuals defined as "different" from the mainstream.

Iris concludes by bringing us back to the focus on disabilities study, cautioning that concern about and attention to the overlapping constituencies of the elderly and those with disabilities within the evolving discipline of disability studies is critical because that is where, she maintains, the greatest potential exists for understanding how public perceptions are shaped and constituted.

Patrick Devlieger traces the history of mental retardation as not only reflecting the history of certain people, but also society's history and the working of culture. According to this perspective, the terms we use to refer to "mental retardation" may be viewed as windows on society, showing the changing definitions over the last century as definitions of "difference".

Adopting an anthropological-semantic approach, Devlieger concentrates on the professional development of terminology of mental retardation to arrive at a larger framework – narratives of mental retardation. "Narratives" can be understood as verbalizations of what the role – expectations and practices – of individuals with mental retardation in society should be. For example, the term "idiocy" must be seen in the context of a late-nineteenth century society with low expectations and technical capabilities, and giving no thought to the potentially harmful effects of social-environmental factors on intelligence and behavior.

By means of semiotic analysis, Devlieger views the changing terms used to denote mental retardation over the last century as insightful for learning about the dynamics between disability as "difference" and as "similarity" within a socio-cultural context. Citing evidence from the popular media, textbooks, and dictionaries, Devlieger also shows the importance of diffusion of narratives, beyond their mere production. Perhaps, he proposes, we are getting to the point where narratives that focus on the match between the environment and the individual with retardation will result in identification of elements in that environment that could be improved, rather than continuing to look for the site of the disability within the individual.

Devlieger agrees with Albrecht that when relating mental retardation to society, other dichotomies besides integration-segregation exist, including the mood of society (e.g., liberal vs. conservative) at a given time, the dominant metaphors of American culture (productivity, individualism), and the varying dominance of different professional groups on behalf of individuals with retardation.

In the concluding chapter of Part 3, Gerald Gold expands the theme of community beyond geographic boundaries into the postmodern age in a discussion of an ethnographic study of an electronic or virtual support group for multiple sclerosis. Gold's study, completed over a two-year period during which he was both a participant and a reflexive observer, examines the effectiveness and limitations of a virtual support group (MSN-L) as revealed through the topics posted and discussed. Indeed, through various threads an emerging MS agenda began to appear.

The distinguishing feature of support groups – whether face-to-face or electronic – are the reported similarities between participants that create and reinforce a community. That is, the voices of those who live with or near the disability become a source of authority and authenticity. While electronic support groups share many of its characteristics, they are not based on the face-to-face model, primarily because they usually are independent of territorial restrictions and less dependent on direct medical authority. Further, they extend to most disability groups and both genders, paving the way for a distinctive community.

In discussing the mechanics of the MSN-L, Gold emphasizes its public and private persona – the combination of public postings and private, or backstage messages, which reply to specific concerns or autobiographic accounts. Thus, although some observers suggest that virtual groups do not encourage intimacy and enduring contexts, Gold found that this was not the case with virtual support communities. The ability to participate in a common identity and disability culture is situationally significant both for persons with disability and their significant others who often are part of the same dispersed community. According to Gold, such groups can lead to an embryonic group culture where a fusion of experience and expertise can alter the life course of persons with disabilities.

Examining The Fit Between Deafness And Disability[1]

Susan Foster

At a time when the disability community is defining itself as having a culture and calling for a celebration of differences rather than exclusive focus on inclusion and sameness, why is it that people who consider themselves culturally Deaf often distance themselves from the disability movement? If deafness is not a disability, should deaf persons be entitled to SSI payments, special schools, and the protection of laws such as the Americans with Disabilities Act? For deaf Americans who are also members of minority ethnic or racial groups, what is the dominant determinant of identity? What are the implications of a bilingual, bicultural model of deafness for educational policy and practice?

In this chapter, these and other questions will be tied to questions of "disability as difference" and the emerging field of disability studies. Competing definitions of deafness – both historical and current–will be reviewed, and the impact of these definitions on deaf people will be discussed. Core issues regarding the fit between deafness and disability studies will be explored, including areas of overlap between the deaf community and other communities, as well as areas of distinction.

At the author's university, job announcements are posted through electronic mail. The following statement is routinely included: "Ability to contribute in meaningful ways to the college's continuing commitment to cultural diversity, pluralism, and individual differences strongly preferred. *People who are deaf or hard of hearing, with a disability, are women and/or members of a minority group are encouraged to apply*" (italics added). This statement captures the current debate in the field of deafness – is deafness a disability or is it a condition of linguistic minority status?

At a time when the disability community is defining itself as having a culture and calling for a celebration of differences rather than exclusive focus on conformity and inclusion, why is it that people who consider themselves culturally Deaf [2] often distance themselves from the disability movement? If deafness is not a disability, should deaf persons be entitled to SSI payments, special schools, and the protection of laws such as the Americans with Disabilities Act? What are the implications of a linguistic minority definition of deafness for educational policy and practice? In this chapter, these and other questions are tied to an examination of the "fit" between deafness and disability, and the place of deafness in the growing field of disability studies.

The chapter is divided into three sections. In the first section, three models of disability are reviewed, and the impact of these models on the field of deafness is discussed. In the

---

1 Reprinted from *Exploring Theories and Expanding Methodologies*, Volume 2, Barbara M, Altman and Sharon. N. Barnartt (Editors), Susan Foster, "Examining the fit between deafness and disability", pages 101-123, Copyright (2001), with permission from Elsevier.
2 The upper case "Deaf" is used in this paper to refer to deaf people who share a language, culture, and values, while the lowercase "deaf" refers to the audiological condition of not hearing. Similarly, the uppercase "Disability" is used to refer to a disabled persons who identify themselves in terms of a shared culture, experience, and values.

second section, areas of similarity and difference between deafness and disability are examined. The chapter is concluded with a discussion of the "fit" between deafness and disability, and the implications of this fit for disability studies and deaf studies.

Section one: three models of disability, and the implications of each for deafness[3]

The condition of "disability" has been defined in several ways. In each instance, the model used has had far reaching implications for the ways in which disabled people, including deaf people, are viewed and treated. In this section, three major models of disability are described; they are (1) medical, (2) social construction, and (3) political.

Medical Model: Disability as an Individual Problem

Generally, the medical model assumes that whatever problems the disabled individual is experiencing can be traced to that person, and defined in terms of some form of physical or mental abnormality; in other words, the problems associated with the condition reside *within* the individual. As a result, diagnosis and treatment revolve around the disabled person and involve tests, evaluations, and interventions that are applied to the individual. Such a model also places responsibility for rehabilitation with the disabled person, in that he or she must define him or herself as impaired and willingly participate in the process of diagnosis and treatment. Inherent in the medical model is a belief in the expert and active role of specialists, with corresponding weight and credibility attached to expert opinion. Terms used in the medical model include "diagnosis", "prescription", "affliction", "defect", "stages of acceptance", "rehabilitation", "prevention", and "cure".

The medical model has traditionally been the most widely held model of deafness. Also referred to as a clinical, infirmity, or pathological model, the medical model of deafness is grounded in the belief that the condition represents *failure* of a critical sensory system and is, therefore, impairment. Implicit in this interpretation is the belief that something is broken, e.g., the ear; remediation necessarily involves repair of, or compensation for, the defect. The goal of remediation is generally restoration of the deaf individual, both physically and socially, to the mainstream of society by reducing the differences and enhancing sameness, or conformity.

Within a medical model, deafness is a defect to be avoided, and the focus of remediation is almost always on the deaf individual. It is the individual who is affected, who must be treated (and submit to treatment), who will hopefully be rehabilitated and restored. Whether the treatment is medical (surgery, medicines), technical (hearing aids, cochlear implants), educational (special curricula, individualized education plans), vocational (rehabilitation), or psychological (therapy), the focus is on the deaf person and on oral speech versus American Sign Language (ASL). Diagnosis, prognosis, and treatment are

---

[3] Elements of this discussion also appear in S. Foster, "Doing research in deafness: some considerations and strategies", in P. Higgins and J. Nash (Eds.), *Understanding Deafness Socially*, Second Edition, 1996. Courtesy of Charles C Thomas, Publisher, Springfield, Illinois.

managed by specialists trained in the various professions described above (physicians, audiologists, teachers of "the deaf", speech-language pathologists, counselors). The language employed within a medical model reflects these patterns; i.e., "hearing loss", "hearing impaired", "speech therapy", "communication disorders".

The medical model has had an impact on scholarship and research in deafness. The tremendous growth of the field of audiology after World War II, and the strong links between audiology and medicine, served to strengthen the relationship between medicine and deafness. Many of the causes of deafness have been linked to illness or heredity; for example, the rubella epidemic of 1963-65 resulted in the birth of approximately 8000 infants with some degree of hearing loss (Stuckless and Walter, 1983). Research in audiology and speech-language pathology has played a major role in the field, including studies that are physiological as well as psychological in nature. Much of this work has focused on the function of the auditory or speech systems, the development of medical or mechanical technologies and therapies designed to restore a measure of hearing or enhance the ability to speechread or speak, or the individual's ability to accept and/or adapt to their deafness (Bender, 1981; Liben, 1978; Myklebust, 1964). More recently, specialists working within the medical model of deafness have pursued advancements in the fields of genetic research (linking genes to deafness), miniaturization of hearing aids, and the development of cochlear implants.

Social Construction Model: Disability as a Social Construct

Beginning in the 1960's and continuing through the present, the medical model of disability has been challenged through the works of Thomas Szasz (1961), Howard Becker (1963), Erving Goffman (1961, 1963), Dorothea and Benjamin Braginsky (1971), Jane Mercer (1973), Robert Bogdan and Steven Taylor (1976), Frank Bowe (1978, 1980), and Mike Oliver (1983, 1986), among others. These scholars propose that the experience of people with disabilities can best be understood as a function of interaction between the individual and society, and that the meaning of such concepts as impairment, handicap and disability[4] is socially constructed. Within this model, also referred to in the literature as interpretive, or interactionist, interventions focus on the environment as well as the individual, and the perspectives of persons with disabilities assume positions of authority in defining the experience of being disabled.

The social construction model calls for a critical examination of the design, method and interpretation of disability research. Studies conducted within this model include examination of the environment in descriptions and explanations of the experiences of the individual. The judgement and behavior of professionals and other experts is subjected to the same scrutiny as was reserved in the past only for the disabled person (Scott, 1969;

---

4   In his book *Handicapping America* (1978), Frank Bowe defines disability as "a condition of at least six months' duration that interferes with a person's ability to perform certain major life activities (p. 154) He defines handicap as "an interaction between a disability and a given environment" (p. 154) Thus, a disabled person may be handicapped in one setting but not in another. Critical to the difference between disability and handicap is the availability of appropriate accommodations and the attitudes of those involved in the interaction. Impairment is a definition of disability in which the interpretation of the individual's condition is negative, e.g., something is broken or a system has failed.

Conrad and Schneider, 1980). Popular culture is analyzed in order to better understand the sources of prejudice and stereotypical images of disabled people (Zola, 1987, 1985; Bogdan et al, 1982; Kriegel, 1982). Social attitudes are a focus of study and discussion (Makas, 1988).

Within the social construction model, concepts such as "hearing impairment", "deaf and dumb", and "rehabilitation", are understood as the reflections of social understandings of what it means to be deaf, as well as the perspectives of those who use these terms. Barriers experienced by deaf people in daily life activities, such as shopping, going to school, or attending public gatherings, are considered a function of linguistic and cultural differences between the majority (hearing) and minority (deaf) group. "Bilingual", "Deaf culture", and "linguistic minority" are examples of terms used by those who adhere to a social construction model of deafness.

Applications of this model to research and scholarship in the field of deafness are reflected in rich descriptions of the history, language, and culture of deaf people (Sacks, 1989; Van Cleve and Crouch, 1989; Padden and Humphries, 1988; Groce, 1985; Lane, 1984; Stokoe, 1960), as well as studies of the ways in which deaf people have been portrayed in popular culture (Hafferty and Foster, 1994; Gershon, 1992; Schuchman, 1988). Work has also been done that focuses on understanding the experience of deaf people from their perspectives and in their words. For example, Foster (1989c), Seidel (1982), Becker, (1980), and Higgins (1980) have examined the community and culture of deaf people. Other studies have described the experiences of deaf persons in employment (Emerton et al, 1987; Foster, 1987, 1992; Crammatte, 1968) and education (Foster, 1988, 1989 a,b; Mertens, 1989; Saur et al, 1986).

Political Model: Disability as an Advocacy and Policy Issue

Within the last ten years, criticisms have been raised with regard to both the medical and social construction models. The basis for these criticisms is that both these models are shaped by traditional power relationships between disabled and non-disabled people, with consequent alienation and oppression of disabled people (Hahn, 1985, 1988; Oliver, 1992; Scotch, 1984; Zarb, 1992). The political model, also referred to as emancipatory, reframes the concept of disability in terms of power – i.e., power to define disability, to determine what treatments (if any) should be applied, and the power to claim equal status and rights within the larger society. Within this model, the perspectives of people with disabilities assume greater authority than those of non-disabled experts in the development of agendas for action, study, and policy. Language typically used within the political model includes "emancipation", "civil rights", "control", "power", "empowerment", and "oppression". While culture is an important element of the political model, it is more often framed in terms of relative power and distribution of resources rather than social acceptance or inclusion.

Within the political model, deafness is viewed as a condition of a linguistic minority that has suffered oppression at the hands of the hearing majority. Historically, it is argued, deaf people have had less power than hearing people, so the latter have been able to impose definitions of deafness on deaf people, including definitions of deafness as a disability. Hearing people have also controlled access to resources and have been the guiding force in treatment and policy decisions which effect the lives of deaf people. The political model of deafness suggests that hearing persons can never fully understand the experiences of deaf people, any more than men can fully understand women's perspectives or caucasians understand the perspectives of blacks. As a result, no matter how well intentioned, hearing people should not be in positions of control over the destinies or treatment of deaf persons.

The focus in a political model of deafness often revolves around civil rights, public policy, and control of resources. For example, the Deaf President Now (DPN) movement at Gallaudet University has often been cited as an instance in which deaf students and their mentors fought for and won the right to a deaf leader for Gallaudet (Christiansen and Barnartt, 1995). Similarly, the Americans with Disabilities Act of 1990 (ADA), which guarantees deaf people certain rights regarding communication access and accommodations, was viewed as a "civil rights law" for people with disabilities.

Studies in deafness have been done within a political framework. For example, Baker-Shenk and Kyle (1990) examine conflict between hearing scholars and the deaf community in the field of linguistic studies. They conclude that hearing researchers should become aware of areas in which conflict is likely to arise and make adjustments that empower rather than alienate deaf people. Other researchers have examined the history of deaf people in terms of power and oppression (Lane, 1992) and the role of political activism within the deaf community (Bateman, 1991).

Making Sense of the Models

What should we make of these various, and often competing, models of disability and deafness? One possible interpretation of the models is that they are evolutionary, e.g., the medical model has been superceeded by the social construction model, which in turn is now being replaced by the political model. Inherent in this interpretation is the belief that subsequent models represent an improvement over the model they have replaced.

A second interpretation is that the medical model is the only "real" or enduring model. Within this interpretation, the social construction and political models are discredited as fads which are more indicative of the social and political climate of the 60's-90's. A related notion is that the social construction and political models are promoted by a small core of radicals within disability and deaf communities, and as such cannot be taken seriously or viewed as representative of these communities.

Neither of these interpretations are helpful, nor do they adequately reflect the social and political realities in America today. Major government funding for such programs as the Human Genome Project and the Disability Prevention Program, each of which includes elements related to deafness, indicate that the medical model of disability and deafness remains very powerful. Many deaf people and people with disabilities desire or require medical interventions designed to prevent, improve, or cure their deafness or disability. For these people, medical research, access to rehabilitation services, and the advice of experts are valued resources. On the other hand, there can also be little doubt that the social construction and political models have sparked major trends in this country with regard to persons who are disabled and/or deaf. Mainstream education for students with disabilities, the Americans with Disabilities Act, the Deaf President Now movement, and positive portrayals of deaf and disabled persons in the media are but a few examples of ways in which these models have changed the American landscape with regard to persons with disabilities.

Rather than attempting to identify which model is the most accurate, representative, or useful, it may be more fruitful to think of them as different perspectives on disabilities and deafness. Each may have a useful application under certain conditions, or within certain limits. It is doubtful that any of the models can adequately address all aspects of the experiences of persons who are deaf and/or disabled. It is also probably healthy that there are competing models, since each model encourages proponents of the other models to review and question their assumptions and approaches to disabilities and deafness.

Connecting the Models to Disability Studies

Definitions of "disability studies" suggest that the field is closely connected to the social construction and political models of disability, but not to the medical model. For example, Pfeiffer and Yoshida (1995) make clear the difference between the medical paradigm and the disability studies paradigm when they write, "In the medical model disability is a health question. In the disability studies paradigm disability is a policy and political question" (p. 478). Other scholars have explored the role of disability studies in expanding college curricula and the social construction of knowledge:

> Disability studies challenges the idea that the social and economic status and assigned roles of people with disabilities are inevitable outcomes of their condition, an idea similar to the argument that women's roles and status are biologically determined. But disability studies goes beyond cataloguing discrimination and arguing for social change. It challenges the adequacy of the content and structure of the current curriculum. As with women's studies, disability studies redresses omitted histories, ideas, or bodies of literature and also analyzed the construction of the category "disability", the impact of that construction on society, and on the content and structure of knowledge–fundamental epistemological issues. (Linton, Mello, & O'Neill, 1995, p. 5)

Deafness has clearly been defined from the medical, social construction and political perspectives, as has disability. To the degree that it has social construction and political dimensions, it may fit within the broad disability studies paradigm. Yet many within the Deaf culture would argue against such a fit. On what grounds? And with what implications? These questions guide the remaining sections of this chapter.

Section two: similarities and contrasts between deafness and disability

This chapter began with an examination of some of the major models that have been used historically as well as currently to define disability and deafness in America. In this section we examine the similarities and contrasts between deafness and disability. On what points do they converge? On what points do they differ? The section is divided into two parts. In the first part, areas of agreement, or convergence between deafness and disability, are described. In the second part, those areas in which deafness and disability perspectives differ from one another are examined.

Points of Convergence Between Deafness and Disability

There are many points of agreement, or convergence, between deafness and disability. At the most general level, deafness and disability *share a history of definition and experience* within each of the three models described in the first part of this chapter. For both disability and deafness, the medical model has been (and remains) a powerful defining paradigm. More recently, members of both the deaf and disabled communities have begun to identify themselves as members of minority groups, and draw parallels between their status and that of other historically oppressed groups, such as women and black persons:

> Equally important is the influence of other rights movements. People with disabilities, especially those on college campuses, were often involved in anti-Vietnam era protests. Some were involved in Black civil rights causes, and many of the women were influenced by the feminist movement of the 1970's. Disability rights leaders speak of their realization that the rights embedded in these other movements could and should be expanded to their rights as persons with disabilities. (Brannon, 1995, p. 4)

Just as women and African Americans have defined themselves as having a special culture, history, and political agenda, so have deaf and disabled persons. Many deaf and disabled people have extended these connections to frame political activism such as that reflected in the ADA of 1990 or the DPN movement in terms of a new civil rights movement.

Disability and deafness scholars have developed *similar vocabularies and metaphors* to describe the minority identity of the group. One example is the use of the uppercase "D" in reference to Disability culture and Disabled persons (e.g. Gill, 1995) as well as Deaf culture and Deaf persons (e.g., Padden and Humphries, 1988). Generally, this notation is used to emphasize the minority group and cultural status of the persons so described. In descriptions of deaf persons, it is also used to distinguish within the group between those who consider themselves to be part of a minority culture and those who do not (Padden and Humphries, 1988; Bienvenu, 1991).

A second example is the application of the "colonization" metaphor, and its corollary "paternalism", to the experiences of deaf persons and persons with disabilities. For example, Hirsch and Hirsch (1995) apply this metaphor to persons with disabilities:

> Colonization is a phenomenon that is rooted in the modern world view–colonized people need to be conquered and educated by the colonizers to become part of the modern world... If people with disabilities are the "colonized" people, and the "helping professionals" are the colonizers, the struggle of the oppressed to free themselves takes place within institutions that the colonizers established: residential institutions, group homes, nursing homes, special education, and vocational rehabilitation... While individuals with disabilities are still seen as generally incapable of exercising self government and wielding sovereign authority over wealth and power in the modern world, the medical model and its paternalistic implications that were imposed upon people with disabilities by the helping professions, are being rejected and replaced by a minority group model... People with disabilities are using legal and political means to gain control over service delivery programs, educational institutions, and public policy developments. The "natives" are rebelling against the colonizers and taking power and control away from them. (Hirsch and Hirsch, 1995, pp. 22-23)

Similarly, Lane (1992) describes parallels between Africa's paternalistic colonial history and the oppression of deaf communities:

> Paternalism, whether that of the colonizers in Africa or that of hearing professions concerned with deaf communities, is benighted, unsuccessful, and selfish, but the catalog of its evils does not end there. Paternalism places its beneficiaries in a dependent relation and keeps them dependent for its own psychological and economic

interest. Paternalism deprives its beneficiaries of their history and therefore of the possible lives they can envision. Paternalism corrupts some members of the oppressed minority, forming a class who conspire with the authority to maintain the status quo. Paternalism evades responsibility for its failure by affirming the biological inferiority of the beneficiary. Allowed to endure, paternalism instills the benefactor's values in the beneficiary – the oppression is internalized. And in the end, the beneficiaries despise the benefactors who have so long despised them, and the benefactors decry the thanklessness of their jobs. (Lane, 1992, pp. 38-39)

Yet a third example has evolved from the terms "racism" and "sexism". Bogdan and Biklen (1977) coined the term "handicappism" to describe "a set of assumptions and practices that promote the differential and unequal treatment of people because of apparent or assumed physical, mental, or behavioral differences" (p. 14). Similarly, Lane (1992) defined the term "audism" as "the hearing way of dominating, restructuring, and exercising authority over the deaf community" (p. 43).

The case has been made for both disability and deafness that they are *handicaps only under certain social conditions*. For example, it is not a handicap to use a wheelchair when there are curb cuts, accessible bathrooms, phones placed at appropriate heights, and elevators. When written materials are provided in Braille, blind persons are not at a disadvantage. Similarly, it has been argued that deafness is not a handicap at the local deaf club or when interpreters are available, because the language differences disappear. Indeed, Groce's (1985) study of deafness on Martha's Vineyard recorded a place and time where deafness was not handicapping because all the islanders (both deaf and hearing) knew sign language.

Both deaf and disabled people experience *barriers to learning about their culture(s)*, and generally enter the culture as young adults or adults. One reason for this is that persons with disabilities and deaf persons are generally born to non-disabled or hearing parents. Another has to do with demographics – for many, opportunities to meet and interact with other disabled or deaf persons are restricted. In these cases, a visible Deaf or Disability culture serves as a beacon to deaf or disabled persons (Padden and Humphries, 1988; Gill, 1995).

A major source of controversy in both disability and deafness involves the *role of non-disabled or hearing people* in research, leadership, and political activism. In particular, the political model of disability and deafness has frequently called for restrictions on the roles or influence of non-disabled or hearing people in these activities. For example, in his discussion of an "emancipatory research paradigm", Oliver (1992) suggests that researchers "learn how to put their knowledge and skills at the disposal of their research subjects, for them to use in whatever ways they choose" (p. 111). In discussing the question of research on deaf individuals by hearing persons, Stinson (1993) writes that "as a deaf researcher, I seem to have a weighing system where if something is written by a person who is deaf, it receives extra weight because of the commonality of the deaf experience, even if I disagree with the particular writer's perspective" (p. 19). Bienvenu (1991) proposes that "non-Deaf" people have no right to define what it means to be Deaf: "It's about time we Deaf people declare who we are without having our community defined and described by non-Deaf professionals who more than likely have not taken one course in ASL or American Deaf Culture" (p. 21).

More often, a middle ground has been proposed. For example, a collaborative strategy proposed by Foster (1993) involves the formation of partnerships between deaf and hearing researchers. Woodill suggests that some able-bodied persons can participate in the disability rights movement under certain conditions, e.g. that "they do not assume a leadership position in the movement, they enjoy the support of an organization of disabled people which has asked them for their participation, and they are prepared to learn to see the world from the perspective of a person with a disability" (p. 47). Altman (1994) and Batavia (1994) recommend a separation of roles in their discussions of who can be researchers and advocates. Watson and O'Day (1996) and Foster (1993) describe the potential "downside" of requiring particular physical characteristics in order to be associated with a disability or deaf research project/political movement, e.g., that deaf or disabled persons might find themselves equally restricted in their choices (limited to disability or deaf areas and causes, or evaluated on the basis of their physical characteristics rather than their experience and skills).

Points of Difference between Deafness and Disability

In some important ways, deafness has also been defined, experienced, and described as different than disability. One major distinction involves the proposition that ***culturally Deaf persons constitute a linguistic minority rather than a disability group*** (Lane, 1995a; Bienvenu, 1991). Many arguments have been made in support of this perspective, but the most powerful is probably that culturally Deaf persons generally choose to communicate using ASL[5], and as such they form a language community that has more in common with other linguistic minority groups than with disability communities.

A second, and related, difference between the deaf community and the disability community is *interpretation of PL94-142* and the ensuing trend towards mainstreaming all children with disabilities in public schools (Lane, 1984; Van Cleve and Crouch, 1989; Higgins, 1990; Foster and Emerton, 1991). **While the disability rights movement has focused on inclusion in schools and viewed mainstreaming as a major breakthrough, culturally Deaf persons have interpreted integration as a form of cultural genocide**. The reason is that special or separate schools for deaf students, generally referred to as "schools for the deaf", have been the incubators for and transmitters of Deaf culture. Without them, it is argued, deaf children may have few or no opportunities to meet the deaf peers and deaf adults who will help them to learn ASL and become part of the Deaf culture. As mainstreaming has become the predominant model for educating all children with disabilities, many of the schools for the deaf have lost enrollments, and some have closed, a trend which led Roe and Roe (1993) to describe PL94-142 as "a popular law... that has been a boon for children with physical handicaps but a bane for children with deafness" (p. 146).

A more subtle distinction between deafness and disability is that, in the latter, there has been a greater *correlation drawn between cultural consciousness and political action*. For example, Brannon (1995) notes that "part of the agenda-building process of the disability

---

5 The notion of ASL as the "language of choice" rather than simply a convenient way of communication for deaf persons is critical because it underscores the connection between language and culture, i.e., in choosing ASL, culturally Deaf persons are making a statement about cultural affiliation and identity.

rights movement has been an appeal to cultural concepts to foster group identity, to build coalitions among differing disability groups, and to aid the search for empowerment" (p. 3). Similarly, Gill (1995) describes four functions of Disability culture, each of which is linked to the development of a political as well as social identity; they are (1) fortification, (2) unification, (3) communication, and (4) recruitment. Deaf culture and deaf communities, on the other hand, long pre-existed the deaf rights movement, most probably because the primary bond was shared language rather than oppression or civil rights. Many deaf organizations, especially local groups such as community deaf clubs, have as a primary focus the creation of opportunities for social interaction and fellowship rather than political action[6], and deaf leaders have expressed frustration in efforts to mobilize the deaf community for political activity (Batemen, 1991). Deaf persons are far more likely to gather for purely social purposes than are persons with disabilities, and approximately 86% of deaf married persons are married to another deaf or hard of hearing person[7] (Schein and Delk, 1974).

A review of *major topics covered in disability studies and deaf studies curricula* illustrate the relative importance of advocacy and politics within each field. In their analysis of disability studies courses in the 1980s and 1990s, Pfeiffer and Yoshida (1995) found five topics that were covered in 50% or more of the courses; these are (1) attitudes, (2) advocacy, (3) definitions, (4) developmental disabilities, and (5) politics. A review of deaf studies programs at Gallaudet University and NTID suggests a different focus. At Gallaudet, the introductory deaf studies course is designed to help students "develop a special focus on the sociological, historical, linguistic, and psychological aspects of people with different degrees of hearing loss" (Gallaudet University Course Book, p. 50). Elective courses within the deaf studies program cover three thematic areas–culture, community, and language. Examples of courses offered include "Comparative Poetics: ASL and English" (Culture), "History of Mass Media and the Deaf Community" (Community), and "Bilingual Aspects in Sign Communication" (Language). Deaf studies at NTID is intended to "give students the opportunity to develop a strong knowledge base which includes the American Sign Language, historical, anthropological, linguistic, literary, artistic, and multicultural aspects of Deaf culture and the deaf community" (Preliminary Rationale..., p. 1). Those students who select a concentration in ASL or Deaf Studies will complete coursework in five areas: American Sign Language, Sign Language Teaching, Creative Arts and

---

6   This is not to suggest that deaf persons have not organized for political purposes. For example, the National Association of the Deaf was formed in 1880 in direct response to the Milan Conference and the need to preserve sign language, and the National Fraternal Society of the Deaf was established in 1901 out of frustrations by many deaf people in their efforts to purchase life insurance.

7   Several colleagues who reviewed earlier drafts of this paper said it would be interesting to know the percent of persons with disabilities who married other persons with disabilities. Unfortunately, I was unable to find this figure. However, I did learn that disabled women are less likely to marry than non-disabled women or disabled men (Fine and Asch, 1988), while deaf women are more likely to marry than deaf men (Schein and Delk, 1974). Moreover, it was speculated that "disabled women who marry *after* onset of disability are more likely than similarly disabled men to have a disabled spouse" (Fine and Asch, 1988:21); for deaf couples the situation is reversed, in that 88% of deaf males have deaf or hard of hearing spouses compared to 85.8% of deaf females (Schein and Delk, 1974).

Literature, Advocacy and Community, and Deaf History. While advocacy is a core topic in the NTID curriculum (and there are also several elective course options related to policy and human rights in the Gallaudet curriculum) the emphasis in these programs is clearly on language, history, and art, rather than on politics.

A metaphor for understanding the difference between disability and deafness can be found in the terms that members of these communities have identified as *preferred "ways of naming"*. For example, the generally accepted term for members of the first group is "people with disabilities", in which the primary emphasis is on people, and the identity of disability placed second. The phrase "people who are deaf", however, is generally not the preferred choice by members of the deaf community. A deaf colleague offered the following explanation for this preference:

> There has been a movement in the disabled community to do away with labels and for this reason the handicapping condition of a person should be de-emphasized. Thus people who are deaf would be preferable over deaf people. However, many people in the deaf community do not agree. (It appears that deaf people are often at odds with other groups in the disabled community over various issues.) Anyhow, many deaf people do not feel the need to cover their identity as a deaf person. This phrase... "people who are deaf" seems to be as ridiculous as... "people who are black" or "people who are women" or... "people who are gay..." The preferred terms for these groups would be black people (or African-Americans), women, gay people and so on. I have also noticed among many deaf people (including myself) that we would get upset if there was no reference to a person being deaf if there was a story about him/her in the newspaper. An identity as a deaf person is so important to many of us that we feel offended when the word "deaf" is omitted when we make the news. Again, I know many people in the disabled community find it unnecessary and offensive when the disability is specified in the story, especially when the story has nothing to do with the disability itself. (Thomas Holcomb[8], personal communication, 3/31/96)

So it is with many deaf persons, and in particular with people who consider themselves to be culturally Deaf. Deaf community, deaf children, deaf adults, Deaf President Now (DPN) – in each of these phrases, the term "deaf" is placed first. **This sense of pride and the primary role assigned to being deaf is also at the core of the linguistic minority concept as it is applied to deaf people and the corresponding call for separate education through which the Deaf identity and culture can be developed and preserved.**

Another difference between the deaf and disability communities is the *importance of "place"* for many deaf people (Lane, 1995b; Van Cleve and Crouch, 1989). "That Deaf Americans should feel they have a place of their own, that such a conception is needed to organize the prominent facts of American Deaf history, testifies to quite a different construction of deafness than the one based on disability spelled out earlier" (Lane, 1995b, p. 76). Residential schools for the deaf are only one example of "shared place". Deaf clubs, "tiny reservations of deafness across America, where Deaf people govern, socialize and communicate fluently in ASL when the work day... is over", is another (Lane, 1995b, p. 76). Gallaudet University has also become a special place for deaf people, as the only Deaf

---

8   Thomas Holcomb, Ph.D., is a faculty member in the Ohlone College Deaf Center in Fremont, CA.

university in America. Admissions research conducted with students at the National Technical Institute for the Deaf (NTID), a college of Rochester Institute of Technology serving approximately 1100 deaf students, documents the need of many deaf young adults for opportunities to participate in a community of deaf persons (Foster and Elliot, 1987). As noted by both Lane (1995b) and Van Cleve and Crouch (1989), deaf people have even sought from time to time to establish a deaf state, a kind of utopian vision of a land populated and controlled exclusively by deaf citizens.

An obvious but perhaps underestimated difference between deafness and disability is that *most people with disabilities are not deaf.* This difference maintains a sense of distance between disabled and deaf persons much like that between deaf persons and other hearing persons. As a friend pointed out, "many deaf people still feel disabled or handicapped in the disabled community. For example, the isolating experience would be as severe for a deaf person in a room full of disabled individuals as it would be in a place where there is no other disabled person. For this reason, there is no distinction between disabled people and hearing people for us. They are still "hearing"! It's like when women claim that it is a men's world or black people say it's a white world with no special categories for other minority groups. We see the world as the hearing world, including those who are disabled. (Thomas Holcomb, personal correspondence).

A core distinction between deafness and disability is that, at least *among culturally Deaf people, deafness is not considered a disability*. In this regard, culturally Deaf people may welcome the birth of a deaf child. As Lane (1995a) notes, "American Deaf people... think cultural Deafness is a good thing and would like to see more of it. Expectant Deaf parents, like those in any other language minority, commonly hope to have Deaf children with whom they can share their language, culture and unique experiences" (p. 178). Moreover, most culturally Deaf persons would not choose to receive treatments, such as cochlear implants, which would make them hearing, even if these treatments were guaranteed to be 100% successful (D'Antonio, 1993).

The result of these differences between deafness and disability is that the two have often had what Padden and Humphries (1988) call an "uneasy" alliance. Almost always, the reasons for the alliance are political or economic. For example, deaf and disabled people worked together to ensure passage of the Americans with Disabilities Act of 1990. Many deaf people claim disability benefits or services under present legislation for disabled people. Special education funds, which support students with disabilities in public schools also support interpreters for mainstreamed deaf students and separate programs for deaf students. In discussing a Deaf friend's ambivalence towards using a "handicapped" discount on the subway, Padden and Humphries (1988) make the following observation regarding the awkward relationship between "disabled" and "Deaf":

> "Disabled" is a label that historically has not belonged to Deaf people. It suggests political self-representations and goals unfamiliar to the group. When Deaf people discuss their deafness, they use terms deeply related to their language, their past, and their community. Their enduring concerns have been the preservation of their language, policies for educating deaf children, and maintenance of their social and political organizations. The modern language of "access" and "civil rights," as unfamiliar as it is to Deaf people, has been used by Deaf leaders because the public understands these concerns more readily than ones specific to the Deaf community. Knowing well the special benefits, economic and otherwise, of calling themselves disabled, Deaf people have a history, albeit an uneasy one, of alignment with other disabled groups. But as

our friend on the subway reminded us, "disabled" is not a primary term of self-identification, indeed it is one that requires a disclaimer". (Padden and Humphries, 1988, p. 44)

As Lane (1995a) acknowledges, if cultural Deafness was redefined as a linguistic minority (rather than a disability), many of the currently available entitlements and services would no longer apply. Instead, culturally Deaf persons would be covered under civil rights laws and rulings, and educational provisions designed to support linguistic minority children could be applied to culturally Deaf children. What is not clear is where the lines would be drawn. For example, if separate schools were available for culturally deaf students, what definition would be used to determine eligibility and how would it be applied? Might someone identify themselves as culturally Deaf with regard to schooling, but later claim a disability status, or is the claim to a particular status made once and then maintained for a lifetime? How many people who consider themselves culturally Deaf would be willing to give up economic benefits and legal rights currently available to them as "disabled" citizens? These and other questions must be address if a formal change in status is adopted for any group of deaf persons.

Section three: analysing the "fit" between deafness and disability

The focus in this chapter is the examination of deafness and disability as "same or different". The three models of disability and deafness described in the first section can also be described as a continuum from same to different. The medical model is essentially a conformist model in that the emphasis is on encouraging and enabling the disabled or deaf person to conform to expected standards and levels of performance. The social construction model is an inclusion model, through which society is altered in ways that facilitate the integration of deaf or disabled persons into the social and economic mainstream. The political model is multicultural – disabled or deaf persons seek to discover and maintain a unique identity and culture while ensuring equal rights and opportunities.

In the second section of this chapter we examined points of convergence and difference between deafness and disability, and found considerable evidence to support both sides of the issue. So what's the answer? Are deafness and disability simply variations of the same theme, or are they fundamentally different experiences? Perhaps this question can be more easily answered by examining disability and deafness as multi-dimensional experiences, and by considering the question at three levels – that of the deaf community, the disability community, and the American community.

At the first level, there is tremendous diversity within the deaf community. As Bienvenu (1991) notes, of the 20 million American people with a hearing loss of some kind in America, only about two million are culturally Deaf, i.e. Deaf persons who "share the same language, norms and values". Most culturally Deaf persons are deaf from birth or become deaf before acquiring spoken language (prelingually deaf), use ASL as a first language, support separate schools for deaf students, and participate actively in the deaf clubs. Persons who describe themselves as hard of hearing, advocate oralism, are postlingually deaf, support mainstream schooling for deaf students, and/or do not participate in the deaf clubs are generally not considered culturally Deaf. Age of onset of deafness, language preference, school experience, and parents' hearing status all contribute to the way(s) in which a deaf person thinks of him or herself. When issues of race, ethnicity and gender are added to the mix, the heterogeneity of the deaf community is further underscored. While two deaf persons share the physiological condition of deafness, the similarities may end at that, or they may be built upon other shared characteristics or experiences, such as race, gender, schooling, and so forth.

At the level of disability, deafness is also both "same and different". As noted in the last section, deaf and disabled people share many experiences and circumstances, but they also are quite different in significant ways. Those deaf persons who define themselves as culturally Deaf may see themselves as different from persons with disabilities. However, the larger community of deaf and hard of hearing persons who are not culturally Deaf may identify with the experiences and perspectives of persons with disabilities. It is also possible for deaf persons to incorporate both Deaf culture and disability culture within their identity.

At the level of American society, deaf persons are "same and different" in the same ways as are persons with disabilities. Both groups want access to quality education, opportunities for employment and career advancement, and the ability to enjoy the same level of resources and services as are available to all citizens; in this regard, they are the same as other members of American society. Their differences have to do not so much with the physical characteristics that traditionally have been labeled "disability" or "deafness", but with the models within which these characteristics have been interpreted.

Same or Different? A Multi-Dimensional Perspective

Research on identity of deaf minority persons offers a potentially useful way of thinking about the relationship between deafness and disability. Foster and Kinuthia (1995) conducted in depth, open-ended interviews with 33 deaf minority college students (11 each African, Hispanic, and Asian American students). The broad purpose of the study was to describe the experiences of these students within their families and at school prior to their arrival on campus, as well as their experiences while at college. A subset of questions focused on issues of identity; students were asked to describe how they think about and define themselves, e.g., as black, deaf, male/female, etc.

Students' stories and explanations of who they are suggest that identity can be modified according the demands of the situation. For example, a deaf Hispanic student said that at college he is deaf but at home he is more hard of hearing and Spanish. In his words, "Here [college] I think I am more deaf than at home. Because at home there are not that many deaf... There I think I am hard of hearing... But here I am deaf because [I] use sign language a lot... At home, with my parents, I don't use sign language. I just speak with my voice and speak Spanish". For this student, communication and language circumstances were a determining factor in shaping identity.

In other cases, students' identities were created or permanently reshaped in response to new circumstances. For example, a deaf black student who came to college as a single mother found that she identified more strongly with other caucasian deaf single mothers than she did with black deaf friends who did not have children; while race and deafness were still defining factors in her life, parenthood had refocused her identity.

The circumstance of oppression or discrimination is a third kind of situation that shapes identity. One student said that he thinks of himself as "deaf first" because he feels he will be denied opportunities for employment because he is deaf. Another student said that she thinks of herself as "black first" because that is how others define her: "When I walk into the restaurant, they are looking at me because I'm black. Or, I'm going into the store, they follow me because I'm black, and they think I'm going to steal something".

Implicit in these students' stories is the idea that people have more than one identity. Gender, race, marital status, parenthood, deaf/ASL, deaf/oral–these are but a few of the core identities described by students. One or more of these identities is drawn out in response to the needs and demands of the situation. The Hispanic student is not a hypocrite or unsure of himself because he is "deaf" at school and "hard of hearing" at home; rather, he is adapting to the circumstances and opportunities presented by each situation.

In short, it was concluded that identity is fluid, responsive, and cumulative, changing according to the demands of the situation and evolving over time. This did not mean that the individuals interviewed lacked a "core identity", or sense of who they are. Rather, their identity was multi-dimensional. In her discussion of cultural and language diversity among deaf persons, Parasnis (2000) makes a similar point when she describes self-identity as "a dynamic concept, influenced by psychological, situational, and relational variables".

Is deafness the same as or different than disability? A multi-dimensional and dynamic interpretation of identity would suggest that *it is both*. Just as it is possible for a person to be both "deaf" and "hard of hearing" it is possible for a deaf person to seek inclusion within one situation and segregation within another. A deaf person may choose to work from 8-5 with hearing people, where she or he uses a combination of communication strategies, including speech, writing, gestures and interpreters. The same person may then go to the local deaf club, or home to a deaf spouse, where communication takes place in ASL. Deaf parents may choose a separate school for their deaf child but encourage that child to attend a mainstream university. Deaf advocates may ally with disability advocates to seek passage of legislation, but otherwise distance themselves from Disability culture. A deaf woman who has never used a hearing aid may choose to get one when she gives birth to a hearing child because she finds with the device she is more likely to hear her child cry from the next room.

Implications for Disability and Deaf Studies

Areas of overlap as well as distinction between disability studies and deaf studies curricula should be addressed. For example, many if not most of the topics currently covered in disability studies courses have implications for deaf persons (i.e. race, technology, women, mental health, education, employment). However, it must be recognized that the interpretation of these topics may be very different for deaf people than for people with disabilities (for example, school inclusion). Other topics which are core to deaf studies programs, such as American Sign Language, may not be covered in most disability studies courses. Such gaps should be acknowledged and, where possible, students should be referred to courses or alternative resources for further instruction and information. In the long run, instructors may find it beneficial to devote one or more classes within the disability studies course to the topic of deafness, and to use this time with students to discover, describe, and reflect upon the various ways in which deafness is both "same and different". Such dialogue may lead to further conversations within the field of disability studies about ways in which we are all unique as well as the ties that bind us to one another.

Finally, disability studies curricula must acknowledge and incorporate deafness as both same and different. This includes recognition of the perspective of culturally Deaf persons that they are not part of Disability culture and the reasons for this belief. It must also include the myriad perspectives represented by the other 90% of deaf and hard of hearing people, including the belief by some that deafness is, indeed, a handicap under some circumstances. This does not mean that disabilities studies curricula should promote or support a definition of deafness as handicap, only that they should recognize this belief as part of the broad mosaic of individual as well as collective identities of people who are deaf.

Acknowledgements

This document was produced at the National Technical Institute for the Deaf in the course of an agreement between Rochester Institute of Technology and the U.S. Department of Education. I would like to thank Pat DeCaro, Joan Erickson, and Mike Stinson for reading earlier drafts of this paper and making valuable suggestions. A special thanks to Thomas Holcomb, whose comments were critical in revising the paper and who gave me permission to cite many excellent points from his personal correspondence.

References Cited

Altman, B. (1994). Thoughts on Visibility, Hierarchies, Politics and Legitimacy. *Disability Studies Quarterly,* 14 (2), pp. 28-51.
Baker-Shenk, C., and Kyle, J.G. (1990). Research with deaf people: issues and conflicts. *Disability, Handicap & Society*, 5 (1), pp. 65-75.
Batavia, A. (1994). Representation and role separation in the disability movement: should researchers be advocates? *Disability Studies Quarterly,* 14 (2), pp. 51-55.
Batemen, G.C. Jr. (1991). Perceptions on political activism: definitions and attitudes. *Perspectives on Deafness: A Deaf American Monograph* 7-13.
Becker, G. (1980). *Growing old in silence.* Berkeley: University of California Press.
Becker, H. (1963). *Outsiders: studies in the sociology of deviance.* New York: The Free Press.
Bender, R.E. (1981). *The conquest of deafness: a history of the long struggle to make possible normal living to those handicapped by lack of normal hearing.* Danville, IL: The Interstate Printers & Publishers, Inc.
Bienvenu, M.J. (1991). Can deaf people survive "deafness"? *Perspectives on Deafness: A Deaf American Monograph.* In M.D. Garretson (Ed.) Silver Spring, MD: National Association of the Deaf, pp. 21-28.
Bogdan, R., and Biklen, D. (1977). Handicapism. *Social Policy*, 7 (March/April), pp. 14-19.
Bogdan, R., Biklen, D., Shapiro, A. and Spelkoman, D. (1982). The disabled: media's monster. *Social Policy*, Fall 1982, pp. 32-35.
Bogdan, R., and Taylor, S. (1976). The judged, not the judges: an insider's view of mental retardation. *American Psychologist,* 31, pp. 47-52.
Bowe, F. (1978). *Handicapping America: barriers to disabled people.* New York: Harper & Row.
Bowe, F. (1980). *Rehabilitating America: toward independence for disabled and elderly people.* New York: Harper & Row.
Braginsky, D. and Braginsky, B. (1971). *Hansels and gretels: studies of children in institutions for the mentally retarded.* New York: Holt, Rinehart & Winston.
Brannon, R. (1995). The use of the concept of disability culture: a historian's view. *Disability Studies Quarterly,* 15 (4), pp. 3-15.

Christiansen, J. and Barnartt, S. (1995). *Deaf President Now! The 1988 revolution at Gallaudet University.* Washington, DC: Gallaudet University Press.

Conrad, P. and Schneider, J. (1980). *Deviance and medicalization: from badness to sickness.* St. Louis, MO: The C.V. Mosby Company.

Crammatte, A.B. (1968). *Deaf persons in professional employment.* Springfield, IL: Charles C Thomas.

D'Antonio, M. (1993). Sound and Fury. *Los Angeles Times*, Sunday November 21, 1993. Home Edition, Los Angeles Times Magazine, p. 44

Emerton, R.G., Foster, S., and Royer, H. (1987). The impact of changing technology on the employment of a group of older deaf workers. *Journal of Rehabilitation of the Deaf,* 21 (2) pp. 6-18.

Fine, M. and Asch, A., Eds. (1988). *Women with disabilities: essays in psychology, culture and politics.* Philadelphia: Temple University Press.

Foster, S. (1987) Employment experiences of deaf RIT graduates: an interview study. *Journal of Rehabilitation of the Deaf,* 21 (1), pp. 1-15.

Foster, S. (1988). Life in the mainstream: reflections of deaf college freshmen on their experiences in the mainstreamed high school. *Journal of Rehabilitation of the Deaf,* 22 (2), pp. 27-35.

Foster, (1989a). Educational programmes for deaf students: an insider perspective on policy and practice. In L. Barton (Ed), *Integration; Myth of Reality?* London: The Falmer Press, pp. 57-82.

Foster, S. (1989b). Reflections of deaf adults on their experiences in residential and mainstream school programs. *Disability, Handicap and Society*, 4 (1), pp. 37-56.

Foster, S. (1989c). Social alienation and peer identification: a study of the social construction of deafness. *Human Organization*, 48 (3), pp. 226-235.

Foster, S. (1992). *Working with deaf people: accessibility and accommodation in the workplace.* Springfield, IL: Charles C Thomas.

Foster, S. (1993). Outsider in the Deaf World: Reflections of an Ethnographic Researcher. *Journal of the American Deafness and Rehabilitation Association,* 27 (3) pp. 1-11.

Foster, S. (1996) Doing research in deafness: some considerations and strategies. In P. Higgins and J. Nash (Eds.) *Understanding Deafness Socially.* Springfield, IL: Charles C Thomas, pp. 3-20.

Foster, S. and Elliot, L. (1987). Why students decide to attend NTID at RIT: an interview study with first year college students. Technical Report, National technical Institute for the Deaf at Rochester Institute of Technology, Rochester, NY.

Foster, S. and Emerton, G. (1991). Mainstreaming the deaf student: a blessing or a curse? *The Journal of Disability Policy Studies*, 2 (2), pp. 61-76.

Foster, S. and Kinuthia, W. (1995). The development of cultural identity of deaf persons of Black, Asian, or Hispanic heritage. Paper presented at the 1995 annual meeting of the *New York State Sociological Association*, Hobart and William Smith College, Geneva, NY, October 28, 1995.

Gallaudet University Course Book, Washington, DC: Gallaudet University.

Gershon, H. (1992). Reasonably deaf: television's representation of deafness. Paper presented at the annual meeting of the Society for Disability Studies, Seattle, WA, June 17-19.

Gill, C.J. (1995). A psychological view of disability culture. *Disability Studies Quarterly*, 15 (4) pp. 16-19.

Goffman, E. (1961). *Asylums: essays on the social situation of mental patients and other inmates.* New York: Anchor Books.

Goffman, E. (1963). Stigma: notes on the management of spoiled identity. London: Penguin.

Groce, N. (1985). *Everyone here spoke sign language: hereditary deafness on Martha's Vineyard.* Cambridge, MA: Harvard University Press.

Hafferty, W.F. and Foster, S. (1994). Decontextualizing disability in the crime mystery genre: the case of the invisible handicap. *Disability & Society*, 9 (2) pp. 185-206.

Hahn, H. (1985). Toward a politics of disability: definitions, disciplines, and policies. *The Social Science Journal,* 22, pp. 87-106.

Hahn, H. (1988). The politics of physical differences: disability and discrimination. *Journal of Social Issues,* 44, pp. 39-47.

Higgins, P. (1980). Outsiders in a hearing world: a sociology of deafness. Beverly Hills, CA: Sage.

Higgins, P. (1990). *The challenge of educating together deaf and hearing youth: making mainstreaming work.* Springfield, IL: Charles C Thomas.

Hirsch, K. and Hirsch, J. (1995). Self-defining narratives: disability identity in the postmodern era. *Disability Studies Quarterly,* 15 (4) pp. 21-27.

Kriegel, L. (1982). The wolf in the pit at the zoo. *Social Policy,* Fall 1982, pp. 16-23.

Lane, H. (1984). *When the mind hears: a history of the deaf.* New York: Random House.

Lane, H. (1992). *The mask of benevolence: disabling the deaf community.* New York. Alfred A. Knopf.

Lane, H. (1995a). Constructions of deafness. *Disability & Society,* 10 (2), pp. 171-189.

Lane, H. (1995b). Reproductive control of deaf people and the deaf search for a homeland. In *A Deaf American Monograph,* M. Garretson (Ed.), Silver Spring, MD: National Association of the Deaf, pp. 73-78.

Liben, L.S. (1978). *Deaf children: developmental perspectives.* New York: Academic Press.

Linton, S., Mello, S. & O'Neill, J. (1995) Disability studies: expanding the parameters of diversity. *Radical Teacher,* 47, pp. 4-10.

Makas, E. (1988). Positive attitudes toward disabled people: disabled and nondisabled persons' perspectives. *Journal of Social Issues,* 44 (1) pp. 49-61.

Mercer, J. (1973). *Labeling the mentally retarded: clinical and social system perspectives on mental retardation.* Berkeley: University of California Press.

Mertens, D. (1989). Social experiences of hearing-impaired high school youth. *American Annals of the Deaf,* March, 1989, pp. 15-19.

Myklebust, H.R. (1964). *The psychology of deafness: sensory deprivation, learning, and adjustment.* New York: Grune & Stratton.

Oliver, M. (1983). *Social work with disabled people.* Basingstoke, United Kingdom: MacMillan.

Oliver, M. (1986). Social policy and disability: some theoretical issues. *Disability, Handicap & Society,* 1, pp. 5-18.

Oliver, M. (1992). Changing the social relations of research production? *Disability, Handicap & Society,* 7 (2) pp. 101-114.

Padden, C. & Humphries, T. (1988). *Deaf in America: voices from a culture.* Cambridge, MA: Harvard University Press.

Parasnis, I. (2000). Cultural and Language Diversity and Identity: Implications for Deaf Education. Proceedings of the 19th International Congress on Education of the Deaf, July 9-13, Sydney, Australia.

Pfeiffer, D. and Yoshida, K. (1995). Teaching disability studies in Canada and the USA. *Disability & Society,* 10, (4), 475-500.

Preliminary Rationale Format. Center for Arts and Sciences. American Sign Language/Deaf Studies. Rochester, NY: National Technical Institute for the Deaf.

Roe, C. and Roe, D. (1993). The dismantling of a culture: PL 94-142 and its effects on the education and future of deaf children. *A Deaf American Monograph,* M. Garretson (Ed.) Silver Spring, MD: National Association of the Deaf, pp. 143-147.

Sacks, O. (1989). *Seeing voices: a journey into the world of the deaf.* Berkeley: University of California Press.

Saur, R., Layne, C., Hurley, E., & Opton, K. (1986). Dimensions of mainstreaming. *American Annals of the Deaf,* 131, pp. 325-329.

Schein, J. and Delk, M. (1974). *The deaf population of the United States.* Silver Spring, MD: National Association of the Deaf.

Schuchman, J. (1988). *Hollywood speaks: deafness and the film entertainment industry.* Urbana IL: University of Illinois Press.

Scotch, R. (1984). *From good will to civil rights: transforming federal disability policy.* Philadelphia: Temple University Press.

Scott, R. (1967). *The making of blind men.* New York: Russell Sage foundation.

Seidel, J. (1982). The points at which deaf and hearing worlds intersect: a dialectical analysis. In *Social aspects of deafness, volume 3: the deaf community and the deaf population.* Proceedings of the 1982 Conference: Sociology of Deafness. P. Higgins and J. Nash (Eds), Gallaudet College, Washington, D.C. pp. 131-167.

Stinson, M. (1993). Research on deaf individuals by hearing persons: one deaf researcher's perspective. *Journal of the American Deafness and Rehabilitation Association,* 27 (3) pp. 17-21.

Stokoe, W.C. (1960). *Sign language structure.* Reissued, Silver Spring, MD: Linstok Press.

Stuckless, E.R. and Walter, G. (1983). Students hearing impaired from the 1963-1965 rubella epidemic begin to enter college. *The Volta Review,* (October-November), pp. 270-278.

Szasz, T. (1961). *The myth of mental illness.* New York: Hoeber-Harper.

Van Cleve, J. and Crouch, B. (1989). A place of their own: creating the deaf community in America. Washington, DC: Gallaudet University Press.

Watson, S. and O'Day, B. (1996). Movement leadership. *Disability Studies Quarterly,* 16 (1) pp. 26-30.

Woodill, G. (1994). The role of an able-bodied person in a disability movement. Disability Studies Quarterly, 14 (2), pp. 47-48.

Zarb, G. (1992). On the road to Damascus: first steps towards changing the relations of disability research production. *Disability, Handicap & Society,* 7 (2), pp. 125-138.

Zola, I. (1985). Depictions of disability-metaphor, message and medium in the media: a research and political agenda. *The Social Science Journal,* 22, pp. 5-18.

Zola, I. (1987). The portrayal of disability in the crime mystery genre. *Social Policy,* (Spring), pp. 34-39.

Study Questions

1. Describe three models of disability.
2. Why is it important to understand the various models of disability?
3. Which of the three models of disability has been the most widely held model of deafness? Why?
4. Pick one of the three models of disability and explain its implications for research and scholarship in deafness. Include examples of the kinds of terms this model uses, the kinds of research that have been done, and the ways in which research is conceptualized.
5. Which of the three models of disability do you find the most compelling? Explain your choice.
6. Describe three points of convergence between deafness and disability (i.e., three ways in which concepts and practice in each area have been or continue to be similar). Support your answer with examples.
7. Describe three points of difference between deafness and disability. Support your answer with examples.
8. What are the implications of viewing deafness and disability as the same?
9. What are the implications of viewing deafness and disability as different?
   Do you believe that deafness and disability are essentially the same or essentially different? Defend your answer.

Winks, Blinks, Squints and Twitches:
Looking for Disability and Culture Through My Son's Left Eye

Philip M. Ferguson

One of the hallmarks of the disability studies movement is to explore, recover and celebrate a "culture of disability". What this phrase means is by no means settled, of course. Indeed, it is precisely in the move from talking about culture *and* disability to talking about the culture *of* disability, that the tension between "same" and "different" most clearly emerges. This chapter will argue against hasty attempts to answer the question of what it might mean to speak of a "culture of mental retardation".

My initial focus will be on the history and status of cognitive disabilities within this larger evolution of approaches of disability. Most of my discussion will revolve around three specific policy initiatives of particular importance to research in cognitive disabilities: normalization, inclusion, and independent living. The social values and policies commonly associated with normalization have been much more influential within the field of mental retardation than any other disability. Similarly, some of the strongest proponents of educational and community inclusion come from a background in what used to be called "severe and profound" mental retardation. Finally, the example of independent living provides a very different process where a concept has been transported to the field of cognitive disabilities from it primary origins within the area of physical disability.

Finally, I will return to my attempt to evolve what I refer to as a "relational approach" to disability and culture and describe several identifiable patterns for a cultural interpretation of cognitive disability. I will compare the relevance of these patterns for other disabilities. Predictable, if not inevitably: Lessons will be drawn for the future of disability studies.

For most of modern Western history, the "official" reasons to study intellectual disability have been to learn more about how to make it disappear. As a medical condition, it has been something to prevent or cure. As an educational deficiency, it has been something to remediate or overcome. As an economic and social burden, it has most often been something to rehabilitate or at least remove from society's view. Recently, however, the emergence of the disability rights movement has challenged this predominantly clinical approach in areas as wide-ranging as personal experience, social policy, and cultural interpretation. As a result of this movement, many of us are re/cognizing disability for the first time as both a complex social construction and a significant personal identity. That is, we are simultaneously recognizing and rethinking (literally *re-cognizing*) the interaction of self, culture and disability in the lives of individuals. **With this new approach, usually referred to as "disability studies", the reason to study disability is to make it more visible, not less; more valid as an ongoing part of the human experience; and more legitimate as a topic of study across the humanities and social sciences.**

One of the hallmarks of the disability studies movement is to explore, recover, and celebrate a "culture of disability". What this phrase means is by no means settled, of course. Indeed, it is precisely in the move from talking about culture *and* disability to talking about the culture *of* disability that a tension between "same" and "different" most clearly emerges. This chapter will argue against hasty attempts to resolve this tension by imposing one orientation or another upon the still emerging field of disability studies. I will look in particular at two movements at the heart of disability advocacy over the last two decades or so: independent living and inclusion. Central to this discussion is a consideration of what it might mean to speak of a "culture of mental retardation". Other questions quickly follow: Is there such a thing? Should there be? How might it compare to cultures of deafness, blindness, physical disability? And, what forms and approaches should attempts to answer these questions take? That is, what should disability studies look like? Finally, throughout the chapter, I will ground my reflections on these topics within a narrative approach to events from my son's life.

Blinking Away Definitions: Seeing Disability Through My Son's Left Eye

My son, Ian, is now 28 years old and has multiple disabilities. Over the years he has collected a variety of labels that supposedly specify what those disabilities are: severe mental retardation, spastic quadriplegia, developmental disabilities. Predictably, the educational and adult service systems involved in his life have given labels only to his perceived limitations; there have been no clinical diagnoses for his mixture of odd talents and personal quirks that are the main images I have of him now. What is the technical term for an aficionado of sound effects tapes? Which professional would assess Ian's ability to identify TV sitcoms by the first four or five notes of their theme songs? When does he get graded for the terrific laugh he shows along with a warped sense of humor?

My point is simply that my son's individuality can be easily swallowed up by the scary stereotypes and diagnostic categories that lie behind the official labels. After 28 years, most of what matters to me about Ian is not touched by terms like "mental retardation" and "cerebral palsy". Certainly, the physiological realities giving rise to those terms are there to be reckoned with. Many things that most 28-year-olds find easy to do are impossible for Ian without intensive supports. However, after all these years observing his progress and frustration in dealing with those limits, the question that really bothers me is one that may at first seem superficial: How am I to describe what Ian is doing when he "winks"?

The story goes like this. Several years ago, someone taught Ian to squeeze together the eyelids of his left eye in a rough approximation of an acceptable wink. If you ask him to wink, he will do this behavior. If he sees someone else "wink", he might imitate that action even without being asked. And on rare occasions he might actually produce his winking behavior spontaneously. He almost always laughs or smiles when he does this, and it usually evokes smiles and laughter by those around him as well.

So a brief summary of the situation might note that Ian can close his eyelids together on one eye: he knows the mechanics of winking. He also does it when asked to "wink". That is, he apparently associates the word "wink" with the same physical action (roughly speaking, he is not very coordinated about it) that the rest of us do. He even apparently understands at some level that something about the physical action is humorous, because he usually laughs when he does it. But the question remains: Is Ian really winking? It seems more volitional than an uncontrolled twitch would be. But is he really doing some learned squint or blink? Perhaps his actions could be described as imitating a wink, but without any intentionality behind the physical behavior similar to what motivates others to wink (indicating that one is joking, acknowledging some sort of conspiratorial understanding with another person, flirting, etc.). Or, does Ian's disability overwhelm any cultural context to such an extent that a thin behavioral description of eyelids closing is all that remains available for careful observers?

These are not new questions, of course. Although he never mentions disability, Clifford Geertz's famous essay on "thick description" (Geertz, 1973) relies upon the complexity of winking (admittedly borrowing from Gilbert Ryle's original discussion) to illustrate how even the simplest physical behavior can quickly become embedded in layers of cultural interpretation as we thicken the context surrounding that behavior (from twitching, to winking, to imitating a wink, to practicing imitating a wink, etc.)[1].

This connection with Geertz and the concept of thick description is purposeful. Geertz is not so much interested in winks as he is in how to interpret them as symbols full of cultural meaning. His discussion has relevance to disability studies as well. **As a way to explore the interactions of self and culture within the context of disability studies, an elaboration of "thick description" encourages us to collect and interpret the narratives within which the cultural meanings of disability are initially embodied.**

What might go into a thick description of whether and how someone like my son could be understood to actually be winking? The larger questions that emerge from this involve the changed interactions of personal perspective and cultural context – all of the dimensions that help make a description thick instead of thin – when the participant's very capacity for intentional behavior is somehow questioned, or at least inaccessible.

So, from Ian's winks, I am led to two basic questions. First, what is it that Ian is doing when he closes his eyelids, and how is it similar to or different from what others do? Second, what is it that I am doing when I try to understand what Ian is doing, and how is that similar to or different from what has been done in the past? I take the first question to involve, at least partly, an attempt to define cognitive disability. And I take the second to involve, at least partly, an attempt to define disability studies. Obviously, with both questions, then, I am emulating Geertz's use of the mundane behavior of winking to open up a much broader and more abstract consideration of disability and culture.

Asking for definitions – of disability or disability studies – is often misleading. As often as not, the questions send us off into an epistemological wilderness, hunting for some conceptual trophy that we can mount on the wall at home for all to study and admire. A definition seems to imply an essence – some common meaning that in turn refers to a discrete piece of shared reality possessed by all those objects to which the term correctly applies.

However, a search for definitions need not involve such a commitment to essentialism. The philosopher Wittgenstein reportedly advised his students to avoid this trap by framing the question differently: "Don't ask for the meaning, ask for the use" (cited in Wisdom, 1965, p. 87). In other words: Give up the quest for some smooth but slippery essence that strips away particularities of context in the push for linguistic common ground. Instead, Wittgenstein advises, get back to the rough ground of practice and recognize how people actually interpret

---

1 Geertz also uses an extended discussion of mock sheep raids in Morocco to make his case for cultural interpretation. However, to my knowledge Ian has never participated in a sheep raid, so I decided to stick with winking as my primary example.

their lives in language. Don't define literature for me, tell me some stories. If I notice some family resemblances among the examples, then so much the better.

So, what I hope to do in response to my two questions is not so much to define disability in general or cognitive disability in particular. Much less do I desire to pin down some prescriptive rules for how to do disability studies "correctly". My goal is simpler: to tell some stories, look for relationships, and find enough traction to move forward our culture's interpretations of cognitive disability.

From Twitch to Wink: Finding Self in Culture

> You can't wink (or burlesque one) without knowing what counts as winking, or how, physically, to contract your eyelids… But to draw from such conclusions that knowing how to wink is winking… is to betray as deep a confusion as, taking thin descriptions for thick, to identify winking with eyelid contractions. (Geertz, 1973, p. 12)

One way to rethink ("re-cognize") mental retardation or cognitive disability is to describe how the complex array of possible meanings for a person's behaviors seem drastically curtailed. The social construction of the meaning of language and behavior initially leads to a potentially infinite variety of interpretive possibilities. (Objectivist critics of such constructivist approaches to meaning argue that this relativism cannot be escaped, leaving us with interpretive anarchy where there are no rules to prefer one meaning as more valid than any other.) We move from the babble of possible meanings to the precision of communication through a complex interplay of cultural location, historical period, subgroup conventions, specific elements of immediate context, and personal intention. I am arguing that one useful way to approach cognitive disability is to see it as a preemptive constriction of this communicative process.

To a certain extent, Ian's eyelid movement is just an eyelid movement because it is taken out of this interpretive interplay. It is not suspended in the same "webs of social significance" (Geertz, 1973, p. 5) that the rest of us spin for ourselves. **At its most profound, cognitive disability seems to remove the element of personal agency or psychological intent that pushes the behavior from twitch to wink.** It is difficult, for example, to think of Ian as a sexist when he winks, objectifying women as sexual objects by knowledgeably participating in a traditional behavior of men. It is equally hard for me to impute an ironic or deceptive sensibility to Ian's behavior. In the same way, it is hard for me to envision someone thinking of Ian as a racist, or a capitalist, or any number of other categories typically available to those interpreting the behavior of adult white males in our society. To the extent that I believe some personal understanding of the cultural norms and traditions is important to such interpretations of specific behavior, those meanings seem less available to Ian than to others.

The crisis of representation spoken of so frequently in post-modern discussions of social science and the humanities seems superseded here by an earlier crisis of presentation. The "crisis" arises not from my inability to provide direct access to Ian's understanding of his world, but rather from an uncertainty that a fully furnished world is there to be accessed. If we may accurately portray the social sciences at the heart of disability studies as the interpretation of other people's interpretations (the so-called "double hermeneutic"), then how does one interpret the absence of interpretation?

Telling Stories: Describing Cultural Context

The answer for me comes dressed in the metaphors of the humanities rather than the sciences: I try to "read" Ian's story within a symbolic "discourse" that changes behaviors into actions. It is important to recognize what makes cognitive disability so different in what is still the dominant approach to disability. **It is not so much that we do not see a "person" or "a real human being" when we encounter someone with so-called profound mental retardation. Rather, it is that we do not see any culture. We see no meaning to the behavior: there are words but no discourse; events but no story.** In a way, the challenge for interpretation is that *all* we see is an individual: Rousseau's noble savage, a single person in a cultural void, as close to a de-contextualized existence as possible. The physiology seems to overwhelm the social. We see no religion, we see no politics, no racial awareness or class identity, no moral stance, no economy. We have trouble admitting any intentional awareness of these cultural components that the rest of us use to define each other. What potentially impedes my interpretation of Ian's "winking", then, is not an absence of self but an absence of culture. Without such a cultural context, people with significant cognitive disabilities are neither the same as, nor different from, the nondisabled population. There is no comparative context within which to make the judgment.

However – then culture flows in. By representing my son's life to others I invest it with a narrative, I inscribe his actions with a temporal sequence that starts to transform his eye twitches into winks. When I told the story earlier of how he came to learn to close his eyelids when asked to wink, I was contributing to an enculturation of Ian's life through narrative. In short, Ian cannot wink unless someone wonders aloud if he can. It makes culture relevant to his life, and starts the search for further interpretive symbols. That may not be sufficient, but it seems a necessary interpretive leap for questions of similarity and difference to have meaning to the lives of people with cognitive disabilities. The poet may be right that the world will end not with a bang but a whimper; I argue only that it begins with a wink. "I wink, therefore I am".

A brief aside may be appropriate here. This analysis seems to me to show a path to conceptual co-existence between hard-headed interpretivists and soft-nosed behaviorists. The evolution among enlightened educators from shaping discrete skills to embedding activities in functional settings is at least a partial recognition of the importance of cultural context. At the same time, interpretivists must avoid the impression that successful enculturation of people with significant cognitive disabilities is purely an interpretive exercise in collective pretending. If Ian did not learn some approximation of closing his eyelids, then no amount of "as if" stories would create a persuasive wink. Talking of the necessity of cultural status should translate behavior into meaningful activity, not invent behavior that no one else can see. One of the few ethnographic researchers to focus attention on people with so-called profound mental retardation, David Goode (1980, 1995), has used the metaphor of "behavioral sculpting" to describe this necessary combination of "raw material" and interpretive insight in the ability of friends and family to recognize purposeful actions where others see mere random sound or movement.

Reading Stories: Explaining Cultural Context

> Once human behavior is seen as... symbolic action... the question as to whether culture is patterned conduct or a frame of mind, or even the two somehow mixed together, loses sense. The thing to ask about a burlesqued wink or a mock sheep raid is not what their ontological status is. It is the same as that of rocks on the one hand and dreams on the other – they are things of this world. The thing to ask is what their import is: what it is... that, in their occurrence and through their agency, is getting said. (Geertz, 1973, p. 10)

What gets said, of course, depends on who is listening and in what cultural context. It is not enough to tell stories about people with cognitive disabilities. We must also learn how to explain them. Asking if Ian can wink, and what that might mean, begins the story, identifies his behavior as part of a social discourse. The cultural hermeneutics behind Geertz's treatment of thick description allows me to interpret the "said" of Ian's behavior, not merely what he did or did not mean to say. That is, Ian's wink becomes a social text with meanings.

For people with significant cognitive disabilities, this social dimension is crucial. Ian's ability to wink is not only temporal, it is situational. Ian has to be around people who believe he can wink – in some sense of that term that is meaningful to them. Sartre was wrong. His famous quotation that "hell is other people" conveyed the crushing sense of finitude that simply recognizing the presence of other active humans created for cranky existentialists. I always interpreted his remark to refer more to spatial limitations than to hints of mortality. That simple awareness of the existence of other conscious actors defeated my comforting conceit of solipsistic control of the world and its interpretation. Every time we sit through a frustrating committee meeting with people who refuse to recognize the superiority of our ideas, we get a superficial sense of what lies behind Sartre's epigram. For Ian, though, Sartre seems profoundly wrong. Other people are Ian's salvation; they are essential to the daily elaboration of who he is. Even more than for most of us, other people are a crucial part of who Ian is. **Cognitive disability is the not the absence of self; it is the absence of other people.**

There are two explanatory components to this social expansion of Ian's narrative. First, there is the importance of Ian's community membership, surrounded by supportive friends and family who join him in a choral presentation (as it were) of his personal story. Ian's story must be told by groups with multiple voices. The historical isolation and segregation of people with mental retardation from precisely this kind of community affiliation are part of what has deprived them of a cultural voice. Stories of Ian's presence in the community, his enculturation if you will, thicken the explanation of how he acts in the world. Using the interpretive metaphors of social text allows me to have Ian's friends tell their stories as well. Ian's story must be explained by those around him.

The second dimension of explanation has to do with a type of conceptual thickness. Not only must Ian have other people help tell his stories. He must also have his story placed in a critical, sociohistorical context. The thick explanation of why Ian can or cannot wink would have to attend to the opportunities for people with cognitive disabilities to be perceived as winking by other members of the culture. Interpreting Ian's winking as part of a larger, macrolevel commentary on the emerging social challenge to the medical model of mental retardation reflexively invests his action with greater explanatory richness than he could ever imagine (Watson-Gegeo, 1991). That Ian does not bring an especially acute political consciousness to his action does not prohibit such application: "[W]here an interpretation comes from does not determine where it can be impelled to go. Small facts speak to large issues, winks to epistemology, or sheep raids to revolution, because they are made to" (Geertz, 1973, p. 23).

This sociohistorical context for explanations of Ian's life also locates some important differences between cognitive and other types of disabilities. Attempts to supply a cultural context for critical explanations of Ian's place in society soon confronts the issue that there is no alternative or subculture available to replace or resist the absent culture of dominant society. In this regard, at least, severe cognitive disability differs from a disability such as deafness. Whether or not Deaf people choose to (or are allowed to) locate themselves within such a community, there exists an impressive and distinct tradition of language, heritage, and shared values that is demonstrably different from the mainstream culture. (See Foster's discussion of this point) There is a potential self-awareness of "me as a DEAF person" that such individuals may develop and present to the world. Simultaneously, that reflexive interpretation of an alternative culture by members of the Deaf community themselves provides a thick explanatory context for others to study and interpret as well.

What I am suggesting is that there may be little use in trying to speak of a "mental retardation culture" in the same way that it makes perfect sense to speak of a "Deaf culture", or a "Blind culture", or even a "Physical Disability culture". There is probably something that might be called a "professional" or "bureaucratic" subculture, which often engulfs people with mental retardation. One can find evidence of such patterns of life in many of residential programs operated for people labeled "developmentally disabled". It is a life of rules and programs and procedural rigidity that turns a home where disabled people live into a facility where support staff work. There is perhaps even something of a "family/advocate" subculture. A kind of "support group" identification can emerge among family members, for example, that becomes a haven of familiarity for parents and others who grow tired of explaining, defending, and advocating to a seemingly indifferent outside world.

However, I would argue that these examples are more about people who surround those with significant cognitive disabilities than a culture arising from the mentally retarded population itself. **At most, people with significant cognitive disabilities have been offered the options of fragile assimilation into, or paternalistic parodies of, the dominant culture.** This is a complicated issue, and one that has not received the scholarly attention it deserves. There are important differences in cultural experience relating to how severely intellectually disabled someone is. I do not pretend to deal adequately with the topic here. However, the logic of my argument clearly suggests that distinct mental retardation subculture is not a persuasive possibility. If mental retardation is appropriately understood as the absence (or the progressive diminution) of culture, then the viability of an alternative culture uniquely identifiable with mental retardation (rather than the bureaucracy surrounding it) seems to be an unavoidable corollary.

This contrast in explanatory contexts could itself help explain the relative isolation (with important and increasing exceptions) of critical scholarship and advocacy within the disability studies movement in general from similar and contemporaneous developments within the field of interpretivist scholarship in cognitive disabilities. The historical choices for interactions with culture have been different for people with different types of disabilities. For most, the choices have involved movement between alternative and mainstream cultures. For people with cognitive disabilities, the choices have involved movement from no culture to some culture. The common experiences of oppression, discrimination, and stigmatization that cut across these disability categories do not totally displace these different initial starting points for defining a cultural position. (Surely, this is similar to the different traditions of people of color as opposed to the dominant culture in America. The different historical contexts of African-Americans and Asian- Americans do not undermine their shared experiences of stereotypes and racism, but do complicate their own interactions and cultural positions. Disability is no more cohesive a term than ethnicity in this regard. We should not ignore or diminish the intersectional complexities that exist within the disability community, any more than generalities about ethnic minorities should replace recognition of racial particularities in culture and tradition.)

Winking at Adulthood:
A Relational Approach to Cognitive Disability

Let me pursue these cross-disability comparisons by shifting my focus to stories about something more obviously fundamental to my son's life than winks and twitches. Specifically, I want to use Ian's transition to adulthood over the past decade to examine the cultural implications embedded within two of the more influential policy reforms of that same period: the Independent Living Movement (ILM) and the Community Inclusion Movement (CIM). These two movements are interesting case studies in the different cultural histories of cognitive and physical disability. They seem to me to provide helpful examples of the conceptual tension between core concepts of "sameness" and "difference" that run through the evolving relationship of disability and culture.

Briefly, to forecast my argument, **I find assumptions of both essential sameness and essential difference implicit in the discourse surrounding both the ILM and the CIM, although they emerge within separate dimensions of adulthood.** The unintended consequence of this persistent essentialism is to risk the continued ghettoization of people with the most significant cognitive disabilities to the margins of both the disability community and mainstream culture. This comparison suggests to me the potential strength of a relational approach to disability and culture that chips away at the frozen distinctions of essentialism without dissolving our legitimate differences in some sort of mythical melting pot.

As before, I want to ground my discussion in a narrative slice of my son's life. In many ways, Ian's experiences over the last two decades or so exemplify a generation of dramatic changes in social policy and professional practice in dealing with people with his level of cognitive disabilities. When he was 5 years old, he was legally excluded from the public schools in the state where we lived. One year later (and more than 20 years after the *Brown* desegregation decision, The Education of All Handicapped Children Act (now IDEA) guaranteed for the first time his basic right to a "free, appropriate public education". During his school years, Ian benefitted from professional advances in how to combine a focus on functional skills with an emphasis on keeping him in the most integrated educational settings possible. Finally, just as he got ready to leave school, there was a renewed professional attention to effective planning and coordination to make that transition to adulthood as smooth as possible (Rusch, Szymanski, & Chadsey-Rusch, 1992).

These changed perspectives followed Ian (and others of his generation) as he left school and tried to make his way as an adult. Over the last few years, there has been a dramatic change in how many families and professionals have approached the challenge of designing effective services to help people with disabilities similar to our son's lead an adult life embedded in the community as fully as possible. Through a type of vocational policy called "supported employment", Ian has been able to avoid the segregation of sheltered workshops. An analogous policy in the residential domain – "supported living" – may offer Ian a greater variety of living arrangements to choose from than traditional group homes or other forms of congregate care.

The Day the Canary Died: The Fragile Status of Adulthood

However, translating these reforms into concrete and durable improvements continues to be a frustrating challenge. As I write these words, Ian and I are trying to recover from a disastrous week in which three years of planning and work by my wife and me seemed dangerously close to collapse. The pieces had finally seemed in place for Ian to move into a home of his own, making all of the transition plans, policy waivers, redesigned support strategies, and searches for flexible support dollars seem worthwhile. But within a few days, the outlook seemed dramatically changed. A selective chronology from one day of the week:

9:00 AM: Ian's van dies. His personal assistant cannot get it started even with jumper cables. This means Ian misses work, and is effectively stuck at our house with no transportation. I get the call and come home. The personal assistant is right: the van won't start.

10:30 AM: The mortgage seems critically ill. I get a call from the loan officer handling the mortgage for Ian's new house. Despite a preapproved loan arranged for months with a special trust arrangement for Ian to participate in home ownership, the previously happy investor had suddenly developed cold feet, and would not allow the closing to go forward.

12:45 PM: The pay system collapses. I call in from the car repair garage to get my phone messages. I hear from the person who is coordinating Ian's support plan that the system of flexible state support dollars we had helped design over the past 18 months is falling apart. It looks as though Dianne and I will have to cover salary commitments to Ian's support staff or risk losing them to other jobs that actually pay wages.

1:30 PM The refrigerator won't work. The man delivering the refrigerator to what is supposed to be Ian's new house calls to tell me that it will not fit. It seems that the extra-wide door built to handle Ian's wheelchair changed the dimensions for the refrigerator space. No one thought to re-measure. I am ready for cold storage.

3:45 PM At a previously scheduled meeting with Ian and his support staff, I review the day's events. Ian is in a lousy mood from missing work. His helpers are in lousy moods because their pay arrangements still seem unsettled. We abandon plans to move Ian into his house over the weekend. The meeting adjourns with yet another ad hoc plan for the coming week. I am supposed to be optimistic and cheerful.

8:00 PM: I find Ian's pet canary, Lucy, lying very still on the bottom of her cage. I think of the old stories about coal miners using canaries as an early warning system for the presence of explosive gases. After years of digging our way through the bureaucracy, I wonder if everything is about to blow up.

We survived the week (well, except for Lucy), and prospects look better now. However, the sequence of events and my own growing sense of futility and frustration during that week reinforced an awareness that the longer all of those disruptions and delays persisted, the more fragile Ian's adulthood seemed. Whether the issue is winking or adulthood, the main feature of Ian's disability right now is how contingent his cultural status seems on events that are largely out of his (or my) control.

I want to be clear about the issues I am raising here. First, it is the cultural status of adulthood that seems fragile, not whether Ian is an adult or not. **Being an adult and securing the symbolic status of adulthood within the dominant culture are two very different achievements. In many ways, it is precisely in the gap between the two where cognitive disability resides.**

The second cautionary note flows from the first: the causal direction is important. It is not, in my observation, the type and severity of Ian's multiple disabilities that have cumulatively *caused* his adulthood to be so at risk. Just the reverse: it is the multiple social barriers placed in the way of his adulthood – the breakdown of the narrative rather than any physiological impairments – that construct and define the nature and severity of his disability.

Most frustrating of all, perhaps, is that Ian's difficulties with concepts and language mean that he is largely unable to challenge these threats to his adulthood in his own words. All of us, disabled or not, have had days similar to the one I described above. Certainly, most people with a disability can recite their own horror stories of dealing with a bureaucracy that seems intent on perpetuating their dependence and poverty. What is different in Ian's experiences (and those of others with significant cognitive disabilities) is how he responds to such barriers. Ian does not necessarily recognize the challenges to his adulthood as readily as those of us around him do. Even if he does in some way recognize a challenge, his opportunity to respond effectively may be limited by both his communication and social skills. In other words, part of the issue surrounding his adulthood is how it continues to require my (or some other advocate's) ongoing translation of his complaints and desires.

Finally, I do not want to deny or neglect the very real gains that my son, and many others with similar disabilities, have derived from policy reforms directly attributable to either the ILM, the CIM, or both. His life is embedded in a circle of friends who help tell the stories of his adulthood to a larger society that often remains uncomfortable with his presence. Clearly, Ian's battles to maintain a job and move into a home of his own are very tangible signs of the efforts of a generation of disability advocacy to create a recognized place within those personal and cultural dimensions where the status of adulthood seems to dwell. And in winning some of these battles, however fragile and few the victories seem, Ian and many of his peers have a better life today than we dared envision 25 years ago. Nevertheless, despite these gains, I want to argue that this cultural terrain will remain contested by the dominant society until the essentialist assumptions of both movements are recognized and reframed.

Independent Living and the Personal Dimension of Adulthood

Personal autonomy is the meaning or dimension of adulthood that has probably received the most attention from the fields of special education and adult services. Having control over where I live and with whom, where I work and for whom, these are perhaps the most common markers in our personal lives of our independent living. It is this personal connotation of adulthood that educators and human service professionals usually mean to convey when they speak of the "transition from school to adult life". Over the past decade, the expansion of formal planning for this transition has most often focused on those domains of life that are most clearly associated with personal independence in our society (Rusch, DeStefano, Chadsey-Rusch, Phelps, & Szymanski, 1992).

From its outset, the strength of the Independent Living Movement has also been to concentrate on the personal dimension of adulthood. Perhaps the central contribution of the ILM has been to relocate the sources of economic dependency and social isolation from personal deficits inherent in the disability to cultural and environmental barriers constructed by society. The movement stressed the values of self-determination and autonomy as being well within reach of people with disabilities if only the full range of creative adaptations and accommodations were made available. The key value seemed to be personal control: over where one lived, what one did for a living, and how one got around from place to place.

As several commentators have noted, the structure of the Independent Living Movement was to argue that people with disabilities could succeed in the dominant society if allowed to use alternative means to achieve the same ends. The social critique presented by the movement was with the barriers to these hallmarks of Western individualism – autonomy and self-sufficiency – not the goals themselves. In the words of one of the earliest interpreters of the movement: "While disabled persons have been excluded from full participation in the American economic-political system, they still subscribe to the system's most cherished values and assumptions. They still want to become a part of the system" (De Jong, cited in Williams, 1983, p. 1004).

Adulthood, the argument goes, is essentially the same for disabled people as for everyone else. It is the environmental accommodations that need to be different. As a result, the rules of this predominantly economic game went unchallenged; disabled people were simply demanding a place at the starting line.

Within the disability rights community, some would argue that it is precisely this politically moderate agenda that is behind the relative success of the movement, at least in terms of official policy and rhetoric (Williams, 1983). Certainly, it could be argued that the attitudes and programs flowing from the Independent Living Movement have helped produce a major shift in how our culture thinks of adults with disabilities. The epitome (at least rhetorically) of that shift may be contained in the language of the Americans with Disabilities Act: "[T]he Nation's proper goals regarding individuals with disabilities are to assure equality of opportunity, full participation, independent living, and economic self-sufficiency for such individuals" (Section 2.a.8).

But there is a danger in this success that flows from the very core of the ILM. If the argument is that disabled people are essentially the same as everyone else, then once the barriers to full adulthood are removed, any remaining differences are reified into equally essential "facts of life". Since the ILM does not seriously challenge the social rules of rugged individualism, then if there is a remnant that continues to fail even when access is expanded, its exclusion from culture appears more justified than ever (Ferguson, 1994; Ferguson & Ferguson, 1986). If Ian has to continue to earn his way into adulthood by the measures of personal productivity and self-determination, then his social participation will remain persistently fragile at best, or overtly denied at worst. For people with the most significant cognitive disabilities, the ILM has created a logic that could legitimize their marginalization as the exceptions that prove the rule of essential sameness for other disabled people. Once more, it is the essentialist assumptions of an either-or ontology that reinforces the supposedly inherent "otherness" of some by claiming the inherent familiarity of most.

Deconstructing the discourse surrounding the ILM shows how this exclusionary logic was present from the earliest descriptions of independent living. It is not only the limited success of the ILM that potentially justifies the continued exclusion of cognitively disabled people from the status of adulthood. That exclusion originated in the terms and definitions of who was acknowledged as disabled in the first place. One of the open secrets of the early years of the disability rights movement is its often obvious discomfort with sharing the disability label with the so-called "mentally retarded" population. Just as with the internationally recognized graphical symbol for "disability" (the stick figure in the wheelchair), some of the most prominent spokespersons for independent living place physical disability and disability in a synecdochical relationship where the part stands for the whole (or vice versa). So, in both terminology and practice, the ILM made physical disability synonymous with disability itself. One way to understand the unnoticed implications for people with cognitive disabilities of the essentialist logic within the ILM is that the very terms of the movement did not recognize such individuals as disabled in the first place.

This exclusionary discourse continued even when the first flush of success prompted calls for attention to groups who had previously been excluded from the movement's analyses. When one of the earliest and best known interpreters of "independent living"(De Jong, 1984) described the progress of the ILM, he admitted that its "core constituency" (p. 40) had thus far been limited to young adults with a limited range of physical disabilities. The groups that he found "notably absent" (p. 41) from the movement were elderly people and racial minorities with physical disabilities. At that point, the absence of people with severe cognitive disabilities was not even "notable".

Again, my point here is not that early – much less recent – proponents of the ILM have intentionally adhered to an essentialist defense of personal autonomy as a way to distinguish themselves from an undesirable association with cognitively disabled people. The attractions of searching for some common essence, some objective reality that grounds our identity, are often as unnoticed as they are irresistible. They can be found in equal force, and equal dangers, within the advocacy movements that have explicitly focused on people with severe cognitive disabilities.

Community Inclusion and the Cultural Dimension of Adulthood

While the cultural dimension of adulthood is related to such indicators of personal autonomy as employment and residence, it goes beyond such concrete personal circumstances. It is perhaps even more problematic than the personal definition of adulthood for people with the most significant cognitive disabilities. It involves a more symbolic dimension of citizenship, membership, and reciprocity that I invoke when I speak of someone being "a responsible adult", or "a good citizen".

Unlike the ILM, many of the strongest early proponents of the Community Inclusion Movement came from the ranks of advocates for people with the most significant intellectual disabilities. The CIM's focus on how to secure full adulthood for people with disabilities also changed. While inclusion is often seen as a call for educational integration of students with disabilities, the language of inclusion has been extended by most of its interpreters to include to other domains of life (e.g., Ferguson, Hibbard, Leinen, & Schaff, 1990; Taylor, 1988), including adulthood. Unlike the Independent Living Movement, however, the calls for community inclusion of adults with disabilities emphasized the cultural dimensions of adulthood over the personal.

Instead of a vocabulary focused on personal qualities of autonomy and self-determination, the CIM seemed to focus on the symbols of membership and participation. The argument, however, remained familiar. People with cognitive disabilities are *essentially* the same as everyone else. Therefore, they deserve acceptance as full citizens of their communities in recognition of this essential sameness. Indeed, it is largely through the social dimensions of assimilation that full adulthood will be achieved. As part of the analysis of the symbols of adulthood, the avoidance of symbols associated with disability seemed equally important.

Perhaps the clearest demonstration of this argument is found in the calls for "people-first" language that many self-advocates and others within the developmental disabilities community have made. At least part of the impetus behind the adoption of such terminology is the assertion that whatever differences reside behind the labels of intellectual disability, they should be inconsequential compared to our essential humanness. The linguistic reform is consistent with an implicit ontology that relies on a shared human nature that emerges when the cultural barriers to inclusion are removed. (My argument, here, looks only at the ontology behind the "people-first" language. There may well be ethical and/or political arguments that counterbalance my conceptual abstractions The history of abuse, incarceration, and even extermination at the hands of people who denied their humanity, which has fallen especially hard and often on people with severe intellectual disabilities, make those additional areas of argument particularly relevant. See Devlieger's chapter for a more extensive explanation of the entire history of labeling used for people with cognitive disabilities.)

The risk in the cultural essentialism of some versions of inclusion is that its implicit denial of essential differences from the dominant culture can also deny people with cognitive disabilities access to the alternative cultures and traditions that the larger disability community is beginning to celebrate. In our struggle to surround Ian with the cultural symbols of adulthood, to have him fully included as an adult in his community, my wife and I worry that we are simultaneously isolating him from the equally important benefits of the being included within the larger disability community as well.

If, as I have argued, cognitive disability can be seen as the absence of culture, then gaining the benefits of the alternative cultures emerging within disability studies seems equally as valuable as creating his affiliations within the mainstream culture. Unique strengths, traditions, role models, values, and relationships are available to Ian because he is disabled at a time when that is becoming a source of pride. Surely, the status of adulthood for people with cognitive disabilities should be available without sacrificing a constructed identity as a disabled person as well. Indeed, the dichotomy seems to exist only as long as the essentialist logic posits them as incompatible concepts in the quest for the Truth about the nature of disability.

The Relational Approach to Disability and Adulthood

Essentialism in disability studies is like a fundamentalist religion: the security of the doctrine conceals the leaps of faith required to maintain belief. We seem to need the Manichaean dichotomy of devils and deity. Of course, whether one finds difference to be divine and similarity the road to hell, or vice versa, the solace comes from the clarity of conviction. What is truly hellish in such a theology is a tolerance of ambiguity and change. What is left for an interpretivist agnostic who has his doubts about heaven and hell? If both the personal and the cultural dimensions of adulthood have been captured by essentialist assumptions embedded in the most prominent reform movements of the past 25 years, where should an interpretive approach to disability and culture look for difference and similarity in adult life?

For me, the issue becomes one of how to advocate for Ian's adulthood in ways that do not, through the very act of my advocacy, emphasize how he differs from other adults (including those with other disabilities). Do I emphasize his differences and try to avoid the conclusions of inferiority that society has traditionally attached, or do I emphasize his sameness and risk perpetuating the same social rules and expectations that have already unfairly excluded him? Should Ian's adulthood look the same or different from the dominant cultural models, or from any alternative models presented by other parts of the disability community?

All of these issues are similar to the ones that feminist scholars such as Martha Minow (1990) and Anita Silvers (1995), as well as a few prominent interpreters of cognitive disability (Woodill, 1994; Zola, 1994) have written about. How am I to emphasize the differences that seem constitutive of Ian's identity as a disabled adult without unintentionally perpetuating the grounds for exclusion that the dominant culture has traditionally used to rationalize its denial of my son's adulthood? Minow has summarized this "dilemma of difference" with explicit reference to how it affects people with significant cognitive disabilities and those who advocate on their behalf:

> Social, political, and legal reform efforts to challenge exclusion and degradation on the basis of assigned traits continually run up against the danger either of recreating differences by focusing upon them or of denying their enduring influence in people's lives. This dilemma of difference burdens people who have been labeled different with the stigma, degradation, or simple sense of not fitting in while leaving the majority free to feel unresponsible for, and uninvolved in, the problems of difference… [D]ecisions about housing, education, and employment for individuals with severe mental disabilities add to the dilemma of difference the difficulty of learning what the individuals most affected would themselves want. (Minow, 1990, pp. 47-48)

I can only suggest the outlines of an answer here, and it is not original with me. I find the answer in relationships instead of essences, in the ambiguity and messiness of daily interactions. Much of Minow's "social relations" approach (and also articulately defended by Zola, 1994) seems a promising way to avoid the negative consequences of the "difference dilemma" quoted above, without trying actually to dissolve the tension. For people with cognitive disabilities, ironically, "inclusion within the independent living movement" is one of the practical examples of how this relational advocacy could work. If significant cognitive disability is characterized as the absence of culture, then moving to secure their status in either an alternative or a dominant culture might accomplish the same end of mitigating the negative consequences of being denied a cultural context. Instead of removing or dissolving the tension between sameness and difference (independent living or inclusion, disability culture or community integration), the relational approach avoids the essentialism implicit in the assumptions of the dichotomy.

We must, then, start to approach disability as relational, not essential. To my mind, that does not diminish disability, it does not discredit its centrality to our lives. Everything that tells us who we are, how we are the same and how we are different, is suspended in the webs of relationships that construct our culture. To interpret disability as relational simply shows us where to look, not what we should see. It only begins our search. When I look, I find disability in our affiliations with each other, our celebrations of difference, our struggles for equality. I find it in our cultural achievements and shared aspirations. I find it in our friendships and mutual supports. I find it in the history of our differences and our similarities. I even find it in our debates over who can really participate in the search for the meaning of those relationships: Who is "us" and who is "them"?

I find it most of all in the stories we tell each other about our lives. I find it especially in the stories my son helps me hear and see. I find it, in short, in the wink of an eye.

Acknowledgment

Portions of this chapter appeared in a modified version in the following publication: Ferguson, P. M. & Ferguson, D. L. (2001). Winks, blinks, squints and twitches: Looking for disability, culture and self-determination through our son's left eye. Scandinavian Journal of Disability Research, 3(2), 71-90.

References Cited

DeJong, G. (1984). Independent living: From social movement to analytic paradigm. In R.P. Marinelli & A.E. Dell Orto (Eds.), *The psychological and social impact of physical disability* (2nd ed.) (pp. 39-63). New York: Springer.

Ferguson, D.L., & Ferguson, P.M. (1986). The new victors: A progressive policy analysis of work reform for people with very severe handicaps. *Mental Retardation, 24*, 331-338.

Ferguson, P.M. (1994). *Abandoned to their fate: Social policy and practice toward severely retarded people in America, 1820-1920.* Philadelphia: Temple University Press.

Ferguson, P.M., Hibbard, M., Leinen, J., & Schaff, S. (1990). Supported community life: Disability policy and renewal of mediating structures. *Journal of Disability Policy Studies, 1*, 9-35.

Geertz, C. (1973). Thick description: Toward an interpretive theory of culture. *The interpretation of culture.* New York: Basic Books

Goode, D. (1980). Behavioral sculpting. In J. Jacobs (Ed.), *Phenomenological approaches to mental retardation* (pp. 381-396). Springfield, IL: C.C. Thomas.

Goode, D. (1995). *A world without words: The social construction of children born deaf and blind.* Philadelphia: Temple University Press

Minow, M. (1990). *Making all the difference: Inclusion, exclusion, and American law.* Ithaca, NY: Cornell University Press.

Mishler, E.G. (1995). Models of narrative analysis: A typology. *Journal of Narrative and Life History, 5* (2), 87-123.

Rusch, F.R., DeStefano, L., Chadsey-Rusch, J., Phelps, L.A., & Szymanski, E. (Eds.), (1992). *Transition from school to adult life: Models, linkages, and policy.* Sycamore, IL: Sycamore Publishing Co.

Rusch, F.R., Szymanski, E.M., & Chadsey-Rusch, J (1992). The emerging field of transition services. In F.R. Rusch, L. DeStefano, J. Chadsey-Rusch, L.A. Phelps, & E. Szymanski (Eds.), *Transition from school to adult life: Models, lindages, and policy* (pp. 5-15). Sycamore, IL: Sycamore Publishing Co.

Silvers, A. (1995). Reconciling equality to difference: Caring (F)or justice for peole with disabilities. *Hypatia, 10* (1), 30-45.

Taylor, S.J. (1988). Caught in the continuum: A critical analysis of the principle of the least restrictive environment. *Journal of the Association for Persons with Severe Handicaps, 13*, 41-53.

Watson-Gegeo, K.A. (1991, April). *Toward thick explanation in ethnographic research.* Paper presented at the meeting of the American Educational Research Association, Chicago.

Williams, G.H. (1983). The movement for independent living: An evaluation and critique. *Social Science and Medicine, 17*, 1003-1010.

Wisdom, J. (1965). *Paradox and discovery.* New York: Philosophical Library.

Woodill, G. (1994). The social semiotics of disability. In M.H. Rioux & M. Bach (Eds.), *Disability is not measles: New research paradigms in disability* (pp. 201-226). North York, Ontario: L'Institut Roeher Institute.

Zola, I.K. (1994). Towards inclusion: The role of people with disabilities in policy and research issues in the United States – A historical and political analysis. In M.H. Rioux & M. Bach (Eds.), *Disability is not measles: New research paradigms in disability* (pp. 49-66). North York, Ontario: L'Institut Roeher Institute.

Study Questions

1. This chapter argues that one way to understand the meaning of severe mental retardation in our society is as the perceived absence of culture. Talk about how the concept of "culture" could be used in this chapter so that it can be absent or present in people's lives. Are there other categories of people who might be seen similarly as deprived of a cultural context?

2. The author uses his experiences with his own son as the primary basis for his analysis. What are some of the advantages and disadvantages involved in relying on such personal experiences for conceptual analysis in disability studies?

3. The chapter argues that severe cognitive disability is substantively different than other types of disability in how they interact with culture. Do you think this difference also exists between milder levels of cognitive disability and these other types of disability?

4. The chapter invokes quotations from Geertz's well-known essay on "Thick Description". How would you interpret the meaning of". Thick Description"? How does it connect with what Ferguson refers to as "narrative analysis"? Describe some other research contexts in which thick description and narrative analysis might be usefully applied in disability studies.

5. The chapter argues that the independent living movement and the community inclusion movement have focused primarily on different segments of the disability community but share a similar essentialism in terms of their underlying approach to disability. Do you agree with this analysis? Discuss your reasons.

6. Ferguson briefly discusses the terminological debate over how to refer to disabled people generally, and people with mental retardation specifically. One side in this debate argues for "people first" language. Another side (there may be more than two sides here) argues for what might be called a "disability first" position, where language should show pride in one's identify and heritage as a disabled person by making the label prominent. Talk about this debate and its implications for the imagery of disability in our society.

7. How can someone who is not disabled (even if he or she is a close friend or family member of someone who is disabled) really understand how similar or different a disabled person is? Even if this is possible for some disabilities, is it possible when the disability involved is severe cognitive disability?
8. How is cognitive disability similar or different from other categories of diversity in our society such as race/ethnicity, gender, sexual orientation, class, and others? How much of these similarities and/or differences are culturally explained and how much are unchangeable matters of physiology that cut across culture?
9. If you accept the argument that there is no "essence", "nature", or single correct definition for disability, then relationships become even more powerful ways of shaping the meaning of disability. Choose a domain of life (work, school, leisure, family life, etc.) and reflect on how this relational approach to understanding disability might alter our policies and practices.
10. Again, if you accept the argument that the meaning of disability changes over time and place, then speculate about how this meaning might change in the 21st century. How will disabilities in 3003 be similar and different from disabilities in 2003?

The Common Agenda of Aging and Disabilities: Stalemate or Progress?[1]

Madelyn Iris

"Sameness" and "difference" are powerful concepts for defining two potential life experiences, aging and living with a disability. Growing older is seen as the natural outcome of a long life; but living with a disability is often considered a non-normative life experience. While older people may be staying healthier longer, the largest proportion of people living with a disability are those 65 and older. Thus, the shared concerns of older Americans and those with disabilities will take greater prominence in the decades ahead. Older Americans and people with disabilities, regardless of age, are linked through a set of common interests, including access to supportive and assistive services designed to sustain independent living; access to and reimbursement for health services; and continued public support for income maintenance. Within the policy domain both groups are susceptible to shifting images of those who benefit from public programs, as well as redefinition of who should benefit and for what purpose.

This chapter explores the multiple ways in which older persons and those with disabilities are both similar and different. The chapter begins with an examination of cultural images of the elderly and the disabled, presents a case study of Marie Henderson, an older woman with a chronic disability, describes how the concepts of sameness and difference influence the policy process, and then presents an historical overview of efforts to build a common agenda of disability and aging. The analysis focuses on the underlying causes for success and failure in this effort.

Aging is a familiar experience, the natural outcome of a long life. Although western cultures present mixed and often contradictory images of the value of the elderly in society, those who "age successfully" are admired and we seek their secrets to a long life. **The life course perspective provides us with a chronological framework for imposing order upon the physical processes of aging we see before us every day.** The stages of life take us from infancy, childhood, adolescence, through adulthood and finally, to old age, and are predictable across time, linking us to socially and culturally prescribed normative behaviors and expectations (in Neugarten, 1996) as well as transformations (Erikson, Erikson and Kivnick, 1986, Friedan, 1993). How we take measure of our aging speaks to how well we view our success in achieving the anticipated outcome of our lives.

Disability is different. We rarely anticipate disability, and to be born with a disability or to become disabled along the way to old age, is often considered an adversity, a tragedy, the result of a personal fault or failure of character, or, at the least, bad luck (Shapiro, 1993). **Disability represents a disruption of the life course, altering the normative process without supplying new but predictable expectations.** While in the past people with disabilities were

---

[1] Parts of this paper were previously published in Center on Aging, newsletter of the Buehler Center on Aging, Vol. 6, no. 1, Spring 1990.

almost uniformly discredited (Goffman, 1963), today there are no necessarily known outcomes of disability. Thus, disability creates tension and disturbance in the social fabric. We have little guidance to direct our actions or expectations, and few historical or even contemporary models of what it means to be successful at disability.

Within our society, contrary messages about the meaning and value of both old age and disability abound. First, we distance the individual from his or her uniqueness by creating a class, imposing labels such as "the elderly" and "the disabled". Such labeling gives only minimal acknowledgment to the vast diversity of experience and background that may well produce greater inter-group differences than similarities. Second, while we abhor the conditions of dependence, decline and loss associated with both states, we also idealize certain traits, whether real or perceived. The elderly may be viewed as fonts of wisdom and sources of insight into the true meanings of life, but at the same time we visualize the physical manifestations of aging as signs of decay, decrepitude and incompetence (cf. Cole, 1992). Similarly, we can recall many heroic stories of persons with disabilities, especially those who overcome the limitations of their disabling conditions and achieve goals we can all recognize as valuable. But the flip side of these images is that those who fail to achieve or overcome are perceived as failing to pass beyond the dehumanity of their disabilities (Shapiro, 1993).

These images and the meanings we ascribe to them have roots in our cultural history as well as in our contemporary and technological understandings of both the aging process and certain disabling conditions. But the tensions and dilemmas emerging from these understandings cannot be understood from a single explanatory framework. That is, the relationship between free radicals and physical aging, or tau proteins and dementia, is not sufficient to explain our societal struggle to find meaningful roles for older people that can both accommodate their changing needs as well as profit from their perspective of years. Nor does what we know about the genetics of Down Syndrome, Fragile X or even Alzheimer's disease, change the social or public outcomes of these experiences.

This chapter provides an overview of the movement toward consensus on a common agenda of aging and disability, exploring progress toward coalition building and the barriers to identifying common concerns that emerge from differing values, goals, and language. The common agenda is situated within the framework of the social and public outcomes of public policy and its influence on shaping social and self conceptions of the elderly and the disabled. My focus is on the evolution of the special status of elderly people into a unique class, and the evolving recognition of persons with disabilities as a legal, protected minority, looking specifically at the current political context which pushes the two groups toward a common agenda through specific legislative acts.

Examples from interviews with Marie Henderson (a pseudonym) illustrate the "lived experience" of such agenda building and its obstacles. Marie was interviewed in conjunction with the "Aging in Chicago Project"[2] (Iris and Berman, 1995). Diagnosed with multiple sclerosis while in her twenties, she was now 62 and was experiencing difficulty in navigating the transition between two human service systems in Illinois: the Illinois Department on

---

2 The Chicago Community Trust funded the "Aging in Chicago Project". Dr. Christine Cassel served as Principal Investigator.

Aging and the Illinois Department of Rehabilitation Services. Although both departments offer home care services programs, they are not compatible in goals, methods of assessment, nor in service delivery milieus. Marie's experiences illustrate the impact of growing older with a disability, exemplifying the many tensions and internal dilemmas faced by people with lifelong or adult-acquired disabilities, as they encounter older age.

Although she was an active participant in many programs offered by the state and city departments serving persons with disabilities, Marie may also be typical of her particular cohort in that she eschewed the ideology of the disability rights movement. She strongly objected to the more militant, rights-based approach used by disability activists.

"They're another bunch of, yeah, you do for me because I'm handicapped, yeah. ....I mean, I feel like 'who the heck do you think you are!' That's what I say to them when I see them on TV and they're protesting with the banners and everything. 'Who do you think you are'"!

Marie Henderson presents a complex model of aging and disability, which defies a uniform explanation or classification. She is an active user and seeker of both aging and disability services, yet refuses to align herself conceptually or ideologically with one or the other group. Instead, she reflects back to us the problematic nature of understanding the totality of individual identity as a function of a single characteristic such as chronological age or a particular impairment.

The Concepts of "Sameness" and "Difference"

Understanding the ways in which individuals are viewed as the same or different, rests upon the identification of some feature or characteristic that appears meaningful or significant to the problem or situation at hand. Features or characteristics selected as important for classification may change as the problem, purpose, or appropriateness of our classification shifts. For example, when I was a child, being a girl or a boy was often the single criterion for determining which sports you played at school. While sex-segregated sports still exist, gender per se is no longer a sufficient discriminator; rather separation of boys and girls may made based on differences in physical characteristics, such as relative strength or weight.

Categorization is an important developmental task, essential to bringing a sense order to the natural world and providing meaningful and shared understandings of life experience (Lakoff, 1987). Categorization draws upon the recognition of shared and somehow distinctive characteristics among the members of the class. At the same time, the creation of a class also implies potential recognition of a "counter-class". For example, current Medicare eligibility recognizes the distinctive feature of chronological age to create a class of eligible persons 65 and older. By including certain persons younger than 65 but with disabilities in the eligible category, the program and its proponents recognized certain qualities of similarity that transcend age. Those in the group are presumed similar, those not in the group are different, by virtue of some criteria recognized as socially meaningful.

What makes a criterion acceptable as a means of classification varies and lies at the heart of understanding the significance of the concepts of same and different. Criteria for classification tell us what is important according to a system of values, and what, as in the case of Medicare, may stand as a proxy for a host of other, defining characteristics. Once institutionalized, these criteria are often difficult to change, as they embody myriad meanings.

Thus, when we examine the importance of the concepts of sameness and difference in disability and aging, we can appreciate the role of public policy in shaping our values and understandings

The concepts of "sameness" and "difference" are manifested through the policy agendas and advocacy efforts of both the aging and disability communities, as well as in the lives of older persons themselves, including those with disabilities. From a policy perspective, these concepts represent the complex nexus of a set of ideological values, such as inclusion, entitlement, accommodation, and specialization versus generalization, and a set of negatively associated cultural values, such as frailty, dependence, impairment, and neediness. At the heart of this analysis of the similarities and differences coexisting across these groups, are two commonly perceived ideological differences: a focus on integration versus separation, and the appeal to entitlement versus civil rights (see Minow, 1990).

Historically, public policy and program development within the aging services network has emphasized the need for special accommodation of the elderly, through income maintenance, social services, health care, and housing. Such accommodation is generally cast in a model that creates parallel or even unique services and contexts, designated specifically for older adults. The principle underlying the appeal for the creation of such a model is that of entitlement (Neugarten, 1982). Older people are viewed as past contributors to the welfare of society and the well being of younger persons. In their older age, they have earned a position of uniqueness, and a special place in the social system. Justification for entitlement is framed as an argument based on numbers: the U.S., and other western nations as well, are experiencing an historically unique phenomenon, the rise of an older class, necessitating reevaluation of the needs, place and role of the elderly in our society. **Today, the "demographic imperative", generated by increasing numbers of older people living into advanced old age, is a favored metaphor in support of continuing special attention to the needs, place, and role of the elderly in our society.**

In contrast, the philosophical underpinnings of the disability rights movement emerge out of notions of equality and accommodation, leading to integration and equal status. The appeal of this philosophy is to civil rights, and the model for action is that of the U.S. civil rights movement of the 1950s and '60s (Shapiro, 1993), including civil disobedience through sit-ins, demonstrations, and grass roots activism. Most importantly, the disability rights movement calls for self-advocacy and empowerment of people with disabilities. The goal is a barrier-free environment, both physically and attitudinally, so that people with disabilities of whatever sort can move freely in the world with equal access to the same opportunities and social spaces as those available to all other individuals.

The power to achieve these goals will come through the creation of a significant political bloc, uniting all persons with disabilities via a perceived set of common interests. As with aging advocacy, the disability rights movement relies upon the recognition of an historically unique social class which unifies a diverse and disparate group of individuals on the basis of only one of potentially many individually meaningful characteristics. To be successful, people with disabilities must perceive of disability as a more powerful defining characteristic than gender, race, religion, or age. But the lack of a singular set of shared, culturally or socially meaningful, behaviors and attitudes makes it difficult to achieve this goal (see Foster, this volume).

However, while some people are born with a disability, most acquire a disability some time during adulthood. In fact, more than half of people 65 and older are disabled (Torres-Gil, 1996). Since only about 20% of the U.S. population overall is reported to be disabled, this means that most of those considered to have a disability are also elderly. Older people hold a self-concept shaped years earlier, with layers of identity built up prior to becoming disabled.

Taking on the shared perspective of the disability rights movement may be difficult or even parenthetical to older and more meaningful concepts of who and what they are. In fact, rather than ascribing status as a disabled person, a disability may seem to say more about who they no longer are, rather than who they have become.

Marie Henderson's experience illustrates the difficulty older people experience in this process of self-definition; even with viewing themselves as part of the group we call "the elderly. Following hospitalization for severe circulatory problems she was transferred to an extended care center for rehabilitation. In the interview she commented upon her change in status:

> "One thing I wanted to say is when I went into the hospital I felt as old as the people that were in the hospital, and they were all in their 80s....I felt like I was young when I first got sick and then I'd say to myself, remember you're not young anymore. I'd say to myself, you're an old bag, act like it. That's the way I was in the hospital".

Within the environment of the extended care facility, Marie experienced herself as transformed, shifting her identity from that of a younger, disabled person to that of a now deteriorated personality ("old bag").

While researchers and scholars have speculated about the social and cultural significance of a growing population of older people and the meaning of this growth (Callahan, 1987; Silverman, 1987; Cole, 1992; Friedan, 1993), both individually and socially, it is difficult to find a literature that grapples with the same set of issues from the perspective of a growing population of persons with disabilities. While individual life stories and case studies are often presented as exemplary models of life with a disability, only a few confront the meaning of disability in a broader sociocultural or philosophical context (Zola, 1982; Murphy, 1990) and little has entered the public sphere (Berube, 1996). Thus, there continues to be an absence of a larger, public discussion on the meaning of disability within the fabric of American social life.

Despite such differences, **there is a growing trend to unify the interests of older people and those with disabilities.** In doing so, it is necessary to overcome some long-standing historical barriers. For example, anticipated and expected social roles differed greatly for those who grew older and those who were disabled. The place of the elder within the pre-industrial family structure was more complex than usually acknowledged, but is now often sheathed in a cultural mythology in which elders held positions of esteem based on their accumulated wealth, control of property, and positions in a male-dominated hierarchy within the church (Achenbaum, 1978; Cole, 1992).

In contrast, people with disabilities, including cognitive impairments, physical disabilities, and especially mental illness, have long been stigmatized. Devlieger's analysis of the language of mental retardation (this volume), illustrates this quite aptly. The place of the disabled in society was dominated by a model of charity but with social distance best represented by the creation of the asylum. Such culturally engrained attitudes and even language continue to influence our thinking about these groups, and hence justify the exclusion or inclusion of those who are the "other".

A number of questions flow from this analysis. For example, if those with disabilities are "charity cases", "imbeciles" or "mental defectives" or if they represent punishment for past sins, known or unknown, then how do we, as a society, incorporate a vision of equal rights for persons with disabilities (Minow, 1990)? If we continue to mythologize the "good old days" when the elderly were respected and held a seat of honor at the family table, then how do we recognize the need for continuing public support of older adults, and recognize our social obligations to meet the needs of this highly diverse group of people? Finally, how do we deal with diversity – since neither of these groups is internally homogeneous, along almost any dimension, including race, income, age, degree of disability, or the need for services?

Demographics

Before answering these questions, it is important to understand why they are important. Generally, when addressing a problem within the framework of public policy, demographics provide an overriding rationale; questions become important when the answers apply to large numbers of a powerful or potentially powerful political constituency. Such is the case here. As more and more people avoid death at earlier ages, and in addition, live longer, researchers predict higher incidences of disability in later life (Crimmins, Saito and Reynolds, 1997). Thus, we might expect to see a coalescing of interests between the aging and the disabled.

Throughout the literature on our aging society, researchers and scholars invoke the power of the "demographic imperative". In 1990, approximately 13% of the U.S. population was sixty-five years of age or older. This figure represents a significant jump in the numbers of elderly, but most importantly, it includes a rapid rise in the number of people aged eight-five and over. In fact, it is estimated that by the year 2020 about 17% of the population will be sixty-five or older, and the numbers will continue to grow for another ten to fifteen years, as the post World War II "baby boom" reaches older age. Within this group, we will see a greater rise in the number of very old people, so that by 2050, as many as half of all older people will be over age seventy-five (Siegel and Taeuber, 1986).

Such increases in sheer numbers of older people, when combined with an increased life expectancy, mean that more and more people will be living to an older and older age. However, with increased longevity comes potentially higher risk of disability, including impairments in mobility, hearing, vision, and cognition, as well as loss of function due to medical conditions such as congestive heart failure, stroke, chronic obstructive pulmonary disease, and other age-associated illnesses. Ansello estimates that there are already 5.5 million people sixty-five and older with visual impairments or blindness; nine million who have hearing impairments or are deaf, and another six million who have communication impairments of some sort due to a late-life onset (Ansello, 1988).

The U.S. is also experiencing growth in the numbers of people who age with a pre-existing disability. The development of more sophisticated methods for saving lives in emergency situations has had a significant impact in shaping this outcome. For example, Shapiro (1993) notes that during World War I, only four hundred men survived with wounds that paralyzed them from the waist down, and of these, few survived to reach home. However, during World War II, two thousand such men survived and most are still alive, now older adults. During the Korean and Viet Nam conflicts even greater numbers survived with more devastating injuries. The power of the Paralyzed Veterans of American as a political interest group and advocacy association attests to the impact of such survival rates.

New drugs and interventions have also increased the likelihood of surviving a traumatic spinal cord injury or previously terminal illness. For example, the use of insulin as a routine treatment for diabetes has contributed significantly to the numbers of people who are living into old age with what used to be a fatal condition. Many cancers and cardiac conditions have been transformed into chronic conditions. As a result, there are now approximately 35 million to 43 million people in the U.S. living with a disability, and one-third or more are sixty-five or older (Shapiro, 1993; Torres-Gil, 1996).

In addition, Ansello estimates that there are now as many as half a million older people with developmental disabilities or mental retardation and that this number also will continue to increase over the next decades. Increases in life expectancy, both at birth and across the life span, for persons with developmental and other disabilities, will clearly have a significant impact on the number of people who reach older age with a disability in both the near and distant future.

Thus, **the number of Americans who could consider themselves disabled is significant: as many as one in seven (Shapiro, 1993). Should such individuals choose to unite around a unified agenda, their influence on public policy would be impressive.** For this reason alone, it is important to consider the history, policies, and philosophical positions that have kept these individuals from joining in common cause, and to explore the process now underway that seeks to bring them together.

Public History

There are long-standing historical traditions for providing support, through public and private mechanisms, based on cultural visions of the elderly and disabled that emerged out of the ethical and moral precepts of a westernized Judeo-Christian tradition, and predate the evolution of modern public policy as we know it (see, for example, Brakel, Parry and Weiner, 1985; and Gartner and Joe, 1987). As Koff and Park note, in colonial times the elderly poor, the disabled and the mentally impaired were often lumped together and provided care through the local almshouse, which itself received support from both public taxes and private donations (1993). Thus, in the earliest formulations of public policy, Americans were predisposed to see the needs and goals of the elderly and the disabled as more alike than different, and a similar institutional structure was believed adequate and appropriate for both groups.

However, twentieth century public policy has reshaped our perceptions of the elderly and the disabled, and created both incentives as well as barriers to the development of a common set of understandings. In their analysis of aging policy, Koff and Park (1993) describe the intimate tie between public policies, individual and social values, and the relationship between policy, public will, and historical context. This brief review of several of the most important congressional acts designed to provide financial assistance, services, and programs to older adults, illustrates a major theme of this chapter: **that public policy both codifies as well as influences our individual and social perceptions of those served.**

Old Age Policy

Within the realm of aging policy, much emphasis is placed on creating programs to assist and compensate for the perceived effects of aging. Programs like Social Security and SSI provide financial support, while a programmatic structure like the aging network, established by the Older Americans Act, serves as a universal, national mechanism for service delivery and support.

The history of social security, its grounding in the after-effects of the industrial revolution, and its subsequent emergence as a consequence of the Great Depression are well documented (Achenbaum, 1986; Koff and Park, 1993). Social determinations of the value of older age began to change due to several causes. These include the shift from an agrarian to an industrial economy, which disenfranchised the elderly land owner as the holder of the major source of wealth and power, and an increasing life expectancy that rose from an average of 40 years in 1850 to 47 by 1900 to approximately 60 years in 1935 (Siegel and Taeuber, 1986). Associated with this increased life expectancy was a portrayal of old age as a time of increasing illness, decreasing vitality, and loss of mental competence due to an inevitable state of senility. Old age became a disease in itself. As Koff and Park (1993) note, chronological age became the marker for determining an individual's place in society, rather than individual needs or differences. A new social class, the elderly, evolved based on the single characteristic of age alone, but with a wide-ranging association to increased impairment, frailty, and social and financial need. This created a precedent for viewing the elderly as a distinct sub-group of the larger population, now somehow different and distinct from who and what they had been before. It is only recently that scholars, policy makers, and program developers have come to realize and appreciate the tremendous diversity that exists amongst older persons, a diversity that may well serve to factionalize rather than unite these individuals.

Social Security has a long and complicated history, with roots in several social movements, and passage supported by increasing evidence that the elderly were at special risk for poverty and economic dependence. For example, in 1890, two-thirds of all men over age 65 had been working, but by 1930, less than half of men this age or older were still employed (Koff and Park, 1993:51). Although there was considerable resistance to the idea of a public pension program for American workers, the onset of the Great Depression swung the balance in favor of this innovative social program and the Social Security Act was passed in 1935 under the leadership of Franklin Delano Roosevelt.

For purposes of political expediency, and to ensure its passage, in its initial form the act encompassed a three-pronged approach to the creation of a national 'social security' program with a strong emphasis on aid to the elderly: old age assistance for the needy elderly, old age insurance, and unemployment insurance. Within just a few years the act expanded to offer protection to numerous other groups, including spouses, widowers, children of deceased workers. The 1939 amendments included provisions for payments to the children of disabled workers and to parents of children with disabilities (Koff and Park, 1993).

Over the years the Social Security Act has been amended numerous times, either with minimal adjustment to benefits and policies or with sweeping changes. 1965 stands out as a vanguard year for change, with passage of Medicare and Medicaid, Titles XVIII and XIX, respectively. Together, these titles create a program of national health insurance for three classes of individuals: the elderly (those over sixty-five); the indigent, and those with disabilities. In 1972 the Supplemental Security Income program (Title XX) was passed, consolidating guaranteed income programs to the very poor and those with disabilities.

The Social Security Act, as it now stands, funds a block of programs that unite the interests of older persons and those with disabilities through two mechanisms, financial benefits tied to past income or current need, and medical care, including both acute and long term services. Although distinctions are drawn between benefits paid to retired workers, who have "earned" the right to participation, and those who receive benefits on the basis of inability to work, and therefore, have no "earned" right, it is clear that both groups have vested interests in what happens to social security programs in the future, through adjustments to, or reductions in benefits, taxation of benefits, narrowing of benefits eligibility, etc. Current attacks on the social security system, attempts to portray it as a key contributor to a never-shrinking national deficit, and images of beneficiaries as undeserving, malingering, outrightly fraudulent, or, at minimum, greedy, demand a unified response from both constituencies. In addition to providing financial support to the elderly and the disabled, the federal government has also carved out a role in the provision of health care services to these two groups, through a number of venues, including the Medicare and Medicaid programs.

Prominent public attention was not given to these various roles until passage of the Medicare Act in 1965 and its companion bill, Medicaid. These two pieces of legislation provide for universal access to health care for three significant groups: the elderly, i.e., those sixty-five and older, those with disabilities, and the indigent. Through a two-part system of premium payments, one for in-hospital services (Part A) and one for physician out-patient services (Part B), Medicare offers comprehensive coverage to older adults and some younger people with disabilities. Medicaid covers the cost of a wide-range of services for those who meet low-income eligibility requirements, including a significant number of people with disabilities who receive supplemental security income benefits (SSI). Most importantly, by covering costs for nursing home care, and now, increasingly, for home care services under state-based waiver programs, Medicaid has become a significant funding source for skilled nursing and home care for those in both groups who meet rather stringent income eligibility requirements. In fact, the portion of Medicaid dollars that goes to support long-term care services has grown significantly since its inception, and has come to dominate the public's concern for how to deal with the increasing costs of the Medicaid program.

While people with disabilities and the frail elderly all benefit from both the Medicare and Medicaid program, via access to health services, durable medical equipment, and long term care services, there have been few attempts to develop consensus or even a unified posture of support for these programs. I believe there are several reasons why this is so. First, both Medicare and Medicaid emphasize coverage for acute care services and respond to the needs of those with chronic illness or permanent conditions only via an acute care model: to receive services one must have a definable medical illness. This means that the disabling effects of conditions as diverse as osteo-or rheumatoid arthritis, cerebral palsy, spinal cord injury, mental retardation, chronic back pain, environmentally-induced systemic allergies, dementias of various etiology, and so on, must all be defined as illness or disease.

As a result of this emphasis on acute care services there has been a concurrent dominance of the medical model of both aging and disability. The medicalization of aging and disability is a topic beyond the focus of this chapter, but it is a conceptualization that affects both groups. Significant attention has been given to the latent as well as more overt biases that permeate the medical model of both disability (Zola, 1988; Longmore, 1995) and aging (Cohen, 1988; Estes and Binney, 1989; Minkler, 1990), and both groups are in continual danger of the backlash effect associated with the tendency to view those with chronic and/or disabling conditions as victims of poor lifestyle choices or a multi-risk circumstance such as poverty.

The movement toward managed care provides a timely example of how common threats to the well-being of both the elderly and the disabled, through access to health care and related services, could serve to formulate a common agenda. Recent debates on universal access to health care have emphasized the clearly strong public opinion that rising health care costs need to be contained, and that the American health care system is in a "crisis". This crisis has its roots in two sources: increasing costs of health care for the elderly and increasing demand for high-tech interventions and solutions to health related problems.

Managed care is seen as one solution to these problems. Managed care limits costs through strict control of patient access to services, clearly defined protocols of treatment, and other efficiencies. In many states Medicare and Medicaid programs offer managed care options. The implications of this model are significant, both for older persons, who are amongst the highest users of health care services, and those with disabilities, who may require regular and ongoing services and especially, high cost items such as motorized wheel-chairs, augmentative communication devices, remote environmental controls, portable respirators, etc. While it is not yet evident how well or how poorly managed care will serve these two populations, it is clear that neither group is paying nearly enough attention to the issues.

For example, resolutions concerning health and long term care passed by the delegates to the 1995 White House Conference on Aging did not specifically address issues of managed care, though they did call for maintenance of personal choice and autonomy regarding health care decisions. During a November, 1995 post-conference televideo on linkages between the aging and disabilities communities, issues related to health care and access were not debated, although both disability activists and aging advocates participated. At the 1996 American Society on Aging Conference, June Kailes, a disability rights activist and policy consultant, exhorted the audience to unite around the issue of managed care, describing it as a singular threat to adequate health care for both older adults and those with disabilities (see also Iris, 1996). Thus far, however, little action has been taken.

One singular difference that arises in any consideration of how public policy and legislative actions serve to unite or separate those with disabilities and those who are aged, is that of philosophy and ideology regarding disability and remedy. These differences are reflected well in several pieces of legislation that were implemented with specific populations in mind. For example, the Older Americans Act (OAA), passed in 1965 created the structure for the aging services network that survives till today, and its provisions are founded largely upon the perception of the elderly as a population in need. As originally enacted, the act sought to ameliorate the condition of the elderly through compensatory services in-home assistive services, congregate services such as recreation and meals delivered through a network of senior centers, with minimal attention paid to job placement or retraining. As an "ameliorative" response, as Berkowitz (1987) uses the term, the OAA compensates for a situation through external resources or adjustments, rather than correcting for it, by strengthening the position of the individual. Berkowitz describes the latter position as an "investment".

A unique outcome of the OAA is that in tandem with the now customary and in some cases mandatory retirement age of sixty-five, and along with access to health care via Medicare, it has created a new class of individuals based solely on the characteristic of chronological age. That is, in contrast to other social support programs, Older Americans Act programs, Medicare, and Social Security benefits are not needs based. Thus for the first time in American history, an age-based class structure has been fully formalized and the interests of the elderly, as denoted by birthday, are differentiated from those of all other age, racial or minority groups, at least from the perspective of the policy makers and advocates. In addition, unlike Medicare and the comprehensive social security programs, access to Older Americans Act programs are restricted by age. Thus, there is no opportunity for forging a common bond with other invested parties or constituencies.

Disability Policy

The underlying ameliorative philosophy of the Older Americans Act, and the concomitant emergence of the elderly as a unique social class, contrasts sharply with the more corrective vision of the disability rights movement and its advocacy efforts. The history of rehabilitation services and federally funded programs emphasizing vocational training and rehabilitation is as complicated as that of Social Security and services for the aged. Multiple service systems, replication of services for the general public and for veterans, through the Department of Veterans Affairs, and philosophical differences regarding the purpose and value of the programs all contribute to this complexity. However, 1973 marks a watershed in the history of disability policy, with passage of the Rehabilitation Act which established the Rehabilitation Services Administration, housed within the Department of Health, Education and Welfare. The Rehabilitation Act mandated services to those with severe disabilities and established programs for independent living, emphasizing preparation for community living over job preparation (Berkowitz, 1987).

But most importantly, from an historical perspective, the Rehabilitation Act laid the foundation of the disability rights movement. Section 504 of this legislation established the principle of equal rights and nondiscrimination for those with disabilities. Although the origins of Section 504 are obscure (Berkowitz, 1987), this brief paragraph created a principle of equality around which all persons with disabilities could coalesce and provided the philosophical underpinning for all subsequent advocacy and disability rights efforts, culminating in passage of the Americans with Disabilities Act (ADA) in 1990, the premier civil rights legislation for the disabled.

Generally, the provisions of both Section 503 and the ADA are perceived as specific to persons with disabilities, but in fact the focus upon non-discrimination and equal access through accommodation can be seen as a boon to many varying constituencies within the U.S., including the elderly. As private and public spaces are modified to decrease environmental barriers, through ramps, elevators, widened doorways, etc., many individuals benefit, beyond those with physical or sensory disabilities. Older adults have greater access along with younger persons with similar disabilities of perhaps different etiologies. In addition, accommodation in the workplace could facilitate the hiring of older persons as well as younger persons with disabilities, regardless of cause.

However, these principles of equality in access and accommodation do not seem to have captured the imaginations of older people with disabilities, regardless of level of impact, and many still do not see ways in which the implications of equal rights and access can apply to their own situations. In fact, there has been a continuing public disaffection with the principles espoused by the ADA, and disability rights activists have not been able to create a groundswell of public opinion for their position. The envelopment of the disability rights movement within the cloak of civil rights, and the ascription of minority status to those with disabilities, has served as a nexus for negative public opinion. The current backlash against equal rights and equal opportunity as mandated through legislation, litigation and civil rights opinions, has hit the disability rights movement with a force equal to that directed at proponents of racial equality. **Since there has never been an attempt by the elderly to become a legally recognized minority population, this one position serves as perhaps a permanent demarcation between the two groups, and may be the biggest barrier to creating a common consensus or at least a shared agenda through coalition building.**

Building Coalitions

Coalitions are premised upon the belief that disparate groups share a common concern in at least one area. While competing interests may prevail at different times, at some point in time a single issue focuses attention on mutual concerns, creating a shared agenda. Once the issue is resolved, or deemed irresolvable, the coalition may disband or simply fade away.

The predominant model of consolidation and linkage between the elderly and the disabled is that of coalition building. Such coalition building, however, is asymmetrical in its implementation. While local and national coalitions have emerged, either through grass-roots efforts or as a result of funded programs, they have generally brought together individual or organizationally based disability rights advocates and aging services systems representatives as well as direct service providers. The asymmetries or imbalances that result reflect the very different institutional nature of the two systems. The independent living movement, which became the breeding and training ground for disability rights advocates and advocacy, is organized around individuals. It evolved as a collection of grass roots, localized organizations, staffed and run by people with disabilities, and it spoke directly to their issues and concerns (Berkowitz, 1987; Shapiro, 1993). In contrast, the aging services network is a network of providers, generally not elderly themselves, who advocate on behalf of older adults, but at the same time, on behalf of their own programs and system. Only a few organizations, like the Grey Panthers, or even the American Association of Retired Persons (AARP), actually can claim to be consumer-based advocacy organizations, regardless of their particular politics or policy positions. As a result, a number of inherent problems prevent a true coalition from emerging (Iris, 1990).

Over the last decade numerous attempts to reach consensus on the shared concerns of older adults and persons with disabilities have taken the form of national conferences or symposia, beginning as early as 1985 when the Institute for Health and Aging of the University of California-San Francisco and the World Institute on Disability (WID) in Oakland, California jointly sponsored a national conference at the Wingspread Center in Racine, Wisconsin (Mahoney, Estes and Heumann, 1986). What is perhaps most interesting about this conference, aside from its historic role as perhaps the first national conference on a common agenda, is that Carrol Estes, in her welcoming remarks, framed that common agenda in terms of shared problems: particularly, lack of universal health care and the problems of a health care system focused primarily on the provision of acute care rather than serving the on-going needs of those with chronic-illnesses.

Despite the passage of over ten years, these concerns still stand as perhaps the most important for those with disabilities and the elderly as a whole. Although numerous such conferences and conference publications followed (National Council on Aging, 1988; Ansello and Rose, 1989; American Society on Aging, 1992), there has not been significant progress toward the creation of a meaningful national coalition based on a shared agenda (Binstock, 1992). As Torres-Gil notes (1995), it was only in May 1994 that the National Coalition on Aging and Disability was formed. This coalition assumed the lead in devising a series of post-White House Conference on Aging events, in order to sustain momentum and generate growing interest in the movement. One organized activity, an interactive teleconference held in November 1995, failed to provide meaningful mechanisms or structures for continuing collaboration at the local level.

Even when faced with specific problems in local, state, and national arenas the obstacles to coalition building may be more powerful than common interests. The debate over the catastrophic health care act in 1988 is one example in which, despite common interests of both aging and disability groups, they failed to present a united voice and the importance of catastrophic care coverage for younger persons with disabilities was never fully addressed either locally or in national forums. Had disability activists taken a more vocal stance and recognized the potential long-term benefits of this bill, there might have been a different outcome, and some provisions of the act might have been salvaged. A few years later aging advocates were active sponsors of the National Long Term Care Campaign but it was difficult to generate interest amongst disability groups (Binstock, 1992), probably because "long term care" is still considered a euphemism for the nursing home.

Two other examples of how coalition building has not yet served to identify common issues or jointly address shared interests are the problems related to establishing mainline accessible transportation services and low-income, public housing. A number of years ago, in Chicago, ADAPT, a disability rights group advocating for accessible public transportation, used sit-ins and other forms of civil disobedience to force the Chicago Transit Authority to buy lift-equipped buses as an alternative to, but not a replacement for, dial-a-ride services. While ADAPT was successful in achieving its goal, it was with little or no support from aging advocacy groups or from older persons themselves. In fact, many older people opposed the effort, believing that special services would be discontinued. For a variety of reasons the need for an accessible, integrated, readily available transportation system was not perceived as a shared concern by older adults. Even today, with increasing numbers of bus routes being served by lift-equipped buses, usage by the elderly remains low, despite significant efforts to familiarize potential users with the service and facilitate access.

Further, in terms of public housing, concerns over age-integrated housing have actually generated considerable animosity towards persons with disabilities on the part of older residents (Kailes, 1996). Low-income accessible housing for persons who use wheelchairs is in high demand across the country. In Chicago, for example, attempts to integrate a number of senior housing buildings by offering adapted apartments to persons with disabilities have met with much opposition, as younger people with disabilities feel stigmatized by having to live in "senior buildings" and do not share interests or life-styles with their older neighbors. In return, many older people feel it is inappropriate to have younger people in their buildings. The problem has been exacerbated by the fact that some of the disabled peopled offered such housing are disabled due to a mental illness. Older people feel especially threatened by the presence of such people in their buildings, a reflection of the continuing and powerful stigmatization of mental illness, and aging advocates have taken steps to "protect" their constituents from these perceived threats.

In another example greater opportunities for community-based living were created through the passage of the Fair Housing Amendments Act in 1988 (P.L. 100-430), an act supported and lobbied for by disability rights groups, in part to ensure their right to develop small group homes in residential communities. Yet, although the bill has many potential benefits for older, impaired adults, aging consumer and family-support groups did not take a vocal stance in support of this bill. In fact, they feared its passage would mean the end of the age-segregated housing they favored.

These examples highlight issues around which aging and disability rights groups could join together in recognition of their common concerns. However, it would be naive to think that important differences such as those outlined above can be easily overcome. The history of effort over the last decade or more is evidence of the difficulties that continue to plague this union.

There are a number of well-founded reasons why a unified agenda or common platform has failed to emerge, despite the years of rhetoric and mutual interest. First, it is fallacious to assume that either population group operates with a unified agenda of its own, or even recognized shared concerns within its own constituency. There is clearly no such thing as an "aging agenda" which encompasses positions relevant to all segments of the older adult population. In fact, diversity within the aging segment of the population continues to grow. For example, the "oldest-old", i.e., those eighty-five and over, may have interests distinct from those who are younger, and minority elderly, both African-American and Hispanic, may represent needs and interests quite distinct from those of the white population. Indeed, gerontologists themselves are just beginning to grapple with the implications of confronting such multi-dimensional heterogeneity (Grigsby, 1996).

Finding a set of common issues that unites all persons with disabilities may be even harder as disability itself is an elusive category. There is no public, scholarly, or even legal consensus as to what constitutes a disability, or how affected one needs to be before becoming "disabled" (LaPlante, 1991). As Ferguson notes elsewhere in this volume, the association of disability with the independent living movement and individual autonomy has served to exclude rather than include many persons with non-physical impairments.

Thus, interpretations of difference, as the essential constituent of a disability are varied and complex (Minow, 1990). However, as disability becomes more and more politicized, more problems arise that could potentially splinter rather than unite the movement. Since the passage of the ADA greater numbers of advocacy groups have sought protection from discrimination and access to benefits on the basis of disability. As a result, the category label "disability" has become more and more unbounded, more internally diverse, and thus less meaningful and useful for understanding disability. For example, persons with infectious diseases such as tuberculosis and AIDS are now protected from discrimination on the basis of disability. How similar are their concerns to the concerns of those with congenital disabilities such as cerebral palsy or mental retardation? Seen in this light, there is a danger of "protectionism" or territorialism, as well as a desire to exclude for the sake of uniformity. In such circumstances, similarity will be narrowly ascribed within a particular group or even sub-group, and the principle of distinctiveness and difference will predominate.

Differences in scope and orientation toward public policy and service delivery systems have affected how well aging and disability groups can expect to work together. Aging advocacy groups generally direct their efforts toward national policy, since their concerns lie primarily with Social Security, Medicare, and long-term care coverage under Medicaid. Disability advocacy groups, in contrast, have generally acted within the realm of state and local policy-making, focusing on how services are funded and provided at the local level, including state positions on Medicaid, personal assistance services, transportation and job training.

It is only recently that we have seen greater movement toward the center for both groups. Aging advocates and the elderly themselves are now more likely to adopt the language of the disability rights movement in areas such as home and attendant care services (Sabatino and Litvak, 1992; Simon-Rusinowitz and Hofland, 1992). ADAPT, organized in a loosely structured network of grass roots chapters, has shifted its focus to the national arena and the Health Care Financing Authority, advocating for greater expenditures under Medicaid for community services as opposed to institutional care only.

Differences in acceptance of the medicalization of aging and disabilities also cause some profound disparities between the two groups. Although older adults and aging advocacy and service-providing groups have moved away from a chronological definition of age, they have not yet fully rejected a definition based solely on a set of functional criteria linking health to ability. Here, greater levels of impairment imply greater dependence on others for physical care, along with a decreasing ability to partake of, learn from, or just enjoy common activities such as social interaction, recreational activities, and, of course, jobs. Today, there is a growing focus on the concept of aging well, implying the ability to age without the limitations of disability or chronic illness (Lawton, 1991).

When this medical model linking well-being to health and ability is applied to disability in younger persons, it not only rankles, but is viewed as entirely inappropriate as well as demeaning and discriminatory. The idea of linking a disability to a state of illness, and consequently to a state of dependency, is thoroughly rejected by disability activists. As Zola (1988) and others have noted, (Mahoney, Estes, and Heumann, 1986), disability is perhaps better defined as a social category or status arising from society's rejection of the imperfect and the disturbing. In its extreme form, this position postulates that disability stems solely from social attitudes and environmental barriers, and thus rests entirely outside the individual (Hahn, 1996). This position is in striking contrast to the continuing reliance of the aging service system upon chronological age as the defining factor in acquiring the status of "old", even though, at the individual level, older adults define age as a state or mind or the absence of good health (Iris and Berman, 1995; Cagan, et.al., 1996).

The differing goals of the elderly and disabled are quite explicit in their relative positions on work and job-related training. In a society that continues to define personal value and achievement in terms of economic success and status in the labor market, the issue of work and labor for both older adults and persons with disabilities is highly charged. Most older people have retired from work, and if they do work, it is usually in part-time or volunteer positions. Older people with impairments or disabilities are most unlikely to seek employment. However, younger persons with disabilities are very much focused on gaining employment, and thus must confront barriers such as discrimination, inaccessible workplaces, and lack of job training and other educational opportunities. These are simply not concerns for most older adults, whether impaired or not.

Some of the greatest and perhaps most profound differences are seen when we examine self-definitions and concomitant social perceptions. For example, though we may still search for a non-pejorative set of terms by which to refer to older persons, we can always fall back on the convenience of referring to this population group by a single attribute: chronological age. Those to whom this attribute applies have been able to unite around a number of important issues in the policy arena, including Social Security benefits, health care, and social services. No matter what their differences, they perceive a set of common interests based on age alone.

No comparable marker or set of unified goals unites the population of persons with disabilities, and certainly nothing draws together the interests of the older person with disabilities and those of his or her younger counterparts. In fact, social attitudes, prejudices, and biases against certain types of disabilities, such as mental retardation or mental illness, persist across all sectors of the population, and are as likely to be expressed by persons with other types of disabilities as those without (see Ferguson, this volume).

Most importantly, there are differences in language that continue to inhibit true coalition building. The language of aging has long incorporated a focus on the "unique" needs and concerns of older people (in contrast to the "special" needs of younger persons. The implication is that older adults have particular needs that require special, and thus different, types of interventions and services. For example, "senior housing", "senior services", and "senior centers" are an accepted part of the language of older adults. Older adults with impairments are usually referred to as "frail and "impaired" rather than "disabled". "Care" for older people, is provided by "caregivers", while younger people obtain "assistance" from "attendants". Discussions over language may seem old, but they continue to occupy us as we grapple with the impact of words on perception and the evolution of the beliefs and attitudes which underlie our individual private and public behaviors (Cohen, 1988; Minkler, 1990).

Clearly, **neither persons with disabilities nor the elderly are entirely immune from sharing our society's negative stereotypes or stigmatization of either group: older people do not want to be associated with the 'disabled", and younger persons with disabilities do not, individually, see a set of common interests with those who are older.** People in either group, if they even accept a shared status at that level, may only see common interests as a "sameness" in specific examples of lived experience. Conceptually, they remain "different". Thus, it may not be reasonable to seek a consensus at the individual level. Instead, coalition building may need to go on within the domain of policy, filtering down through individual hierarchies to specific localities.

This analysis has significant implications for predicting the success of continuing attempts to define and establish a unified agenda, in which older people and those with disabilities can see greater degrees of sameness through shared concerns and positive outcomes through policy-making. Certainly, adherence to extreme positions on the part of either population will continue to keep aging advocacy groups and disability rights activists from recognizing that a single voice might achieve much in the areas of greatest importance: long-term care, home care, health services, and benefits programs. Putting aside the desire for individual gain and working toward the establishment of common principles for advancement is an ambitious project, requiring confrontation of entrenched attitudes and prejudices, and ascendancy of the principle of likeness.

The Potential for the Future

In this chapter I have explored both some of the commonalties that unite people with disabilities with those who are old, and a number of issues and fundamental purposes which differentiate them. I have focused on how the creation of public policy, manifested in laws and programs, has shaped our cultural images and public representations of these two groups. Although it might appear there are more differences between them than likenesses, it is helpful to remember that there is a powerful glue that could hold them together: this glue is the common threat from the outside.

Such threat emanates from the continuing public debate that questions our understanding of a common social good, and challenges the communitarian motivations that underlie most social policy programs. These threats emerge as cuts in existing benefit programs, greater restrictions on eligibility criteria, a generalized, growing conservatism that argues against public support for any minority or group of individuals defined as different from the mainstream, and public misperceptions of the aims and goals of those served, i.e., the greedy geezer image and the malingering disabled.

In recognizing such threats, political expediency may override difference, aided by the growing sophistication and maturity of the disability rights movement within the political arena, increasing numbers of elderly and disabled, and hence greater numbers of people with common interests. In addition, as time passes, disability activists will reach older age in larger and larger numbers, bringing a new sense of empowerment and redefinition to what it means to be old and disabled. Over time, we can expect to see increasing self-advocacy by seniors as they shift from the model of the "frail elderly" to one of self-empowerment and self-advocacy.

Within the evolving discipline of disability studies, concern and attention to the overlapping constituencies of the elderly and those with disabilities is critical, because it holds the greatest potential for understanding how public perceptions are shaped and constituted. Demographics alone demands that disability studies concern itself with the dynamics of the aging process and the concomitant aspects of disability and impairment which emerge over time. However, beyond this, there are considerable gains to be made in understanding how meaning evolves in the face of disability, by examining how our society has approached the problems of aging and sought to solve them through public action.

References

Achenbaum, W.A. (1978). *Old age in the new land.* Baltimore: Johns Hopkins University Press.

Achenbaum, W.A. (1986). Society security: visions and revisions. New York: Cambridge University Press.

American Society on Aging. (1992, Winter). Generations. San Francisco: Author.

Ansello, E.F. (1988). The intersecting of aging and disabilities. *Educational Gerontology,* 14, 351-363.

Ansello, E.F. and Rose, T. (1989). *Aging and lifelong disabilities: partnership for the twenty-first century. The Wingspread Conference Report.* Palm Springs, CA: ElderPress.

Berkowitz, E.D. (1987). *Disabled policy: America's programs for the handicapped.* New York: Cambridge University Press.

Berube, M. (1996). *Life as we know it: a father, a family and an exceptional child.* New York: Pantheon Books.

Binstock, R.H. (1992, Winter). Aging, disability, and long term care. *Generations.* 83-88.

Brakel, J, Parry, J. and Weiner, B. (1985). *The mentally disabled and the law.* (3rd ed.) Chicago: American Bar Foundation.

Cagan, E., Iris, M., Marcus, M. And Miller, A. (1996). *The White Crane model of health promotion and well-being for older adults.* Health and Aging. Illinois Department on Aging and Illinois Department of Public Health. Chicago, Il, November.

Callahan, D. (1987). *Setting limits: medical goals in an aging society.* NewYork: Simon and Shuster.

Cohen, E.S. (1988). The elderly mystique: constraints on the autonomy of the elderly with disabilities. *The Gerontologist,* 28, Supplement, June, 24-31.

Cole, T. (1992). *The journey of life: a cultural history of aging in America.* New York: Cambridge University Press.

Crimmins, E., Saito, Y. And Reynolds. S. Further evidence on recent trends in the prevalence and incidence of disability among older Americans from two sources: the LSOA and the NHIS. *Journal of Gerontology: Social Sciences,* 52B(2):S59-71.

Erikson, E., Erikson, J. and Kivnick, H. (1986). *Vital involvement in old age.* New York: Norton.

Estes, C.I. and Binney, E.A. (1989). The biomedicalization of aging: dangers and dilemmas. *The Gerontologist,* 29, 587-596.

Friedan, B. (1993). *The fountain of age.* New York: Simon and Shuster.

Gartner, A. And Joe, T. (1987). *Images of the disabled, disabling images.* New York: Praeger.

Goffman, E. (1963). *Stigma: notes on the management of spoiled identity.* New York: Simon and Schuster.

Grigsby, J.S. (1996). The meaning of heterogeneity: an introduction. *The Gerontologist,* 36, 145-146.

Hahn, H. (1996). Bridging the gap between aging and disability studies. American Society on Aging. March 17th.

Iris, M.A (1990) A common agenda for aging and disability. *Center on Aging,* 6:1-3. Chicago: Buehler Center on Aging, McGaw Medical Center, Northwestern University.

Iris, M.A. and Berman, R.L.H. (1995). *Qualitative study of aging in Chicago. Final Report.* Aging in Chicago Project. The Chicago Community Trust. Chicago.

Koff, T.H. and Park, R.W. (1993). *Aging public policy: bonding the generations.* Amityville, NY: Baywood.

Lakoff, G. (1987). *Women, fire, and dangerous things: what categories reveal about the mind.* Chicago: University of Chicago Press.

LaPlante, M. (1991). The demographics of disability. In J. West (Ed.), The Americans with disabilities act: from policy to practice. *The Milbank Quarterly,* 69, supplements 1/2, 55-77.

Lawton, M.P. (1991, Winter). Functional status and aging well. *Generations,* 31-34.

Longmore, P.K. (1995). Medical decision making and people with disabilities: a clash of cultures. *Journal of Law, Medicine and Ethics,* 23, 82-87.

Mahoney, C.W., Estes, C.L. and Heumann, J.E. (1986). *Toward A unified agenda: proceedings of a national conference on disability and aging.* San Francisco: Institute for Health and Aging.

Minkler, M. (1990). Aging and disability. *Journal of Aging Studies,* 4, 3, 245-260.

Minow, M. (1990). *Making all the difference: inclusion, exclusion and American law.* Ithaca, NY: Cornell University Press.

Murphy, R.F. (1990). *The body silent.* New York: W.W. Norton.

Neugarten, B. (Ed). (1982). *Age or need? public policies for older people.* Beverly Hills, CA: Sage Publications.

Neugarten, B. (1996). *The meanings of age: selected papers of Bernice L. Neugarten.* D.A. Neugarten (Ed.), Chicago: University of Chicago Press.

Shapiro, J.P. (1993). *No pity: people with disabilities forging a new civil rights movement.* New York: Random House.

Siegel, J.S. and Taeuber, C.M. (1987). Demographic dimensions of an aging population. In A. Pifer and L. Bronte (Eds.), *Our aging society: paradox and promise.* New York: W.W. Norton and Company.

Silverman, P. (1987). *The elderly as modern pioneers.* Bloomington, IN: Indiana University Press.

Simon-Rusinowitz, L. and Hofland, B. (1992). *The impact of varying perspectives on client autonomy in long-term care: home care for the elderly vs. Attendant services for the disabled.* Unpublished.

Torres-Gil, F.M. (1995, Nov/Dec). Building federal bridges. *Aging Today.* vii.

Torres-Gil, F.M. (1996). Foreward: health care reform, long-term care, and the future of an aging society. *Journal of Aging and Social Policy,* 7(3/4), xiii-xviii.

Zola, I.K.(1982). *Missing pieces: a chronicle of living with a disability.* Philadelphia: Temple University Press.

Zola, I.K. (1988). Aging and disability. *Educational Gerontology,* 14, 365-87.

Study Questions

1. What are your images of aging? What signs do we acknowledge in our society as markers of aging? How universal and how generalizable are these?
2. What are your images of a person with a disability and what markers of disability do you look for? How culturally embedded are these markers and how appropriated are they today?

3. What are your ideas about the concept of inclusion versus separateness? Do you think older people should have access to separate services and programs based solely upon their chronological age? Do you think all persons with disabilities should expect full inclusion and how much accommodation should society be expected to provide?
4. Language plays an important role in helping us process our perceptions, formulate ideas, and give them verbal expression. What is the role of language in helping shape a common agenda of aging and disability?
5. What is the "demographic imperative and why is it important when thinking about a common political agenda for persons with disabilities and the elderly?
6. What are some of the critical issues in health care reform that could serve to unite aging and disability rights advocacy groups? What are the underlying issues and what barriers currently exist to creating a common agenda? How can these barriers be overcome?
7. In what ways does public policy for the elderly create a class of citizens based on theirsameness or difference vis-a-vis other subpopulations? What obstacles to maintaining the current position are likely to emerge over the next several decades?
8. Why is Section 504 of the 1973 Rehabilitation Act such a critical piece of legislation in the history of disability policy? What principles of sameness or difference does it espouse? In what ways do these principles coincide or differ from those that underlie aging policy programs such as the Older Americans Act?
9. What intragroup differences hinder the creation of a common policy agenda for both those with disabilities and those who are elderly?
10. What recommendations do you make to further the evolution of a common policy agenda? What are the critical issues to address and in what manner?

From "Idiot" to "Person with Mental Retardation": Defining Difference in an Effort to Dissolve It

Patrick J. Devlieger

The history of mental retardation in the United States over the past century is characterized by a continuous flow of definition of the phenomenon that become reflected by such terms as "idiots", "feebleminded", "mentally defective", "mentally deficient", "mentally subnormal", "mentally retarded", and currently "persons with mental retardation". Mental retardation as a difference to be defined meets the continuous challenge of finding a terminology that adequately responds to new societal developments.

The answer to this never-ending search for the right definition of the phenomena that mental retardation represent can be sought at different levels, including the social and political climate and the development of knowledge. The development of different terms will be described in association with a historical context and the prominent players.

Specifically, the two concurrent dimensions, "social" and "intellectual", that are prominent in the formal definitions of mental retardation will be analyzed. Here I argue that favoring the importance of one over the other contributes to portraying persons with mental retardation as rather "different" or "same".

The history of mental retardation as reflected in a sequence of terms is insightful for learning about the dynamics between disability as "difference" and as "similarity". I argue that this dynamic can be understood as the creation of new differences in an effort to absolve those that have earlier been created. I connect this dynamic to a basic distinction between "difference" and "similarity" as it operates in American culture, thus demonstrating how disability becomes a phenomenon that reflects American society.

Many disadvantaged groups in the United States have created a space in which their voice is heard. Such has been the case for women, ethnic groups, and lately gays and lesbians. By contrast, a climate in which the voice of people with mental retardation can be heard has only slowly and indirectly emerged.

The history of individuals with mental retardation is one of changing definitions of difference conceived by others, rather than a group of people finding their own identity, their own history (Ryan & Thomas, 1987). Thus, their history is more one created by people who assume responsibility on their behalf, predominantly professionals and parents. As a result, the formation of groups of people with mental retardation, such as "People First" and "Self-Advocates Becoming Empowered" is most recent. Rather, society has more often imposed the formation of groups upon them, similar to what happens to children, in order to manage problems related to individuals with retardation.

The history of mental retardation not only reflects the history of certain people, but also society's history and the working of culture. In this history, the creative power of society is at work. The questions raised in this chapter are specifically related to the nature of the reality that is imposed on persons with mental retardation. This immediately brings up the language used to characterize and refer to them. The array of terms used over the years inevitably prompts such questions as, "Why are so many terms used in this field"?, "What is the underlying meaning of a given term and how does this meaning degenerate over time"?, "How do these terms relate to their historical context"?, and "How does one term replace another"?

Consider, for example, that the expressed meaning of "mental retardation" as a term is tied in with a particular history of the United States. That is, to understand "mental retardation" in context, one needs to know about parents' struggle against perceived demeaning connotations in the term "deficiency", the contribution of the testing movement to classifying and controlling the population, and a widely accepted recognition that the origin of the social problems related to "mental retardation" is found not in the individual but in the environment. This history of the term also explains that it cannot easily be transferred to other times and places and that it is not very popular outside the United States (Fernald, 1995). Also consider the fact that "mental retardation" is not widely used by persons labeled as such. When referring to themselves, they ignore the label or replace it with one that has more positive connotations such as "client" or "consumer," terms that were introduced by service agencies (Devlieger, 1995).

From such observation one may understand the creation of terms as to denote "difference" in the context of unequal power relations. Changing definitions, therefore, are instructive about American society. This is consistent with the overall objective of an anthropological study of disability: to contribute to our knowledge of social life within a particular sociocultural setting (Bruun & Ingstad, 1990). In other words, the term "mental retardation" may be viewed as a window on society (Sarason & Doris, 1979) as well as a commentary on society. The argument that mental retardation is related to changes in society is well established in the literature. For example, authors have described mental retardation as a social invention (Sarason, 1985); a metaphor (Blatt, 1987) or a socio-cultural concept (Langness & Levine, 1986).

In trying to bring clarity to the confusing array of terms used historically to denote "mental retardation", such as "idiot", "feeble-minded", "defective", "deficient", "subnormal", and the transformations of the term "retarded", I will work in two opposite directions – one attempting to contextualize, the other searching for deeper meanings. Both operations are part of a historical anthropology, relying on some of the achievements of semiotics. Woodill (1994) argued that "in order to better understand the roots of inequality, marginalization and disadvantage faced by persons with a disability, we must research the meaning and origins of the words and images about disability that form part of the cultural codes we all take for granted and in which we are all immersed" (pp. 203-204). He outlines a research program in social semiotics that includes the study of images of disability in popular culture, the representation of disability in professional discourse, and the study of the development of disability culture as its important mission.

This chapter will further pursue Woodill's work, concentrating on the professional development of terminology related to mental retardation. Contextualization is sought by connecting the terms with a particular historical period, expectations of society, important players, and underlying philosophy. From this direction, a larger framework emerges, that of narratives of mental retardation; that is, a story that describes the coherency of expectations and practices deemed appropriate for a person with mental retardation in a particular time.

While narratives can be understood as viable representations of reality, they should not be equaled with reality itself. Nor do attempts at describing narratives at any given time reflect an effort to recover the one true narrative that really reflects reality. Rather, multiple narratives co-exist and interact with each other and in a framework of power, and therefore have implications, over time, for additional connotations and changes in meaning. Changes in narratives could be described as "the liberation from a proliferation of meaning, from a self-multiplication of significance. Things themselves become so burdened with attributes, signs, allusions that they finally lose their own form" (Foucault, 1988, p. 18). The tools being used to reconstruct these narratives include terminology and the changing American definitions of mental retardation over the last century as definitions of "difference".

In a professional narrative of disability, we are concerned with the way disability is communicated as a story. This is a linear sequence that includes a beginning, a middle, and an end. The beginning of the story is a frame of thought, a way of describing how the disability can be understood. The middle is an explanation that connects the frame of thought with a particular context from which the meaning of disability becomes apparent. Finally, the end of the story of disability consist of the practical implications that result from the frame of thought and the meaning of disability. For example, in a narrative of "normalization," disability can be framed as the need for all individuals to have the same access and participation in a context, for example a school, as comparable individuals in a given socio-cultural context. The middle of a narrative of explains how normalization can work in the context of school, through the development of "least restricted environments". The end of this professional narrative provides the practical implication of developing restrictive environments, providing the modalities of access, and so on.

In analyzing terms of mental retardation as narratives, I emphasize the coherency of meanings in a unified structure that makes these meanings intelligible. For example, I try to reconstruct how "idiot" can be understood as part of a larger nineteenth-century narrative, a time when its metaphorical force may the greatest. I also trace the changing nature of meanings and ultimately their overturn, as they are superseded by newer definitions of difference. For example, individuals with mental retardation were at times confined to limited space, sexually controlled, and their life time perspective was not expected to match that of ordinary adults. These various meanings attached to mental retardation can only become meaningful in a narrative that outlines the mutual roles and expectations of person and culture, perhaps emphasizing the danger of persons with mental retardation and the consequent need of society to itself. Contrasting narratives that emphasize definitions and expectations in which individuals with retardation are expected to be part of mainstream life are tied into other narratives of civil rights and individual contributions and responsibilities. Changes in the fortunes and misfortunes of the persons with mental retardation have varied with changes in behavior technology, social and economic conditions, shifting values, new knowledge, and the predominant social ethos of the American way of life (Begab, 1975). Understanding narratives presupposes an incorporation of this knowledge.

To summarize, **"narratives" can be understood as verbalizations of what the role of individuals with mental retardation in society should be.** Narrative as a cultural product comes very close to what Foucault (1988) describes as the action that divides (p. ix), and not the science elaborated once the division is made and calm restored. In other words, the development of new narratives of mental retardation leads to new action that makes earlier action obsolete. In later writing, Foucault (1973[1966]:xx-xxi) elaborates with a domain between the codes of a culture and scientific theories, which has an intermediary but fundamental role. He writes,

> It is here that a culture, imperceptibly deviating from the empirical orders prescribed for by its primary codes, instituting an initial separation from them, causes them to lose their original transparency, relinquishes its immediate and invisible powers, frees itself sufficiently to discover that these orders are perhaps not the only possible ones or the best ones. It is one the basis of this newly perceived order that the codes of language, perception, and practice are criticized and rendered partially invalid. (pp. xx-xxi)

"Narratives" should be interpreted as the expression of newly perceived order in language that becomes known as "discourse". According to Foucault, "we think within an anonymous and constraining system of thought which is that of an epoch and of a language" (1973, p. 15). While this is true, it is also true that such discourses can be challenged and dissolved. That process in itself, however, reveals some of the most fundamental characteristics of the construction of mental retardation in American society, which I will argue can be understood in the construction of new understandings of difference while dissolving old ones. Both the dimensions of the intellectual and social characteristics of mental retardation play a crucial role in this process.

In working from the opposite direction of contextualization, I formalize the terminology related to mental retardation by reconstructing its semantic constellation, using a semiotic square as an analytical tool, following the work of semiotician Algirdas Greimas (Nöth 1995) and earlier similar applications of this method by Stiker (1989).

In this analysis, two types of logical relations are represented. The first type is a binary category, where a key term s1 (assertion) is opposed to s2 (negation); the second type is one of contradiction, which is termed as absence of meaning; that is s1 is contradicted by _s1_ and s2 contradicted by _s2_. The result is a four-term constellation in which a new type of relation, implication or complementarity, appears between the terms s1 and _s2_ and between s2 and _s1_. For example, s1, "life," is contrary to s2, "death," because each term implies the contrary of the other.

```
(Assertion)                           (Negation)
(e.g. "life")                         (e.g. "death")
   S1  ←——————— Contrariety ———————→  S2
    ↑          contra    diction      ↓
    |              ╲    ╱             |
 complementarity    ╲  ╱         complementarity
    |              ╱  ╲              |
    |          contra    diction     |
    ↓                                 ↓
   S2                                S1
(Non-assertion)                   (Non-negation)
(e.g. "non-death")                (e.g. "non-life")
```

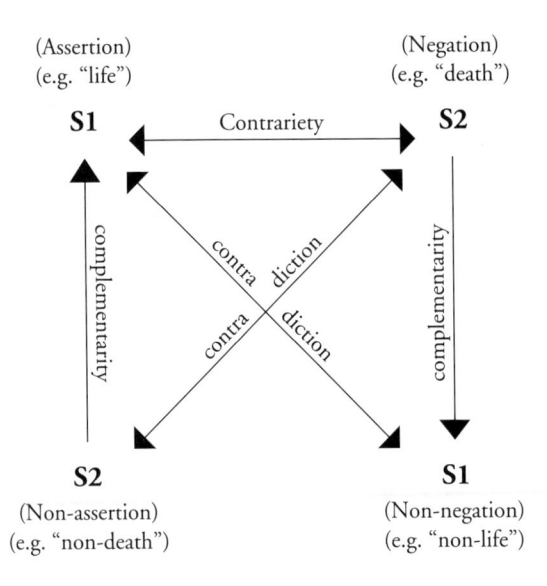

Figure 1: Greimas's semiotic square.

On the other semantic axe, a logical relation of contradiction is described in terms of a presence or an absence (e.g., s1, "life," is opposed to _s1_, "non-life" (In which "life" is absent). Considering a constellation of three terms, on two axes, s1-s2 and s1-_s1_, this may be expanded by the contrary of s2, which is _s2_ ("non-death"). A new type of logical relation emerges in this four-term constellation, implication or complementarity, which appears between the terms s1 and *s2* or s2 and *s1*. This logical relation can be understood as: "life" implies the absence of death, "non-death". The semiotic square in Figure 1 summarizes this constellation.

Apart from contextualization of narratives and the deep structures of used terminology, a number of other questions arise in a study of the social and historical semiotics of disability. One can ask, for example, about the reasons for new narratives, how new narratives of mental retardation supersede old ones, and how they are diffused from a core group of people to the general population. I will touch upon these questions. For example, I will show how textbooks, newspapers, and dictionaries of different eras communicated changing narratives, and how they became common knowledge.

In the context of the overall theme of this volume, "similarity and difference", **new definitions of mental retardation as difference attempt to go beyond earlier created definitions of difference. New definitions of difference absolve older ones that have become "polluted" by accumulated negative connotations. Again and again, the defined differences become outmoded by the changing times and the new definitions.** In the social production of difference, there is a continuous playing off of "similarity" as a correcting force.

In identifying several narratives that include a key term, I will emphasize coherency, thereby somewhat neglecting the presence of a multiplicity of terms at any one point in time as well as the co-existence of narratives. The creative power that is inherent from the construction of difference could be retained from this analysis. All this, however, neglects the development of terms and narratives as they become overburdened and finally lose their form. This is the process of similarity, which is not to be identified in terms of entropy only as a natural process of degradation of meaning. Rather, difference and similarity are complementary processes. While new differences develop, other terms and narratives move to the background. I attempt to track down the workings of similarity by following the process of distribution of knowledge through various written media, such as newspapers, textbooks and dictionaries. The interesting differences among these media is the speed of diffusing information and the longevity of the information. For example, the speed of transmission is faster for newspapers than for textbooks or dictionaries. The longevity of the information takes opposite rankings for the three media.

Without trying to be exhaustive nor comprehensive, an attempt was made to determine how the various narratives were communicated to larger audiences. Three written media: newspapers, textbooks, and reference books (e.g., dictionaries, thesauruses, and encyclopedias) were considered. To understand the diffusion process in newspapers, we looked at the *New York Times Index*. For textbook, only works in psychology were considered.

Defining Difference:
Terminology and Narratives in Mental Retardation

The reconstruction of narratives through an exploration of terminology and definitions of mental retardation simplifies our understanding, while at the same time revealing significant trends helps put current definitions, classifications, and policy initiatives in context. **Essential to understanding the language we use is to find out what the motives behind its use have been in the past.** Were newly invented terms intended to benefit the individual with retardation or society? Were they meant to demystify a problem, or to prevent confrontation through euphemistic or cosmetic obfuscation?

Although I will associate dominant narratives with particular historical times, this does not mean that these narratives were completely absent in later periods. Elements of the underlying narratives have co-existed with older narratives. The shift is partial and reflects a temporal dominance. Further, in addressing narratives in terms of curability/educability or incurability/unteachability, we are informed by the severity of the disability rather than disability category. Support for this argument can be found in the institutional history (e.g., Ferguson, 1994). While variations in narratives are possible, my purpose is more illustrative of the post-structuralist argument, namely, that "we think within an anonymous and constraining system and thought which is that of an epoch and of a language" (Foucault, 1973, p. 15). Departing from this argument, however, I also believe in human agency, and the dissolving of language in a conspiracy with history.

Language is an important tool both in science and public discourse. The history of mental retardation is complex because it involves many different areas of scientific and professional interest, most importantly education, medicine, social work, and psychology, which have taken more dominant interests over time. The language that is developed within these scientific and professional areas grows and erodes as new ideas and practices develop. Older terms become offensive within public discourse. Such is the case for terms such as "idiot" and "mentally deficient". Within the current American popular vernacular, the term 'handicapped' may be the most commonly used. However, in scientific and professional circles, the "disabled" may be more dominant. Some of the names are created in the illusory search for a designation that is neutral or euphemistic, for example "exceptional child".

"Idiot" and the Educational Narrative

Early pioneers such as Itard, Seguin, Howe, and others focused their efforts on the educational remediation of deficiencies. Due to limitations in identification, the concept of the retarded was one of being severely damaged. The potentially depressing effects of social environmental factors on intelligence and behavior were not considered (Begab, 1975). Rather, "idiocy" must be seen in the context of a society of low expectations and technical capabilities.

The label during most of the nineteenth century was "idiot" which, according to one of Webster's (1986)[1] definitions, is an "ignorant or unschooled person". Seguin used the term to identify those in need of physiological education and treatment techniques that stimulate human functions.

---

1 One of the characteristics of dictionaries, compared to, for example, newspapers, is their reluctance to change. They are a "slow" medium that may incorporate different historical meanings. Therefore, multiple definitions may be found in a contemporary dictionary that actually reflect narratives of different historical periods. This is the case for defining "idiot" as an "ignorant or unschooled person".

The semantic constellation of the term "idiot" is represented through the use of a semiotic square (Figure 2). The term idiot is defined as "difference" in the Saussurian sense of distinguishing opposites in the central semantic axis. This opposition needs to be read in terms of society's emphasis on the effects of schooling. The non-idiot implies being schooled. Being unschooled, therefore, implies the possibility of being an idiot. The deep structural meaning of the term comes out of the contradiction between the idiot and the non-idiot in the implication of schooling. In the contradictory meaning of "idiot", the meaning of schooling is lost. If "idiot" emphasized the intellectual dimension, it was due to the failure of education, perhaps exacerbated by a society in chaos demanding order. In turn, some authors worked to distinguish idiocy from insanity, developed an educational classification, and replaced "idiocy" with the more generic term "feeble-minded" (Barr, 1904).

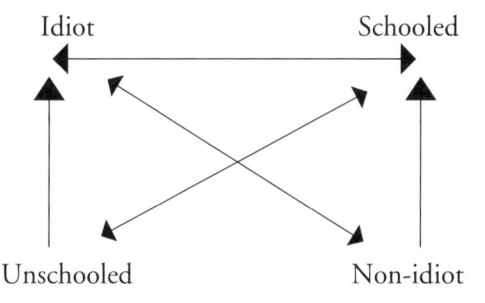

Figure 2: Semantic constellation of "idiot".

"Feeble-Minded" and the Success of the Medical Narrative

Around the end of the nineteenth century, the educational narrative became overshadowed with more reactionary tones. Wilmarth (1906) wrote,

"For years, it has been asserted in the gatherings of those experienced in the care of dependent and defective people, that the opportunities for this class to unnecessarily burden the taxpayer must be curtailed. The feeling is extending, that, with many a one whom we educate to the limit of his capacity and send out to make his own way, we have launched a boat without a rudder and we have no knowledge as to where it may land."

A change from a concern for caring about individuals with mental retardation to one for protecting society from them was evident. The term "idiot" became eroded around the turn of the century and was gradually replaced by the term "feeble-minded", which became central in Goddard's work. The term reflects the narrative that mental retardation constitutes a threat to society (Smith, 1985). The term was used much in the medical realm, and includes the myth that mental retardation is incurable. Interestingly, classification of persons with mental retardation, then called "mental defectives", became based on pathology, the only satisfactory basis for a scientific classification (Singer, 1910).

It also became clear around 1890 that the idea of the institution for the feeble-minded as an educational project had to be abandoned. The shift from educational to custodial care can to some extent be traced in the naming of the institutions of that time, such as the Rome State

Custodial Asylum for Unteachable Idiots at Rome, New York (Davies, 1930; Ferguson, personal communication, 1997).

The shift from an educational to a medical narrative is mostly clearly exemplified in Henry Goddard, a physician, who contributed significantly to shaping a new narrative on mental retardation, essentially outlining the threat that individuals with mental retardation constituted for society. This narrative received support within broader movements in society. First, Goddard (1912) contributed to the eugenics movement with the scientific claim that mental retardation is hereditary. Ironically, by accentuating the moral responsibility, Goddard also outlined the incapacity of the medical profession to "treat" mental retardation. Second, the threat of individuals with mental retardation was accentuated by the threat that great influxes of immigrants into the United States caused and the idea that many of these immigrants were mentally retarded. Third, the testing movement contributed to an alarmist trend as Binet and Simon created a new, definable category of retardation, known today as mild retardation. Goddard labeled this group "morons" in 1910.

The semantic constellation of the term "feeble-minded" as weakness of the mind finds its opposite in the strong-minded as righteous mind, a moral assertion that comes under the authority of the medical profession who in its own way brings new order (Figure 3). Thus, the non-feeble-minded is one who safeguards society by non-involvement in criminality, alcoholism and the effects of diseases, all which were associated with the "feeble mind," of which mental retardation was the clearest expression.

The spread of the term "feeble-minded" into a wider public discourse can partly be derived from its presence in the *New York Times-Index* where it appears for the first time in 1908. Although the term changes at various times to "defective," "mentally defective", and "mental deficiency", it was not eliminated from the *Index* until 1978. The description under "feeble-minded" reads in 1977: use "mental deficiency". Although the term may only have been used in professional circles for a few decades, its long presence in the *Index* indicates how slowly a term can die before it is found to be no longer useful as a referent of public discourse. A similar argument may be made for the term "mental deficiency", which remained in the *Index* long after it had been abandoned in many professional and public arenas.

In a textbook on abnormal psychology of 1932, the emphasis is on the clinical characteristics of mental retardation, as exemplified in terms such as "underdevelopment of cortical neurons". The same classification is still used, starting with the most severe form (idiocy), which also indicates a medical orientation to mental retardation in the way it suggests "treatment" (Moss & Hunt, 1932).

The erosion of the meanings of feeble-mindedness and the confusion that arises from using the term simultaneously with "mental deficiency" and from using the terms too loosely prompted several textbook authors to attempt to clear up the confusion. Such is the case in a 1934 textbook on abnormal psychology, which suggests continued use of both terms, but also recommends using them both as forms of "amentia", relating to a young age of onset, as opposed to some forms of "dementia", relating to a later age of onset (Dorcus & Shaffer, 1934). Interestingly, the age-of-onset criterion led to one of the constituting elements of modern definitions of mental retardation.

Another textbook attempted in 1937 to withhold the term "feeble-mindedness" as an organizing term, but described the multiple dimensions of the term such as legal, medical, and so on. Fisher (1937) examined the social significance of feeble-mindedness, indicating that "the feebleminded individual is more prone to the commission of anti-social acts" (p. 492). He describes that three methods for preventing feeble-mindedness: supervision, segregation, and sterilization, of which the last method "holds the greatest promise of an ultimate solution of the problem" (p. 492). The argument that society has a place for them sweeping streets, hauling garbage, and other unpleasant tasks is rejected as being absurd and steeped in self-complacant egoism (Fisher, 1937). In the 1940s, "feeble-minded" seems to be losing its strength in textbooks to be replaced by "mental defective" (Gray, 1941, 1951; Landis & Bolles, 1946). In some textbooks, mental retardation is discussed for the applied role of psychologists in court and in clinical situations (Gray, 1941; 1951), which suggest an expanded understanding beyond the medical profession.

```
    Feeble-minded              Strong-minded
         ◄──────────────────────►
         ▲  ╲                ╱  ▲
         │    ╲            ╱    │
         │      ╲        ╱      │
         │        ╲    ╱        │
         │          ╳          │
         │        ╱    ╲        │
         │      ╱        ╲      │
         │    ╱            ╲    │
         ▼  ╱                ╲  ▼
   Non-strongminded        Non-feebleminded
```

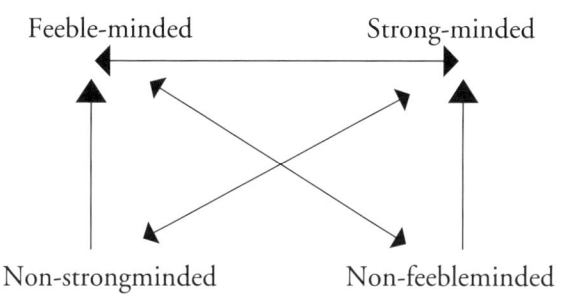

Figure 3: Semantic constellation of "feeble-minded".

"Defective" and the Transformation of the Medical into a Psychological Narrative

The point that demarcates the end of the educational narrative is the application of intelligence tests to a larger proportion of the population. As mental retardation becomes measurable, the moral authority of physicians gives way to the scientific claims and administrative roles of psychologists. While in the "idiot" and "feeble-minded" narratives the emphasis was on the mind in its learning and moral capabilities, the defective narrative radically moves into the social costs of mental retardation. According to Begab (1975), the application of intelligence tests to army troops in World War I revealed an alarming number of young men performing at a mentally subnormal level. Overnight, historically speaking, mental retardation became recognized as a social problem of the highest magnitude. (p. 5)

The term "defective" perhaps most clearly reflects the connotation that individuals were of no use in the context of the war. However, feeble-mindedness was still the most commonly used term in professional discourse.

The social dimension of mental retardation also was strongly emphasized in government reports such as "The Kallikaks of Kansas" (Kansas Commission on Provision for the Feeble-Minded, 1919). Such reports emphasized the menace of individuals with retardation because of its supposed hereditary status among social misfits. The report says:

> There are many indications that somewhere from 10 to 30 percent of criminals are feeble-minded and have fallen into the criminal life because of defective mentality. It is quite probable that an equal or larger proportion of the persons in almshouses and in the ranks of

prostitution are also feeble-minded. If then, in round numbers, one-fourth of these classes are replenished from the mentally defective group, feeble-mindedness is a menace to society because it is contributing such a large percentage of these groups which are making us trouble all the time.

The report concludes that "something must be done to prevent this stream of bad protoplasm from coming into the world and from overwhelming us with social problems".

At this point, a fissure had slipped into the professional narrative that has continued to be problematic to the present time. Although the problem of mental retardation was early defined as being "social", the identification of individuals with mental retardation and the measurement of levels of retardation in terms of the "social dimensions" have been problematic. Specifically, it was difficult to predict whether individuals were going to be productive members of society or present a burden. However, has been possible in terms of intelligence, and although the ultimate problem was the social dimension, measurement has been done in terms of intelligence. A link between social adaptability and intelligence has been presupposed and given rise to a great deal of professional discussion since. This also becomes clear in the semiotic square representing defective as difference (Figure 4). The perfective contradicts the defective in the way the conditions are fulfilled that lead to social incorporation. The link between bodily wholeness and societal functioning is emphasized.

Defective — Perfective

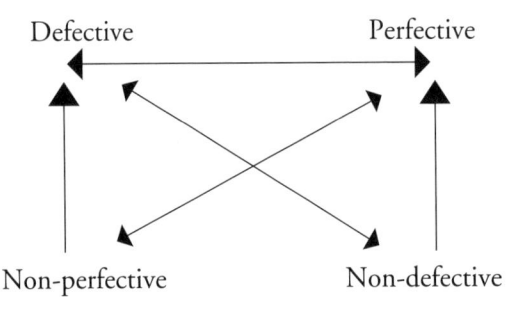

Non-perfective — Non-defective

Figure 4: Semantic constellations of "defective".

The practical implications of being "defective" are well known – sterilization and institutionalization, a tight sealing off from society. This ultimately paved the way to a new turning point. **Some of the public's concern about people with mental retardation dissipated with the growth of institutional facilities and the practice of segregation and control through sterilization** (Begab, 1975). This may only have impacted a small percentage of persons with retardation. However, social changes in the overall population, resulting from the onset of the Great Depression, opened the possibility for alternative explanations. That is, during this time, larger segments of society failed and were not fitting in, making immigration and feeble-mindedness less popular as explanations of social failure. Social arrangements and economic explanations became more dominant, giving way to the New Deal, socialism, and a take-off of the labor movement.

As mentioned earlier, the *New York Times Index* is an invaluable tool to assess when terminology appears and disappears in the public arena. For example, between 1913 and 1920, the term "defective" was mostly used. The articles on the topic related refer to care, prevention, education, and army statistics. In 1921 a new term, "mental defective", is introduced but the explanation is listed under "defective". Teaching still appears at times, but the new terms are now "immigration", "delinquency", and "sterilization".

Interestingly, from 1928, the influence of the medical profession becomes greatly felt. For example, in 1928, the heading "mental defectives" refers to "eugenics". In subsequent years, the reader is referred to look under "mental diseases", "eugenics", and "sterilization of the unfit". This trend continues well into the late 1930s, but in 1935, "mental defective" is replaced by "mental deficiency and defectives". From 1938 onwards, other than purely medical interests become more prominent, reflecting public attitudes and an interest in the well-being of individuals with retardation. Thus, medical interest shifts toward trying to find medication and therapy to help persons with retardation.

From 1948 onwards, there is increased educational programming and interest from parent groups. Further, programming for professionals, such as psychologists and social workers, to prepare them to work with individuals with retardation is enhanced in the mid 1950s. In 1962, President Kennedy's support of the combat of mental retardation becomes the most important topic, followed in 1963 with huge funding action and research programs that continued throughout the 1960s. From 1972 until 1978, the inhuman conditions at Willowbrook state school and the deinstitutionalization movement received the most important coverage.

In a textbook on abnormal psychology, Morgan (1928) states that "since intellectually defective persons were first studied because they failed to adapt, the social criteria are the oldest" (p. 5) The author goes on to situate the new developments in intelligence measurement in social terms, stating that these will lead to "measure intelligence and prepare an individual so that he can meet social situations" (p. 315). Using the term "feeble-mindedness", Morgan relies on Goddard's classification, which included the labels "morons", "imbeciles" and "idiots". He argues that the shift from a medical model to statistical norms of intelligence resulted in a different perspective of who is "feeble-minded". He further states that, according to the medical paradigm, whose tool is clinical-diagnostic, "all persons are regarded normal except the few who are extremely abnormal" (p. 5). This example show clearly how new authors use old terms and classifications and transform their connotations. In this case, the medical connotations to the term "feeble-minded" are being reduced and an alternative narrative is imposed.

"Deficient" and the Transformation of the Psychological Narrative

With the calming down of alarmist reactions in society, the development of testing continued, further deepening the fissure in the narrative between the social and the intellectual. Davies (1930) states: "The undue alarm seems to have been at least in part founded on the erroneous assumption that feeble-mindedness and intellectual subnormality are one and the same thing. Much confusion about the social implication of subnormality may be avoided by carefully distinguishing between the two" (p. 369). The terminology that is introduced during this period is "mental deficiency".

Doll (1947) accepted the substitution of "mental deficiency" for "feeble-mindedness" as "a concession to euphemism". However, he pointed out later in the same paper that the major difference between the two terms is that whereas feeble-mindedness may not be curable, mental deficiency may. From Davies' and Doll's accounts, it is clear that the link between terminology and narrative is developed over time and continues to develop. Equally apparent, narratives are rarely singular; rather competing narratives exist. In addition, certain terms and connections may be latent for some time, for example the notion of subnormality in Davies' account, without becoming prominent. These findings however support the continual production of culture and the creative power inherent in notions of difference.

The consolidation of the shift from a medical to a psychological ordering of the chaos benefitted from the simplicity of measurement and decision-making derived from the intelligence quotient (IQ).

Traditionally, mental deficiency and feeble-mindedness have been terms used to designate a symptom-complex, a clinical syndrome, a diagnostic condition characterized by a correlation of characteristics and validated by multiple criteria. But in the past quarter-century IQ measurement has been advocated in place of the clinical requirement of valid differential diagnosis. (Doll, 1947, p. 420)

In the process of this consolidation of control, the IQ emphasized the intellectual over the social dimension.

According to Webster (1986), mental deficiency is "failure in intellectual development resulting in social incompetence that is considered to be the result of defect in the central nervous system and to be accordingly incurable". This definition reflects well the supposed link between the social and intellectual and the references to central nervous system and incurability reveal its roots in the medical field. Interestingly, the White House Conference on Child Health and Protection (1933) proposed the term "mental deficiency" to refer to retarded intelligence and social competence and "feeble-mindedness" to refer to retarded intelligence and social incompetence. This dichotomy was not widely adopted, however, and "mental deficiency" gradually replaced "feeble-mindedness" during the 1940s (see Scheerenberger, 1983), although its use lingered on during the 1950s and even the 1960s. In "mental deficiency," the intellectual and social components of mental retardation became integrated as dimensions of the same concept.

The radicalness in emphasizing intellectual and social components leveled off in the terminology and became clear in the semantic constellation of "mental deficiency" (Figure 5). Being "sufficient" is a relative notion that incorporates a greater complexity of conceptualization. It incorporates context, that is, what is sufficient in one context may not be sufficient in another, as well as gradation, that is, being more or less sufficient. Thus, it is considered a greater possibility to move between the categories of deficient and sufficient. In this respect, it is important to note that those who favored the narrative of "mental deficiency" considered the condition to be reversible.

Interestingly, some textbooks started to point out that the definition of mental deficiency may be different in different countries. For example, Landis and Bolles (1946) pointed out that in England social competence is the most important criterion, whereas in most of the United States an essential criterion is the intellectual status as shown on an intelligence examination. Such differences are pointed out in other textbooks later (e.g., Harmatz, 1978).

"Mental Retardation" and the Incorporation of the Parent Movement

The involvement of parents in the 1950s, followed by major federal government involvement initiated by President Kennedy, countered the objectivity of the testing

movement. Further, media coverage in newspapers, photo magazines, and on television of the tainting of institutional services, e.g. of Willowbrook, contributed to a major change.

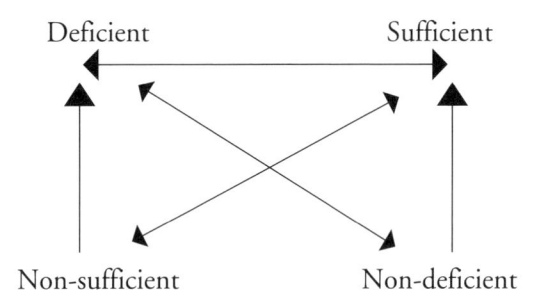

Figure 5: Semantic constellation of "deficient".

Despite changes in the public arena, the professional-scientific narrative continued to be influenced by the fissure between the social and intellectual, however. For example, Sloan and Birch (1955) pointed to a too great of an emphasis on the intellectual aspects of mental retardation in the past and noted that this overemphasis was reflected in terms such as "mental deficiency" and "feeble-mindedness". They argued that quantification of degree of retardation becomes a matter of indicating the subject's level in a number of different areas of function.

This fissure between the social and intellectual dimensions of mental retardation became formalized in the 1959 definition of the Association of Mental Deficiency. To be considered mentally retarded, a dual criterion of reduced intellectual functioning and impaired social adaptation was required. In addition, a further concession to the dominance of the testing movement was reflected in the classification of individuals with mental retardation. Thus, the tripartite classification of mental retardation – moron, imbecile, and idiot – was abandoned in favor of a five-part structure based on the number of standard deviations from the mean (Heber, 1959; Scheerenberger 1983).

Within this period, the emergence of two terms needs to be mentioned: "mental subnormality" and "mental retardation". The term "mental subnormality" stressed that certain social and cultural variables have a strong correlation with mental retardation. This idea gained in importance as a result of the civil rights movement in the 1960s. And it had an impact in terms of greater attention to milder forms of retardation in the 1960s, as seen in greater emphasis in federal legislation, in research reported in journals, and in the distribution of

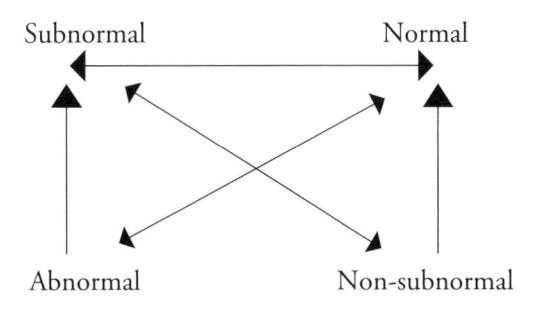

Figure 6: Semantic constellation of "subnormal".

services rendered by state agencies (Haywood, 1979). However, the term "mental subnormality" as such did not survive.

The term "mental retardation" as it eventually came to replace "mental deficiency" needs to be related to the support of parents. Important shifts included a definition in terms of other individuals, a deficiency which is not necessary absolute, and the idea that it is not incurable. Indicative perhaps of the very late response of the professional and scientific disciplines to the demand from parent groups to change terminology is the late change in the name of the association and the journal of the American Association on Mental Retardation. The association did not change its name from mental deficiency to mental retardation until 1981.

The term "mental retardation" was introduced in 1981 in the *New York Times Index*. It reflects the outcome of deinstitutionalization and, interestingly, refers to the term "handicapped" (for inclusion). In the later part of the 1980s, especially from 1986 on, social concerns increase – in general, and specifically as they relate to young adults with retardation. The issues include employment and coping in adult life, but also child abuse, child custody, kidnapping, education, labor, murders, sex crimes and shootings.

The impact of IQ measurement on the definition and classification of mental retardation is communicated in textbooks in the 1970s. However, neat labeling of different levels of retardation according to IQ distribution in the normal population however ended up with the conclusion that 16% of the general population would be classified as mentally retarded. Costin and Hermanson (1976) corrected such a conclusion by saying that "in practice, only the lowest four levels are usually included" (p. 133)

The control that was exercised through IQ measurement transpired into some textbooks. For example, Harmatz (1978) noted that "mental retardation is a less controversial topic than other types of abnormality" and offers "after all, unlike most psychologic disorders, mental retardation can be diagnosed on the basis of objective tests of intelligence".

Mental Retardation as Handicap and as Disability

As a result of parent group interest and pressure, and the personal involvement of President Kennedy, the federal government in the early 1960s moved actively to redress the long-standing neglect of individuals with retardation. The progressive climate of the 1960s allowed questions to be raised both about the nature of the problem and its solutions. The involvement of the media as well as publications about life in institutions such as Willowbrook led to an overall condemnation of institutionalization as a solution for the care of individuals with retardation.

But the 1960s also revealed a different perception of the problem. For the first time, it was recognized that perhaps the origin of the social problem was not necessarily located within the individual with retardation but might be found in the social environment. Although the nature of the problem was still considered to be truly social, society's maladaptation to the situation of the individual became visible, a perception that influenced issues in the 1980s and the 1990s. In seeking an alternative to institutionalization by placement in the community, it was recognized and documented that society was not very well prepared to accommodate individuals with retardation (Begab, 1975; Edgerton, 1993).

The civil rights movement influenced in several ways the by-now traditional discussion of the social and intellectual dimensions of mental retardation. It was recognized that according to the 1961 definition of the American Association of Mental Retardation (AAMR) (Heber, 1961), as many as 16% of the American population could be classified as having mental retardation, including greater proportions of the bilingual/multicultural populations. A debate evolved whether definitions should be solely based on psychometric evaluations (Mercer, 1973). While supporters argued that intelligence tests, unlike adaptive behavior, were the only valid tool for diagnosis, their argument did not survive, partly because it could not be accepted that mental retardation was an unchangeable condition. In addition, opposition sparked by the civil rights movement noted that many children from minority groups were misdiagnosed.

In the AAMR's definition of 1973 (Grossman, 1973), mental retardation includes both an intellectual and a social dimension. That is, the "concurrent" existence of both dimensions is necessary to classify someone as mentally retarded. Specifically, the definition reads: "Mental retardation refers to significantly subaverage general intellectual functioning existing *concurrently* with deficits in adaptive behavior, and manifested during the developmental period" (Grossman, 1973; italics added). A major revision in this definition was psychometric which resulted in a drop in the estimated percentage of individuals with retardation from 16% to 3% of the total population. Although this effort may reflect attempts to resolve the fissure in the conceptualization of mental retardation, the problem of measurement remains unresolved. IQ testing remained the major criterion.

Perhaps the most important characteristic of the present professional narrative is found in attempts to prepare the social environment to better accommodate the individual with mental retardation. **The match between the environment and the individual with mental retardation is prominent in the latest revision of the definition of mental retardation** (AAMR, 1992; Turkington, 1992). As the new definition is a statement about functioning, the conceptual model is not medical or psychopathological, but functional. That is, the present definition of mental retardation "shifts the emphasis from measurement of traits to understanding the individual's actual functioning in daily living" (AAMR, 1992, p. 9).

Similarly, within the professional arena, the functionality of an individual with mental retardation becomes most important. That is, the end-productivity rather that the process again becomes important. Further, the inclusion of individuals with mental retardation supports destigmatization.

Although in the recent definition of mental retardation, the dichotomy between the intellectual and the social still remains, perhaps a new turning point is announced with the operationalization of the social dimension of mental retardation. That is, although measurement of intelligence remains important as an initial measurement, it is emphasized that it can only be a starting point. Thus, the way seems to have been paved for measuring in social (and not intellectual) terminology a problem that is fundamentally perceived as social.

The semiotic square reveals something else (Figure 7). The semantic opposition between retarded and advanced brings the narrative into the larger discourse of modernity: nonretarded is the condition of being incorporated into an advanced world. It is also necessary to consider how "mental retardation" has been transformed by bringing it into the larger frameworks of "handicap" and "disability". With handicap, mental retardation was defined in terms of opportunities and equality, deriving meaning from the civil rights discourses. **Confronted with the framework of "disability", the relativity of ability and the shifting of the locus of incompetence toward the environment supports the idea that difference-as-incapacity can be dissolved, as for example, in the recent efforts of inclusion.**

```
            Retarded              Advanced
              ◄─────────────────────►
              ▲  ▼             ▲   ▲
              │    ╲         ╱     │
              │      ╲     ╱       │
              │        ╳           │
              │      ╱     ╲       │
              │    ╱         ╲     │
              ▼  ▲             ▼   ▼
          Non-advanced         Non-retarded
```

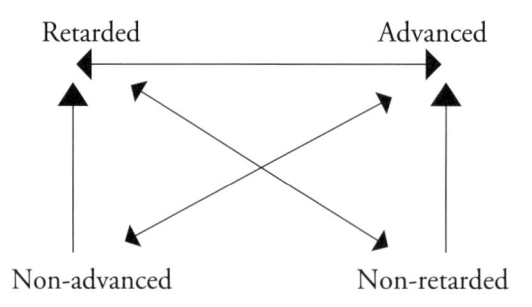

Figure 7: Semantic constellation of "retarded".

Discussion: Defining and Dissolving Difference

A semiotic analysis of "difference" is enlightening by revealing the semantic constellation of meaning that surrounds a certain term. In other words, we come to appreciate how the definition of difference is congruent with deeper structures of thought that relate to sociocultural contexts. That, however, is only part of the analysis. Difference dissolves in two important ways: by *redefining it* and by *distributing it.*

In defining difference within the larger framework of narrative, Dossa (1992) distinguished between two narratives: the old narrative of segregation, leading to confined forms of space and time and the new narrative of interdependence, achieved through cyclical forms of space and time. In a larger historical framework, it is now clear that when relating mental retardation to society, other dichotomies besides the integration-segregation exist, thereby helping to explain the social phenomena of a certain time period.

The first is the mood of society, which can be more conservative than liberal, more reformist than restrained. Second, persistently dominant metaphors of American culture remain helpful: the economic cost-effectiveness of a particular solution; conceptions of productivity (the belief that individuals with retardation can or cannot produce); and theories of dependency (warehouse or rehabilitate, include or exclude). Third, in the case of mental retardation, professional groups have at various points shown more or less optimism about the fate of individuals with retardation. These fluctuations reflect paradigmatic shifts from educational, to medical-psychological, to cultural-functional domains. That is, connotations and meaning are debated as issues are debated within professional organizations concurring with practice, ultimately leading to change in terminology.

In the history of mental retardation, many different professions such as education, medicine, social work, and psychology have occupied a dominant presence at some point in time. Lately, advocates have been instrumental in promoting fresh terminology. Boggs (1994) argued that the need for such changes is recurrent, like the moves at the Mad Tea Party. Indeed, their impact has been one of creating "order" during a certain period, in the sense proposed by Foucault (1973). It has been argued, for example, that medicine as well as education has acted as a main instrument for excluding people with mental retardation from society. To categorize persons with mental retardation as "defective" or "subnormal" is to describe them entirely in terms in their supposed pathology – what is wrong with them (Ryan & Thomas, 1987).

In the same vein, Sarason and Doris (1979) argued that mental retardation is a concept developed in response to perceived social problems and used to justify action. The most frequent action taken within the social context is diagnosis: the attempt to describe, understand, and assess as a basis for action. Diagnosis is a pathology-oriented process activated by someone who thinks something is wrong with somebody else.

Perhaps, in the history of mental retardation the latest developments will make questions about society more possible. For example, Ryan and Thomas (1987) proposed that there have been two directions of reform in which the issue of difference has been central. One has tended to minimize the differences between individuals with retardation and other people, resulting in a move toward integration and inclusion. The other has emphasized differences, resulting in segregation and exclusion. However, both sides of the argument share the same assumption: the problem lies in the nature of individuals with retardation themselves. The question of what is wrong with a Western society that has been so unwilling to accept and integrate these people has been much more difficult to ask. However, we may now be at the point where such questions become more legitimate. That is, narratives that focus on the match between the environment and the individual with retardation may result in identification of elements of that environment that could be improved.

Semiotics is a theory of signification. According to Greimas, it "becomes operational only when it situates its analyses on levels both higher and lower than the sign" (cited in Nöth, 1995, p. 315). In the application of the semiotic square, the deep structural character becomes evident because its four semantic values do not always have a corresponding lexical equivalent in the surface structure. The coherence of the terms allows one to describe the coherence and homogeneity of texts. Greimas borrowed the term "isotopy" from nuclear physics to describe the coherence of texts.

The structural coherence is an important theoretical aspect that adds to our understanding of the existence of different terminologies in the course of the history of mental retardation. However, such understanding must theoretically be complemented by an understanding at yet a deeper level of content dimensions and an understanding of both the diffusion of meanings and their shifts over time, especially the degenerative effect of terms related to mental retardation. I will now touch only briefly on those issues.

The social and the intellectual components are the two content dimensions that have continuously been involved in the construction of the concept of mental retardation in American society. Both dimensions have taken on different degrees of importance at various times and may help explaining the tension between mental retardation as "difference" and as "similarity".

Clearly, intelligence has had different impacts on the concept of mental retardation over the course of history. For example, Seguin had in mind "a lack of similarity" and proposed education as the tool to restore this lack of similarity. This "lack of intelligence" became transformed to "sign of difference" in a time where the unfit needed to be separated from the rest of the population for the "good of society". Such multiple uses of intelligence as a sign of a lack of similarity or a sign of difference "work" in the context of the larger frame of society. Thus, narratives that portray mental retardation as difference incorporate broader streams of societal consciousness.

As for degenerative shifting of meaning in terms related to mental retardation, it is possible to turn again to semiotics for a better understanding. Peirce coined the term "semiosis" to indicate the possibility that every sign can create an interpretation, which in turn is the referent of a second sign, thus resulting in a series of successive interpretations ad infinitum (Nöth,

1995). Terms that signify the condition of mental retardation go through successive interpretations until their meanings add so much connotations that they are unfit for new narratives.

Apart from the production of narratives, their diffusion is also of interest. The American Association of Mental Retardation has been instrumental in both. We looked at popular media, textbooks, and dictionaries as different instruments of diffusion narratives. Other instruments of diffusion such as policy documents and films that were omitted from the analysis must be taken up in further research. Perhaps due to the nature of these instruments, the lag time and the scope of impact differs greatly. Television may reach large audiences and have great momentary impact, but it is known that it does not last very long. Although print media shares some of the same characteristics, it has been shown that outdated terminology shows up in newspaper indexes for long periods of time before it is given up. Textbooks may be a much slower instrument of diffusion, but the impact in practice tends to be felt more. Finally, dictionaries are still slower and may from a research perspective be the most promising instrument for the study of the development, accummuluation, and erosion of the meaning of a particular terminology.

Understanding the workings of similarity and difference as semiotic processes related to the phenomenon of mental retardation, or any other identified "difference". is an ongoing historical and cultural phenomenone – one of finding new frames of order. Language is the primary tool to create this order, giving local and historical meaning to disability as phenomenon.

Acknowledgments

The development of this chapter benefitted considerably from a seminar in American history at the University of Illinois at Champaign-Urbana, and discussion and comments from Phil Ferguson.

References

American Association on Mental Retardation. (AAMR). (1992). *Mental retardation: definition, classification, and systems of support.* Washington, DC: Author.
Barr, M.W. (1904). Classification of mental defectives. *Journal of Psycho-Asthenics,* 9, 29-38.
Begab, M.J. (1975). The mentally retarded and society: trends and issues. In M.J. Begab & S.A. Richardson (Eds.), *The mentally retarded and society: a social science perspective* (pp 3-32). Baltimore: University Park Press.
Blatt, B. (1987). *The conquest of mental retardation.* Austin: PRO-ED.
Bruun, F.J., & Ingstad, B. (Eds.). (1990). *Disability in a cross-cultural perspective.* (Working Paper No. 4, 1990.) Oslo, Norway: University of Oslo, Department of Anthropology.
Costin, F., & Hermanson, R.H. (1976). *Programmed learning aid for abnormal psychology.* Homewood, IL: Richard D. Irwin.
Davies, S.P. (1930). *Social control of the mentally deficient.* New York: Crowell.
Devlieger, P. (1995). *On the threshold of adult life: Dis-course and life course of mental retardation in American culture.* Unpublished doctoral dissertation. University of Illinois at Urbana-Champaign.

Dexter, L.W. (1957). A social theory of mental deficiency. *American Journal of Mental Deficiency, 62*, 920-928.

Doll, E.A. (1947). Is mental deficiency curable? *American Journal of Mental Deficiency, LI*, 420-428.

Dorcus, R.M., & Shaffer, G.W. (1934). *Textbook of abnormal psychology.* Baltimore: The Williams & Wilkins Company.

Dossa, P.A. (1992). Ethnography as narrative discourse: community integration of people with developmental disabilities. *International Journal of Rehabilitation Research, 15,* 1-14.

Edgerton, R.B. (1993) [1967] *The cloak of competence: revised and updated.* Berkeley: The University of California Press.

Ferguson, P.M. (1994). *Abandoned to their fate : social policy and practice toward severely retarded people in America, 1820-1920.* Philadelphia: Temple University Press.

Fernald, C.D. (1995). When in London...: differences in disability language preferences among English-speaking countries. *Mental Retardation, 33,* 99-103.

Fisher, V.E. (1937). *An introduction to abnormal psychology.* New York: The MacMillan Company.

Foucault, M. (1973). [1966] *The order of things: An archaeology of the human sciences.* New York: Vintage.

Foucault, M. (1988). [1961]. *A history of insanity in the age of reason.* New York: Vintage.

Goddard, J.J. (1912). *The Kallikak family.* New York: Macmillan.

Gray, J.S. (1941). *Psychology in use.* New York: American Book Company.

Gray, J.S. (1951). *Psychology in use* (2nd. ed.). New York: American Book Company.

Grossman, H.J. (Ed.). (1973). *Manual on terminology and classification in mental retardation.* Washington, DC: American Association on Mental Deficiency.

Heber, R.F. (1959). *A manual on terminology and classification in mental retardation.* Pineville, LA: American Association on Mental Deficiency.

Heber, R.F. (1961). *A manual on terminology and classification in mental retardation* (2nd ed.). Monograph supplement to *American Journal of Mental Deficiency.* Springfield, IL: American Association on Mental Deficiency.

Harmatz, M.G. (1978). *Abnormal psychology.* Englewood Cliffs, NJ: Prentice-Hall.

Haywood, H.C. (1979). What happened to mild and moderate mental retardation? *American Journal of Mental Deficiency, 83,* 429-431.

Kansas Commission on Provision for the Feeble-Minded. (1919). *The Kallikaks of Kansas.* Topeka: Author.

Landis, C., & Bolles, M.M. (1946). *Textbook of abnormal psychology.* New York: The MacMillian Company.

Lasch, S. (1977). *Haven in a heartless world: the family besieged.* New York: Basic Books.

Langness, L.L., & Levine, H.G. (1986). *Culture and retardation: Life histories of mildly mentally retarded persons in American society.* Dordrecht: D. Reidel.

Mercer, J. (1973). The myth of 3% prevalence. In R.K. Eyman, C.E. Meyers, & G. Tarjan (Eds.), Sociobehavioral studies in mental retardation. In *Monographs of the American Association on Mental Deficiency* (No. 1).

Morgan, J.B. (1928). *The psychology of abnormal people.* New York: Longmans, Green and Co.

Moss, F.A., & Hunt, T. (1932). *Foundations of abnormal psychology.* New York: Prentice-Hall.

Nöth, W. (1995). *Handbook of semiotics.* Bloomington: Indiana University Press.

Ryan, J., & Thomas, F. (1987). *The politics of mental handicap.* London: Free Association.

Sarason, S.B. (1985). *Psychology and mental retardation: perspectives in change.* Austin: PRO-ED.

Sarason, S.B., & J. Doris. (1979). *Educational handicap, public policy, and social history: A broadened perspective on mental retardation.* New York: Free Press.

Scheerenberger, R.C. (1983). *A history of mental retardation.* Baltimore: Paul H. Brookes.

Singer, D. (1910). The classification of mental defectives. *Journal of Psycho-Asthenics, 15,* 3-16.

Smith, J.D. (1985). *Minds made feeble: the myth and legacy of the Kallikaks.* Rockville, MD: Aspen Systems.

Stiker, H.-J. (1989). Catégories organisatrices des visions du handicap. In J.-M. Alby & P. Sansoy (Eds.), *Handicap vécu, évalué.* Grenoble: La Pensée Sauvage.

Turkington, C. (1992). New definition of retardation includes the need for support. *APA-Monitor, 24,* 26-27.

White House Conference on Child Health and Protection. (1933). *The handicapped child. Report of the committee on physically and mentally handicapped.* New York: The Century Co.

Wilmarth, A.W. (1906). To whom may the term, feeble-minded, be applied? *Journal of Psycho-Asthenics, 10,* 203-219.

Woodill, G. (1994). The social semiotics of disability. In M.H. Rioux & M. Bach (Eds.), *Disability is not measles: New research paradigms in disability* (pp. 201-226). North York, Ontario: L'Institut Roeher Institute.

Virtual Disability: Sameness and Difference in an Electronic Support Group

Gerald L. Gold

This chapter focuses on the making and meaning of computer mediated support groups or virtual support groups for persons with disability. These are interpreted as communities that are composed of expansive networks of weak ties (Garnovetter, 1981) that facilitate the rapid, wide scale exchange of information and at times, personal assistance. These wide networks provide significant support for a dispersed population of persons with disability and their significant others. Those who join the virtual community often have limited accessibility to information on disability and chronic Illness (MS can be both) or on medical or alternative therapies and hospital services. Moreover, the virtual support group is not limited to scheduled meetings and places. Like face-to-face groups, virtual support groups include persons with experiential authority (Borkman, 1990, p.20) and become a focus of resistance to the negative gaze of outsiders.

This chapter uses participant observation to study MSN-L, a virtual support group for multiple sclerosis, were participant identity is constantly negotiated in public and private communications. The volume of the first obliges the observer to sample message threads and select what is relevant to her situation. The secrecy of the second can only be sampled through experience.

The topic of a message thread becomes the focus of community attention. The immediacy of replies builds a network where participants interact on a first-name basis as though they are in daily contact. In this way an MSN-L agenda is continuously reconstructed. Following a thread leads to common narratives (sameness) and to a distinctive MS agenda (difference).

Much of the communication takes place backstage, in private posts where the boundaries between experiential and professional authority are blurred. Although most messages have detailed signature lines, they circumvent barriers such as body shape, age, gender and class. List participants become part of an imagined community of persons living with MS. The conclusion discusses the inability of this seeming unity to lead to political action and deal with national differences in the agenda of disability support.

Disability support groups act as forums that interpret disabilities by providing a nonmedical and nonclinical milieu to discuss relationships, biomedical options or the value of alternative medicines. Face-to-face groups are the conventional forums for support, but despite some obvious advantages of direct interaction, they are small and can only be accessed at fixed times within a delimited geographic range. This contrasts with the egalitarianism of virtual support where there is ideally an electronic commons that circumvents differences in rank and gender.

The focal point of this chapter is an example of a virtual or computer mediated support group for disability that is a cluster of identity and are the basis of a community that can be an accessible place for persons with disability. Though there has been considerable recent research with virtual communities, little of this focuses on support groups of disabled persons and their everyday practices. The significance of virtual support for persons with disability is partially in the physical difficulty of assembling dispersed persons into groups. However, it is also related to the recent organizational metaphor of a disability consciousness and the genesis of the concept of disability culture (Brown et al., 1995).

Recent research on communities in cyberspace emphasizes the capacity of virtual networks to benefit from the strength of weak ties, an idea that was initially introduced by Garnovetter(1982) in studies of urban networks, though the metaphor is equally applicable to global support communities (Milena and Wellman, 1996). Others emphasize the altruism of generalized reciprocity in virtual communities which characterizes the giving of information and support without the expectation of immediate return (Rhinegold, 1994, Kollock, 1997). As this essay demonstrates, members of virtual disability communities seek not only the social support and knowledge of others but also information on which treatments are available, a discussion of medications and side effects, and the names and telephone numbers of suppliers (with prices).

Virtual communities can be dispersed over broad distances and may never lead to direct social interaction, a point that is directly related to the strength of virtual disability where computer mediated communication bridges physical barriers to accessibility. In this chapter, I will discuss a widely dispersed virtual support community for multiple sclerosis, in which I am both a participant and an observer. Drawing on this ethnographic experience, the discussion looks at the operation of a virtual support group by analyzing the content of support messages and considering how participants construct an MS agenda or plans to cope with the effects of this disability.

The effectiveness of virtual support for disability is illustrated through several brief case studies. The conclusion suggests some of the similarities, and differences between this community and other disability support communities. Also considered, is the meaning of computer mediated communication among persons whose primary contacts may be with their immediate families, a small group of friends and clinics or a few medical professionals.

This focus is particularly relevant in the context of virtual disability that is one of an imagined community (Anderson, 1991) [1983] without apparent spatial boundaries or a linear concept of time. It is this ethnographic and reflexive approach that characterizes this account of MSN-L, a virtual support group for multiple sclerosis that I will use as a model of virtual disability. Before discussing the ethnography of a virtual support group, it is useful to discuss what I am defining as support and as virtual support and the relationship of participation in the virtual disability community to medical practice.

Support Groups

Both face-to-face and virtual support groups share common characteristics though they have different origins and function in distinctive contexts.[1] Moreover, both types of groups incorporate public and private networks of communication. Within the virtual support group, informed persons with disability can be symbolic equals or medical practitioners and health professionals Though it is important to emphasize that participants in a virtual support group

---

1   Humpreys and Rappoport suggest that self-help groups could be seen as "normative communities and political action organizations (1994, p. 217) rather than as a single type of group(1994, p. 217).

are invisible to each other in a setting which is distant from the isolation of the ward or the symbolic barriers of the doctor's office (Zola, 1983) [1972]. Even when physicians are absent, the clinician's discourse of 'medicalization' is constantly- present within the tropes of everyday exchanges. However, this chapter illustrates the increasingly important actions of persons within virtual support groups to influence and shape narratives of support.

One of the distinguishing features of all support groups is the reported and 'imagined' similarities which create and reinforce a community. **In this way, "experiential authority", the voices of those who live with or near disability, "becomes a source of authority that is independent of other aspects, in contrast to the experiential knowledge of professionals which translates into authority and power within their professional roles, not separate from them@** (Borkman, 1990, p.20). Within the support group, persons with disability participate in a microcosm where " lived experience occupies center stage" (and is not) "incidental to an occupation (Borkman, 1990, p. 20)". In most research, this insight into the relationship of outsiders to those with experiential knowledge refers primarily to interaction-based support groups where meetings are at regular intervals, often under the supervisory gaze of representatives of a charitable or public service organization, or the scrutiny of medical professionals. That medical presence is largely absent or implied within virtual support groups.

The Virtual Support Group[2]

E-mail from the group moderator or learning how to interact by observing other posts, provides a guideline for the process of on-line communication: posting, modes of reply, roles of conduct or netiquette, and dealing with flaming or personal attacks which characterize some on-line communication. Other general considerations that arise include the creation of a database of frequently answered questions (or FAQ) and styles of leadership.

The face-to-face support group with its emphasis on experiential authority is a constant model for virtual support where the support model becomes intertwined with the expected characteristics of other virtual communities. Moreover, time and events in a virtual disability support group may not be permanent and messages are not always easily re-playable (Sproul and Kiesler, 1990, p. 128). The agenda of a virtual support group may carry a sense of urgency as participants question medical authority to seek cures and solutions. In this way, virtual support nurtures a fast-paced community that may not replay past encounters, and many narratives are requests for assistance or political support.

The message thread becomes a focus for an information exchange where lay participants may assume the role of medical professionals. The props of professional health providers become invisible and a well-informed person with disability can provide a comprehensive discussion of medical and paramedical alternatives. Signature lines and departmental affiliations are not a guaranteed seal of authenticity. The emphasis is on the message and valued

---

2 Support groups are only one type of virtual community and as I suggest in this chapter virtual support groups are modeled after both virtual community and face-to-face support groups.

information often comes from informed, non-medical members of the virtual community. These persons, often drawing a disability pension, may be able to accumulate a bank of Medline abstracts, data on alternative medicine, diet or exercise, information on assistive devices, vehicle modification and details of government programs for the disabled. It is the ability to generate this information, often in response to a query or a message thread, which reinforces the experiential authority of some participants within the virtual community.

Fieldwork with a virtual support community

This chapter makes use of participant observation to understand the social construction of MSN-L a virtual community in which I participated both as an anthropologist and as a person with MS. In my required introductory biography and other communication, my role as a social anthropologist was made apparent though interaction with the group was both on-line and in some private visits with members and with the group organizer overseas. At all times, my role has consistently been as a participant and as an observer. Observations are based on everyday list behavior and there were no interviews or questionnaires. Most of the data in this study is publicly-available internet information, though names including the list name are pseudonyms. Private conversations are reported in a manner that protects the identity of list members. Fieldwork with MSN-L was primarily completed on the screen of my office computer, where individual identities assume a realism that does not resemble the anonymity of a simulation where players are not deeply concerned about the topics of everyday conversation. In those groups – MOOs and MUDs, participants are players in role-playing games who use pseudonyms to disguise age and identity or gender. To my knowledge, most if not all participants who actively host communications in this community use their real names and often discuss their place of work and home environment. Moreover, many participants with MS logon with their spouse or significant other, contributing narrative (often it is difficult to tell which person is speaking). It is the first fieldwork that I have done where the person undertaking the study is one of those studied and where almost all interaction and observation was in cyberspace. This study, completed over a two-year period, underscores the effectiveness and limitations of a virtual support group for what is both a disability and a chronic illness.

As is often the case in participant observation, the issue of research access is complicated by the absence of an authority structure and formal criteria for leadership. Yet members, who are self-selected, will respond briskly to messages that they judge to be inappropriate or offensive. In a larger context, their response frames the natural history of a virtual support group where members continually move in, and out of virtual support groups. The boundaries of this community may be obscured as more than one support group represents most disabilities like MS, and many community members may participate in several virtual communities.

Though the MSN-L community may normally have about 225 members, about forty of these are frequent-posters, influential community members, almost all of whom use their real names and have distinctive list personalities. However, MSN-L is not an encapsulated village and its public communications are mirrored or bounced to a Usenet newsgroup. As Usenet readers are not monitored or counted by the host or sending computer, and Word Wide Web search tools bring messages to hundreds of additional readers, hundreds and possibly thousands of readers may read the public messages of a small virtual community.

Despite this openness of public messages, many readers are "lurkers" who do not subscribe to the list and read list messages or 'posts' but never respond. Often, a lurker seeks information for a friend or relative with MS who may never join in list conversation or who may be in a state of denial and rejection of difference (or deviance disavowal (Davis, 1961; Murphy, 1987, p. 123-4). However, as this chapter demonstrates, the virtual disability community, through the intervention of one or more of its members, will attempt to control and define its public identity and members may make occasional use of private, one-to- one, communications which extend or even depart from public discourse. The disability list carries these two personas, public and private. The volume of the first, forces the observer to select and sample message threads. The secrecy of the second extends to private networks and can only be viewed proactively through participant observation.

MSN-L: Virtual Support for Multiple Sclerosis

Data for this study comes from participant observation in two years of screen messages or 'posts' which arrive at the rate of about 35 per day and vary in length from one line to several thousand words. Moreover, in my own reflexive participation as an active member of the support group, I sent about three messages a week to the entire list of about 250 members and about ten private messages yearly to the list manager, and another 50 to other 'members' who posted public and private replies to message threads that I was actively following. In two years I did not see a single private post that had been forwarded to the entire community as a public posting, though that would be uncomplicated (entering a y instead of a n to a query by a computer mailer). With this narrow border between public and private, confidential notes such as a private posting on sexuality (discussed below in greater detail), may be sent mistakenly to the entire list briefly making a private topic into a public one.

Fieldwork includes several face-to-face and telephone conversations as I interviewed the 'list owner,' several active list members in Americans and Canadian cities, including Toronto. However, to dispel romantic notions of fieldwork with an international disability community, on-line' research was more productive than these occasional encounters and public Internet posts were always the more detailed and most candid conversations. Private posts, like interviews, can be exaggerated by metaphors of performance and representation, though the urgency of a MS agenda much of which is directed toward finding a rapid cure may emphasize realist tales (Van Maanen, 1988) at least in public communication.

As an anthropologist, my field became the virtual community on the Internet where experiential and narrative posts generated thousands of pages of electronic notes. At times, I compare fieldwork in cyberia with earlier research in Quebec (Gold, 1990) or in Louisiana or elsewhere in that imagined place I knew as French North America (Gold, 1990.) With the exception of several interviews and encounters, interacting with MS-N is not less insightful, though there is less to observe and all discussions have a written record. As in fieldwork, I did not know initially what to expect. Also, there are continual events in virtual space, some of which are crises and keep me at the microphone until early morning (this research, like this chapter, was done almost completely with VoiceType software). The virtual community is not where I expected to be doing field research, but hours spent reading the list became a field experience. Using indexing software to review and to follow topic "threads", I identified major issues of virtual support but also realized that over two years, the MSN-L agenda had shifted and the voices or members of the list were also changing and constantly questioning and redefining the unwritten criteria for active membership.

Though much talk is directed toward finding the cure for MS, most messages are experiential and deal with daily rituals, symptoms or problems and trips to the clinic. These messages are automatically relayed to 'members' in the USA (about 80%), Canada, England, Germany, Holland, Denmark, Italy, Israel, South Africa, and Australia. The topic of a thread is listed in the message header (e.g. 'getting worse,' 'house'.' or Betaseron, a costly drug which delays the exacerbations of relapsing- remitting MS; Methotrexate, a cancer and arthritis drug found to be effective at inhibiting upper body loss of function in chronic- progressive MS; Amantadine, a Parkinson's drug which prevents fatigue, a serious problem in MS); medicinal uses of Marijuana; the powers of grape seed extract and of primrose oil. A 'member' who does not wish to read all messages can scan headers, select and read or reply to specific threads. Reading all posts and replying to several can require several hours which limits the number of virtual communities that can be effectively-engaged by one person. Over two years, at least 50 members post weekly, and some of these might be multiple messages. The virtual community may have as many as 300 active members; but posting activity is not constant and depends on the issues that are presented in list mail.

Threads and a MS Agenda

In this way, **active participation in MSN-L, like other disability lists, is characterized by continuity where the immediacy of replies and the layering of threads, builds a network where participants interact on a first-name basis as though they are in primary contact with each other on a daily, if not hourly basis**. A major focus of these contacts is the message threads and, indirectly, the making of a MS agenda.

The agenda is continuously modified so that it gradually shifts, in both content and from it's original focus (e.g. a thread focused on Betaseron 'injection tales' can shift to insurance providers). Members limit the number of topics and new threads are difficult to sustain. Even with that degree of consensus, membership in the unmoderated list is open to anyone who contacts the host computer and sends compatible messages. Public messages are accessible to all members or to anyone who monitors public posts through the World-Wide Web. the list manager may occasionally reject objectionable list mail if it is public. However, private mail can be sent without interception, (using the computer address on their message header), whether or not the sender is a 'member' of MSN-L.

Despite this openness, the brief history of MSN-L, illustrates the contradictions and complexity of virtual support and community posts demonstrate how MSN-L develops common narratives and a changing MS agenda that offers a shifting boundary to a virtual community. A few voices write of a disability community, but the notion of a disability consciousness is unexplored. In both of my observers roles, I often wondered whether those list members who are still ambulatory1 deny and overtly fear the disabled body or becoming Stiker's savage and unusual 'other' (Stiker, 1982, p. 15; this volume).

But the overriding themes of MSN-L's global electronic support for multiple sclerosis are directive and reassuring messages: overcoming daily problems, choosing a 'neuro' (neurologist) and dealing with perceived threat to their virtual community. Though one doctor posted extensive advice on bladder problems and other topics, most members deal with these issues by relying on the reported histories of others and these commentators are rarely medical professionals. Moreover, though most support messages refer to other messages and are event-driven and dated, it is the message thread that maintains continuity and an illusion of timelessness.

Within the virtual community or support group, most members monitor their mail daily and respond to individual messages both publicly and privately. However, the sheer volume of mail leads to a mix of long informational posts with shorter conversational notes and requests for help or advice. Reading the message summary screen, before reading a post, a community member can decide from the sender's name, the thread name, and message size, whether it fits with issues of immediate concern. A reader can also determine the status of the message (Is this a direct reply and does it include previous correspondence from this thread?)

Though most electronic support groups are 'un-monitored', they are also subject to continual social control. This reinforces community identity though often it will encourage the defections of active members who are offended, annoyed or frustrated with others and decide to leave the group. This decision may emerge in private messages but it also will be part of a public declaration of departure, often followed by a string of responses pleading with the departing person not to we leave their community.

Lurking and Validating

Shortly after joining MSN-L, the system facilitator, an overseas professor, with MS, asks the new 'member' to 'post' a biographical introduction. In practice, many of new members have already become regular readers, or 'lurkers,' while some long-time members (six months!) feel that they should re-post their biographies for the benefit of "newbies". These self-identification and validating tales are distributed as message posts to all members of MSN-L, many of whom welcome the new 'member' and add their issues of concern to a message thread that often develops out of the validating tale. For example, this introduction by a woman who had not yet been diagnosed with MS, brought a flurry of diagnostic suggestions, but without the appearance of a new thread.

> Thank you for your warm welcome. I am a 45 year old mother of two sons and have a small farm. I have not been diagnosed with MS, but I keep running into the possibility ever since I had some numbness on the right side and would intermittently hear the sound of my heartbeat in my right ear. The neurologist told me I had an inflammation of the nerves in my brain stem – probably caused by a virus – and that it would eventually go away. What he wrote in my records was: "It would appear that she suffered an episode of demylelination and probable plaque formation. It is the first episode that she has had and whether or not she will go on to develop recurrence".

This new member was welcomed to the list but there were no public reactions to the content of her narrative. I did not notice any subsequent posts from her and assume that she either became a lurker or dropped her affiliation with a group that could not be of assistance. Significantly, many of those who visit the virtual disability community do not receive responses to their posts and leave the group shortly after their introduction. This is not a group for everyone with MS: new members are expected to contribute to existing message threads and there are many who do not find the support they were seeking.

Others are informed by list members about the status of their current medical treatment. Writing without apparent reservation, members of the list speak for the 'neuro,' by advising the 'newbie' that they may not find what they are looking for from a neurologist but should consider treatment alternatives. Sometimes, the 'newbie' is directed elsewhere:

Re: "...information on this type of treatment ..".   Comment: I'm sorry, I don't understand. If you are looking for therapies that create functional improvement, I don't think there are many that I can think of. Was that what you meant? Most current MS therapy is directed at symptom management. I'm definitely not the person to provide favorable comments on bee sting therapy.

BTW (by the way), Welcome to MSN-L!

Other validating tales emphasize that MSN-L is their first opportunity to talk about MS to people who will 'listen'. This theme later developed into a separate thread on the significance of the list as a support group.

> It has been one week since I joined the MSN-L and I am very happy that I found this channel for information and support.As (overseas list owner) suggested to me in his warm welcome to the list, I will talk a little about my involvement with MS.
>
> When I was 18 (ten years ago) I had my first exacerbation. It was fairly strong (not being able to walk, etc.). It lasted three days and the doctors didn't find out what was going on. Three years later, suddenly, I got really bad, and then the MS diagnosis came.
>
> During the first couple of years ... I was very worried, afraid that weakness and similar feelings were the beginning of another strong exacerbation. I am Brazilian, and I was lucky enough to get access to the best doctors and hospital in the country (it was the only place in the country with a magnetic resonance machine ...).

A recurring theme of all posts is that MSN-L has become their MS community – a group of similar persons who can respond when others cannot. For example, the following comment is representative of many replies: For example, the following comment is representative of many replies: I feel like I found some people to talk to about aspects of MS that I don't feel like discussing with my family or friends, and I don't have the opportunity (and appropriate "environment") to discuss with doctors. Thank you very much, all of you!

Some introductions are from those who have never been in communication with MS'ers or who live 'normal' lives in which they are unwilling to acknowledge difference: I don't want to intrude on your list – but from reading your posts I have already learned that it is indeed possible to have periods of time which are symptom free ...

Others, about one in six and mostly men, join as caregivers (SO) who speak for their spouse. After several months of posts, however, it becomes difficult to distinguish a person with MS from her SO. This merging of support persons with the disabled and chronically ill reinforces the creation of a single MS agenda. In the lively pace of message swapping, a list-member can lose track of who is who except for the occasional reminder from a SO that they are a voice for someone else.

Community Roles and List Identities

In practice, the unmoderated electronic group has an informal moderator, who maintains the overseas host computer and who contributes frequent opinions, narrative, and private messages. Other members also assume distinctive list- identities2 Notes and are referred to, directly, in comments, or indirectly, if their daily or biweekly post is absent. Some identities are revealed in a name or a signature line such as 'Blue Skies' or a quote in Japanese.

There are assigned and expected roles in the daily communications of the group some of which will be honored and others might be challenged. For example, a plea that elicits immediate response is the perplexed person with MS or a caregiver, with a tale of the newly diagnosed. Other list members assume medical or pseudo-medical roles. For example, list-member A.B., draws on his extensive library of research abstracts and becomes a medical expert who provides background to virtually any inquiry and casts studied rejection to the proponents of fringe cures or unproved theories (e.g. climate-based theory of MS). Yet others who rely on alternative medicine and diet challenge his voice.

MS Tales

Most participants begin with a narrative of eligibility and, once enrolled on the list, even the most vocal and expert of the participants, posts a 'confessional tale' (Van Maanen, 1988, p. 73) that establishes their similarity to others in the virtual community. About a third of the posts, during the first year of fieldwork, provide an update on the availability and effects of Beta Interferon (the first FDA approved drug for relapsing- remitting MS). Others write about methyl-prendisone (Solumendrol), cladibrine or methotrexate. Many commentaries challenge the effectiveness of all medications such as Baclofen, taken for spasticity.

The Beta Interferon posts, accompanied by 'injection tales' and travel routines are experientially detailed. Initially, these narratives were divisive as at least half of the communities are not taking Betaseron, either because it was not released to persons with chronic progressive MS or because they had been persuaded that it is ineffective. Some of this evidence was produced by A.B. working in his brief self- assigned role as role as MSN-L's medical expert (despite the occasional presence of several doctors). Reviewing the neurological publications, A.B. concluded, to many unhappy members that the effectiveness of this high-priced wonder drug was scientifically questionable. Some, following A.B.'s advice, decided not to register for Betaseron. However, in a few months, the opposition dwindled and posts began to include new injection tales and advice on preparing the medication, including rough sketches of bottles. A few resistors, including an influential frequent correspondent, opted for the somewhat less expensive COP1, developed in Israel (Though some Israelis in the community did not support her decision). Meanwhile, Betaseron-users began to send posts about sudden remissions and dramatic improvement.

Another lively thread, which lasted for several months and attracted several dozen posts, is the effect of Cannabis (Marijuana) in substantially reducing spasticity. One poster began buying Marijuana and another reported regularly on two plants (Mary and Jane), growing by his bedroom window. This led to a concerned post, from Germany, about the legality of discussing cannabis on the Internet. But, as Mary and Jane matured, Marijuana-growing gave way to the prospect of MSN-L's summer camp, an imaginary place where things go on as they once did, and everything is accessible.

Significantly, no thread was able to dominate the MS agenda for more than several weeks but the exception is the constant questioning about the effects of medication. While threads such as 'telling the boss,' or 'pee-stories,' and tales of retention and toileting disasters, elicit a fine-grained thread of graphically-vivid discussion, attempts to introduce the topic of sexuality, a subject that is thoroughly covered in printed discussions of MS, were initially avoided.

Topics that enthuse some members, such setting up a FAQ (a bank of 'frequently asked questions') drew complaints from others who insist that a support group should discuss MS-related issues and avoid giving a permanency to a rapidly changing topic. Nevertheless, a British member of the list prevailed in setting up a dedicated FAQ which is never referred to in discussions and which has received few updates. The topics chosen for inclusion in the FAQ emphasize the advice of two persons on medical and nutritional issues and side- step the disability and political dimensions of MS, by including some of A.B.'s essays and the informative advice of Cathy, a doctor of rehabilitation medicine. Moreover, the FAQ does not reflect a large number of the posts on using drug therapies, a continuing thread on employment, insurance, driving, cannabis or camp, and a recent flame war between an outspoken (and severely disabled) member and a new member ('Nutrasweet Betty') over Betty's claim that there is a link between Aspertame and MS.

Even with these omissions the FAQ provides a history to the virtual community and attempts to institutionalize a spontaneous exchange of information as a fixed resource on the World Wide Web (Table 1).

Table 1 -The First MSN-L 'FAQ' (Frequently Asked Questions)

MS Fatigue
Swank diet for MS
Clothing
What's a Kurtzke?
Impairment of Cognitive Function
If it Quacks Like a Duck
I always Wanted to Play the Violin
What Harm Can it Do?
Exercise and MS
Bladder Problems

Backstage: Private Posts

Much of the communication within the virtual community takes place backstage (Foster, 1995; Goffman, 1963), **in private posts which reply to specific concerns or to autobiographical accounts.** Even the medical student, the three doctors and the most prolific posters will use backstage messages if they are concerned about a post or a question and wish to avoid front-stage scrutiny. Many backstage messages are deeply personal or reflect concerns that frequent-posters would not place on MSN-L. Some arrive unexpectedly, as this response to my suggestion that people read Robert Murphy's The Body Silent. Part of the message could have been a public post, but the comments on the list behavior are meant to be private.

Gerry, Just wanted to let you know that I read "The Body Silent". Actually I finished a few weeks ago. Thanks for the suggestion.
I still don't know whether it's a good idea to be a "super crip" or not. There are so few role models in general, though probably a good number on the net. I think Robert Murphy says (and shows by example) that one shouldn't give up the fight and should try to accomplish as

much as possible.   Though we get a lot of conflicting messages on that on the net as well. Such (the medical student among them) who advocate getting a lot of rest ...
Cheers!   Dave

Political Mobilization in Cyberspace

After eight months of participation and fieldwork with MSN-L, two crises demanded a response from the virtual community. In the first crisis, A.B., the resident medical 'expert' threatened to leave MSN-L in reaction to critical comments or "flames". The response was a dramatic mobilization and flurry of messages, one of which came from a doctor, assuring A.B. of his irreplaceable role. The crisis subsided when he continued to post messages. though he stopped posting after beginning a MS virtual support group with a commercial Internet provider. Significantly, another community member, I.M., began posting detailed discussions of MS issues and a series on Doctors respond to Questions about MS. In a short time, I.M. and others, all of whom had access to medical discussions, became the community's resident medical experts. Though several physicians were still community members, others easily assumed the role of a medical voice for MSN-L though the words of A. B. can still be read in the FAQ. This experience may have important implications about virtual support that will be discussed in the conclusion.

A second crisis ensued when Rachel, a literary disability activist with MS, who also is vision-impaired and uses a wheelchair, was ejected physically from her New York apartment and hospitalized. In response to an appeal from the unofficial moderator and a message from a professor at St. John's University, a number of faxes were sent to an official in New York and a fund was started for Rachel's expenses. But the net and MSN-L, which had once received Rachel's activist and literary posts, could not mobilize more than a few persons to assist the writer in trouble. The virtual support group was less effective at political support than in the rapid circulation of messages. Moreover, in a few months Rachel reappeared in MSN-L and both the incident and the abortive mobilization of the support group disappeared into a void of cyberhistory.

The conflict of public and private[3]

These closing remarks deal with two crises in the virtual support group that I think indicate some of the useful directions for further research. The first crisis deals primarily with the dilemma of privacy in communication but also with the need to consider which topics are not discussed within the group narrative and consider reasons for their introduction and suppression. The first example deals explicitly with sexuality but it also could introduce topics such as gender, dating, authority and discussion of degrees of disability, which are also not appropriate to list narrative (see Lyon, 1995). The second example may be the more complex

---

3   Private posts are discussed partially by Lyon (1995).

as it contrasts an engaging public narrative which is optimistic and interrogating, with the private narrative that sinks to despair and defeat.

The most dramatic and personal narratives were consistently received by private E-mail. Two examples bring out the contrast of public and private communication in the virtual community. The first is a woman who is a frequent poster of public messages, but accidentally distributed to the entire list a private message describing the effects of MS on her ability to achieve orgasm. Then, in response to her shame and threat to stop posting, there were multiple appeals for her continuing participation and several posts detailed sexual frustrations in a brief public airing of a topic that was consistently kept offstage.

In the second example, a former computer-programmer corresponded with me on the narrowing of her urban world, difficulties in dressing and grooming and the diminishing rewards of everyday life. Her detailed lament was sent privately while her public persona projected an image of coping and intuition. In this case private despondency never intersected with public response. In both instances, the community members stopped sending regular posts, and possibly could not find virtual support for depersonalizing and disability- related difficulties.

Summary and conclusions

The focus of this chapter is the social construction of virtual community for persons with a disability and specifically a case study of a virtual support group for persons with multiple sclerosis. I have first focused on forms of communication provided by the sharing of online narrative in a virtual community and secondly, on how this virtual group can be a source of support by providing a flow of information on subjects where information is not freely available in an idiom that can be interpreted by laymen. This egalitarianism of the virtual community is antithetical to the specialized and hierarchical environments of medicine and the fragmentation of experience that accompanies the medicalization of disability. But the absence of status or hierarchy does not prevent virtual support from depending on some of the experiential authority that characterizes conventional support groups. It does, however, manifest itself in different ways as authority and experience become objects of reciprocity making them widely available (Kollock, 1997).

A reflexive ethnographic study of MSN-L focuses on focuses on virtual support without a sense of place and with opaque and ill-defined boundaries that are constantly undergoing redefinition. Nevertheless, it is this flexibility that brings together a virtual disability community with fa large number of weak ties of geographically- dispersed persons. Some are isolated by their disabilities, but few would normally have access to one another. Participants in this virtual support group add collectively to the message threads of an imagined community (Anderson, 1991) [1983] and to what I refer to as their MS agenda.

Whereas the voices of experiential authority are significant in many situations, in both types of support group, within the virtual disability group, medical voice is replaceable. MSN-L overcame the loss of its medical expert and eventually of its two physicians members who may continue their presence in the role of lurkers. Not only is much of their advice stored in the FAQ, but other medical voice emerges in text captured frequently by community members and there have been no comments on the departure of the physicians.

In this way, although the virtual disability group had no direct institutional affiliations, its wide network of weak ties assures the constant presence of experiential voices either from the narratives of participants who often deal with medical authority, through reported narratives or from the specialist who occasionally joins the group. This loss of medical authority is never discussed in conversations. Instead, the MS agenda comes from the message thread and is a renewed in a process which does not necessarily recreate earlier narratives.

However, there are gaps in the common agenda and the cultural and social representation of MSN-L. The virtual group includes primarily Americans and Europeans and there are few participants who are not English speakers. Virtual disability, like much of the Internet, may remain Northern or Western rather than cross-cultural. However, as disability studies continues to emerge as a cross-cultural field, it will no doubt look at Internet groups which are a manifestation of the globalization of perspectives on disability. Like conventional support groups their their shared knowledge is experiential, focused on the effects and treatment of disability.

Common experience splinters when communication deals with social security and private insurance plans – none of which are relevant to persons outside the USA. Whether or not these plans are specifically discussed, they are always relevant to the availability of medical care and to individual perceptions of possible action. This difference is strikingly clear in ongoing comparison of MSN-L and a similar community in Canada that includes primarily Canadian participants. The Canadian list never discusses insurance issues but does deal with some of the same experiential questions about living with MS. More interesting, is that the Canadian group actively discussed medical alternatives that ifs participants believe are being ignored – such as the relationship of MS and herpes. But political action is unlikely because like American/overseas counterpart, the gap between a virtual community of persons with MS and the medical establishment is too complex to bridge.

References Cited

Anderson, B. (1991) [1983]. Imagined communities: Refllections on the origins and spread of nationalism. London: Verso.

Borkman, T.J. (1990). Experiential, professional and lay frames of reference. In Working with Self-Help.T.J. Powell (Ed.), Silver Springs, MD: NASW Press

Brown, Stephen E. et al. (1995). Disability Culture … *Disability Studies Quarterly* 15, 4, 2-19.

Davis, F. (1961). Deviance disavowal: The management of strained interaction by the visibly handicapped. *Social Problems*, 9, 21-132.

Foster, D. (1995). *Can we have communities in cyberspace?* Carleton University (Working Papers in Technology and Culture).

Goffman, E. (1963). *Stigma: Notes on the management of spoiled identity.* Englewood Cliffs, NJ: Prentice Hall.

Gold, G. (1990). Finding French America: Quebec anthropology and the definition of a culture area", In Culture and the Anthropological Tradition: Essays in Honor of Robert F. Spencer. R. Winthrop (Ed.), Latham, MD.: University Press of America.

Granovetter, M. (1982). The strength of weak ties: A network theory revisited. In Social Structure and Network Analysis, Peter Marsden and Nan Lin (Eds.), (p.10530). Beverely Hills, CA: Sage.

Humphreys, K. & Rappaport, J. (1994.) Researching self-help/mutual aid groups and organizations: Many roads, one journey. *Applied and Preventative Psychology*, 3, 217- 231. Kollock, P. (In Press). The economies of on-line cooperation: Gifts and public goods in Cyberspace. In. Communities in Cyberspace. Kollock, P. et al. (Eds.), Berkeley: University of California Press.

Lyon, D. (31 May 1995). Cyberspace and Virtual Selves: Change and Critique. [htttp:/www.tees.ac.uk/tcs/socandvirt.html].

Milena G. & Wellman, B. (In Press). Virtual communities: When social networks are computer networks. In Communities in cyberspace, Kollock, P. et al. (Eds.), Berkeley: University of California Press.

Murphy, R.F. (1987). The body silent. New York:W.W. Norton.

Rhinegold, H. (1994) The virtual community: Homesteading on the electronic frontier. New York: Harper Perennial.

Rhinegold, H. (1995). Which part is virtual? Which part is community? [htttp://www.well.com/uk/user/hlr/tomorrow/vcreal.html.]

Sproull, L., & Kiesler, S. (1990). Computers, networks and work". In The computer in the 21st century. Special issue of the Scientific American, 128, 135.

Stiker, H.-J. (1982). Corps infirmes et société. Paris: Aubier-Montaigne.

Van Maanen, J. (1988). Tales of the field. Chicago: University of Chicago Press.

Williams, G.H. (1990.) " Self-help in chronic illness: The case of ankylosing spondylitis. In The social exploration of disability, S.C. Hey, G. Kiger, B. Altman, J. Scheer (Eds.), Salem, OR: The Society for Disability Studies and Willamette University, 125:135.

Zola, I.K. (1983) [1972]. Medicine as a means of social control". In Sociomedical Inquiries: Reflections, inquiries and reconsiderations. Philadelphia: Temple University Press.

Study Questions

1. Discuss the characteristics of virtual support groups from the perspective of their ability to use experiential Authority.
2. Consider some of the possible advantages and drawbacks of virtual support groups for disability. Relate these to the timing of support and the size, experiential authority, availability and physical location of the support group.
3. What are the features of a virtual community? How does this "place" compare to a demographic community?
4. Using this case study or one that you have researched, discuss how medical authority is used within a virtual disability community.
5. How does social control operate within a dispersed virtual disability community? Relate this social control to social attitudes about disability.
6. Discuss one or more of the crises which affected MSN-L. Relate these examples to the social construction of virtual disability.
7. What is the role of a FAQ [frequently asked questions] in a virtual community? Would it be of greato significance to insiders or outsiders seeking medical vs. experiential information? Why?
8. Discuss the significance of backstage communication within a virtual disability community. Would this field research have been possible without it and how does this communication compare with privacy and rumor in conventional field research?

9. Discuss the operation and function of the message thread in virtual disability. Could the threads combine experiential and medical narratives?
10. How can a virtual support group respond to a crisis in cyberspace? [Use several examples.)

Contributors

GARY L. ALBRECHT, Ph.D., is Professor of Public Health and Professor in the Department of Disability and Human Development at the University of Illinois at Chicago. His current research focuses on studying how persons with disabilities develop strategies to gain access to social services and medical care and construct barrier free environments. Albrecht is also studying how women with disabilities go through the menopausal transition. He is a Fellow of the American Association for the Advancement of Science (AAAS), has received the Elizabeth and Sidney Licht Award for excellence in scientific writing, the Award for the Promotion of Human Welfare, the Eliot Freidson Award for The Disability Business: Rehabilitation in America (Newbury Park, CA: Sage, 1992), and the University's distinguished teaching award. He has recently edited (with Katherine Seelman and Michael Bury) The Handbook of Disability Studies (Thousand Oaks, CA: Sage, 2001). Albrecht finds refreshment in the mountains by skiing, climbing and riding his mountain bike and gains new perspectives by traveling in third world countries.

PATRICK J. DEVLIEGER, Ph.D., is associate professor in the Department of Social and Cultural Anthropology at the KU-Leuven (Belgium) and a visiting research assistant professor in the Department of Disability and Human Development at the University of Illinois at Chicago. An anthropologist and pedagogue by training, Devlieger's main interest is in the interface between culture(s) and disability. Devlieger's disability-related work started in Congo (formerly Zaire) with a research assignment from a group of flying doctors. Later, he worked with the United Nations in eastern and southern Africa in regional disability training and research programs. In the United States he received his doctoral degree in socio-cultural anthropology at the University of Illinois. Devlieger initiated ethnographic work with individuals who have become spinal cord injured as a result of gunshot trauma on Chicagoís west side and subsequently developed a peer-mentor model demonstration program in the Department of Disability and Human Development at UIC. Devlieger and his wife Martine live with their three children in Oud-Heverlee (Belgium).

PHILIP M. FERGUSON, Ph.D., is the E. Desmond Lee Professor of Education for Children with Disabilities in the College of Education at the University of Missouri St. Louis. In that capacity he collaborates with a variety of community based disability organizations in research and advocacy projects around issues of inclusive education in urban schools, family support, and the history of disability in the United States. He is currently working on a history of institutional policy in the Pacific Northwest as well as continuing to explore the interaction of culture and disability in the lives of people with severe intellectual disability. In addition to a number of book chapters and journal articles, Ferguson has published a book and videotape (both with the same title) on the history of intellectual disabilities: Abandoned to Their Fate: Social Policy and Practice toward Severely Disabled Persons, 1820-1920. As mentioned in Ferguson's chapter, his son, Ian, lives in a home of his own in Eugene, Oregon. Ian continues to impresses his parents with his accomplishments and the joy and enthusiasm he brings to life's challenges.

Contributors

GERALD GOLD is professor of anthropology at York University, in Toronto, Canada. He has been working on ìcultural constructs of accessibility, virtual disability and social action, Whatever It Takes: Virtual Support Groups for Arthritis, Crohn's Colitis, Fibromyalgia, Lupus and MS (recently completed manuscript). He also features several courses in disability studies at York University and is one of the organizers of their forthcoming graduate program in disability studies. Besides revealing numerous current manuscripts on disability-related issues, he also participates in disability politics in southern Ontario.

CAROL S. GOLDIN, Ph.D., is director of academic and strategic planning at Rutgers, The State University of New Jersey. Her research interests include stigma, deviance, and disabilities. In her doctoral and post-doctoral research, Goldin used anthropology to explore issues of stigma among the prevocationally blind, prison populations, and chronically ill mental patients, including a group of patients who committed violent crimes but were not guilty by reason of insanity. She has also conducted research on staff culture on mental hospital wards. Her work has been published in Human Organization, Social Science and Medicine, and Contemporary Psychology. Goldin maintains an active interest in organizational culture, identity politics, and disability theories. Her other interests include painting, crossword puzzles, languages and travel. Goldin and her husband, Jerry, a theoretical physicist and researcher in mathematics education, have two grown daughters and three grandchildren.

SUSAN FOSTER, Ph.D., is a professor at Rochester Institute of Technology's National Technical Institute for the Deaf, where she has worked in the Department of Research since 1984. She has published extensively on education and employment of deaf persons, including two books (Deaf Persons in Postsecondary Education, edited with Gerard Walter, Routledge, 1992; and Working with Deaf People: Accessibility and Accommodation in the Workplace, Charles C. Thomas, 1992). Current research projects include educational access and instruction for deaf students, identity development of deaf persons of minority racial or ethnic backgrounds, and the career histories of deaf professionals. She is currently Project Director for two US Department of Education Grants (Fund for the Improvement of Postsecondary Education and Demonstration Projects to Ensure Students with Disabilities Receive a Quality Higher Education). Each of these grants has as a central goal increasing access and inclusion for deaf students in mainstream postsecondary educational settings.

MADELYN IRIS, Ph.D., is an associate professor at the Buehler Center on Aging and Department of Medicine, at the Feinberg School of Medicine. She is also the director of the Northwestern University Ethnographic Field School. Before joining Northwestern, she worked as a qualitative research and program evaluation specialist for eight years after receiving her doctorate in anthropology from Northwestern University in 1981. She continues this work through collaboration and partnerships with community social service agencies on research and evaluation studies. Iris' work in aging and disabilities studies unites several aspects of her personal and professional life. For 14 years she was the parent of a child with multiple disabilities and through this experience became active in several disability-related programs. Her focus is on policy issues and the ways the network of aging service providers and disability rights activists defines a set of common goals and links those goals to actions. Some of Iris' publications include "New directions for guardianship research" (1991) and "Guardianship and the elderly: A multi-perspective view of the decision making process" (1988), both of which have appeared in The Gerontologist. She is currently a member of the board of directors of Health and Disability Advocates, a national organization dedicated to improving health care access for persons with disabilities and low-income seniors, and is president-elect of the National Association for the Practice of Anthropology.

VENTA KABZEMS, Ph.D is currently a principal with Edmonton Public Schools. She has been a school administrator in both special and regular programs from pre-school through secondary levels. Venta has worked as an education and behavior programming consultant with students with multiple and severe disabilities, a classroom teacher in both segregated and inclusive educational settings, and a university lecturer in Canada, the UK and Zimbabwe. She has consulted to private and government agencies on topics related to children and adults with a range of disabilities including mental health. Venta has lived and worked in the southern African region for six years and is currently an external examiner in the Faculty of Science for the Zimbabwe Open University. A self-confessed information junkie, Venta thrives on reading from the professional literature in a variety of disciplines and strives to be sufficiently self-disciplined to write.

DAVID PFEIFFER is resident scholar in the Center on Disability Studies at the University of Hawaii and is a wheelchair user. His doctorate is in political science from the University of Rochester and he has taught on the university level for 40 years. He was involved in numerous activities which impacted federal and state legislation and policies related to disability issues. From 1977 to 1980 he served as the Massachusetts state director for the White House Conference on Handicapped Individuals and from 1979 to 1980 as chair of the National Implementation Advisory Council for the Conference recommendations. In Massachusetts, he helped create a statewide, cross disability coalition of disabled citizens and served as its first chair. He assisted in establishing the Massachusetts Office on Disability and served six years as the chair of its advisory council. He is a former member of the Massachusetts Governor's Advisory Commission on Disability Policy. He was the main leader in the successful effort to amend the Massachusetts Constitution to forbid discrimination on the basis of a disability. He assisted in the passage of numerous laws relating to persons with disabilities. He has over 230 publications on a variety of issues most of them related to the field of disability, including transportation, health care, employment, education, legal and regulatory policy, and public attitudes. He is a past president of the Society for Disability Studies and presently editor of the Disability Studies Quarterly, the Society's journal.

FRANK R. RUSCH, Ph.D., is professor of education at the University of Illinois at Urbana-Champaign. Over the past 20 years he has focused his attention upon issues related to competitive and supported employment, with particular attention being paid to benefit-cost analysis, co-worker involvement, and self-instructional strategies. More recently, he has directed the Transition Research Institute at Illinois and the National Transition Alliance. These two institutes have focused upon systemic change in education at the state and local level. The author of numerous books, chapters and articles, Dr. Rusch has consulted to federal, state, local, and international education groups on such diverse topics as program evaluation, school reform, and best practices. He recently published (with Janis Chadsey) a text entitled, Beyond High School, which is an authoritative overview of school-to-work practices based upon the cumulation of over 15 years of research sponsored by the Office of Special Education and Rehabilitative Studies, U.S. Department of Education.

Contributors

HENRI-JACQUES STIKER is associated with the Université Denis Diderot, Paris VII and with the Ecole des Hautes Etudes en Sciences Sociales. The philosophical interests of his youth led him first toward semiotic questions. He followed A. J. Greimas and was confirmed as a researcher with the Ecole des Hautes Etudes en Sciences Sociales. Circumstances led him to become engaged in the action for persons with disabilities. Parallel to this work, he investigated from an anthropological point of view the discourses by the people involved and in history. From this work evolved several publications and invitations to teach in different universities, in France and in Quebec. Having presented the highest French university distinction, he became associated with the Université Denis Diderot, Paris VII and was invited to lead conferences at EHESS. After having studied the legal, philosophical, religious, and medical discourses of disability, he would like to devote more time to literature and art. But even before this, Stiker plans to publish on disability and modernity.

INDEX

alterity 79
American Association of Retired People (AARP) 160
American Sign Language (ASL) 125
American with Disabilities Act (ADA), 1990 28, 111, 115, 122, 159
applied behavior analysis 63
autonomy 17

backstage post 189, 198
behavioral sculpting 135
bicultural model 111
bilingual model 111

capitalist economy 29
categorical approach 54
categorization 82, 86, 151
civil rights 123, 129
coalition building 150, 159-161, 164
cognitive disability 136, 138, 140, 143, 144
cognitive strategies 65
cohesiveness 87
community 189, 190, 193, 194
Community Inclusion Movement (CIM) 138
competency-deviancy hypothesis 68, 76
competitive employment 69, 76
cross-national values 38
cultural model 14, 15
culture of disability 131
curriculum perspective 58

Deaf culture 114
Deaf President Now movement 115
Deaf Studies programs 120, 125
deficit model 54
democracy 29, 41
demographic imperative 152, 154
deviance 17
difference 12, 25
disability paradigm 26

educational funding 46

educational reform 45, 57
empowerment 114, 120
enculturation 135, 136
entitlement vs. civil rights 152
equality 83
equity vs. equality 28
essentialism 133
ethnocentrism 31
experienced reality 28
experiential authority 191, 192, 200

face-to-face support groups 189, 190
FAQ (Frequently Asked Questions) 191, 198
feeble-minded 175, 177
flames 199
fragility 81

"handicap" 9, 25, 79, 84-86
hard of hearing 111, 120, 123-125

"idiot" 174
illustrations of competence 63, 67, 68, 70
impurity 81
inclusion model 49
inclusive education 23, 56
independent living 19
Independent Living Movement (ILM) 138, 160, 162
Individualized Education Plan (IEP) 48
Individuals with Disabilities Act of 1973, 1983 Amendments to 74
integration 45, 56
integration of differences 79
integration vs. separation 152
intelligence test movement 180
interpretivist research 135, 144
irrationality 83

jesting system 82
juxtaposition of differences 87

labeling 143
linguistic minority 111-114, 119-123

Index

list membership 194
lived experience 131
lurkers 193-194, 200

mainstreaming 119
managed care 157, 158
management of differences 88
marginalization 27
market-driven educational policy 46
Maternal and Child Health and Mental Retardation Planning Amendment 68
Medicaid, 1965 156
medical authenticity 191
medical model 112-113, 116
Medicare, 1965 156
"mental deficiency" 176, 179
"mental retardation" 180
Mental Retardation Facilities and Community Mental Health Centers Construction Act 68
message threads 188, 193, 194, 195, 200
meta-worldy 81
mimetic crisis 87
MS agenda 189, 190, 194, 200

narratives 171-173
normalization 45, 51, 68, 69. 74, 75

Older Americans Act (OAA), 1965 158
one curriculum for all students 48
outcome indicators 74
outcome standards 47

paraprofessionals 50
parent movement 180
personal autonomy 140, 142
political model 114
posts 191, 193-198, 200
power 19

Protestant ethic 29
public policy 158, 162, 164
public portrayal 28
public vs. private 193, 199

realities 27, 37
reasonableness factor 52
recognition of differences 91
redistribution of income 33
Rehabilitation Act of 1973 159
relational approach 131
representation 27
rugged individualism 30, 141

sameness 12, 24, 25
segregated placement 50
self-determination 74, 75
semiotics 172
significant other (SO) 189, 192
social construction model 113, 114
social dimension 181
social needs 53
social policy 47, 48
social safety net 38
Social Security Act, 1935 155, 156
social validation 70, 71, 72, 73, 74
subnormal 181
supported employment 70

thick description 133
transition 66

United States Constitution 27

value structure 28
value system 23
values 27
virtual support group 189-192

World Wide Web 196